T0192960

100 THINGS
SABRES FANS
SHOULD KNOW & DO
BEFORE THEY DIE

Sal Maiorana

TRIUMPH
B O O K S

Library of Congress Cataloging-in-Publication Data

Maiorana, Sal, 1962–
    100 things Sabres fans should know & do before they die / Sal Maiorana.
        p. cm.
    ISBN 978-1-60078-722-5
1. Buffalo Sabres (Hockey team)—History. 2. Buffalo Sabres (Hockey team)—Miscellanea. I. Title. II. Title: One hundred things Sabres fans should know and do before they die.
    GV848.B83M35 2012
    796.9620974797—dc23

                                                                    2012009381

This book is available in quantity at special discounts for your group or organization. For further information, contact:

Triumph Books LLC
814 North Franklin Street
Chicago, Illinois 60610
(312) 337-0747
www.triumphbooks.com

Printed in U.S.A.
ISBN: 978-1-60078-722-5
Design by Patricia Frey
Editorial production by Prologue Publishing Services, LLC
Photos courtesy of AP Images unless otherwise indicated

To long-suffering Sabres fans everywhere.
May you someday sing, "You know we're gonna win
that Cup; you know we're gonna win that Stanley Cup;
me and the Buffalo Sabres, yeah, yeah, yeah"—
and have it actually happen.

Contents

Foreword *by Lindy Ruff*. ix

Introduction. xiii

1   Gilbert Perreault—The Original Sabre. 1

2   The Dominator 5

3   Welcome to the Stanley Cup Finals .10

4   No Goal. 13

5   May Day 17

6   Lindy. 19

7   Flying Frenchmen 22

8   The 1999 Finals. 25

9   Punch 29

10   Soviet Slaughter 32

11   Rico 35

12   Breakfast, Anyone?. 39

13   The Winter Classic 42

14   Thank You, Sabres 45

15   The Defection of Mogilny 48

16   Drury and Briere Bolt 51

17   Continental Flight 3407 53

18   The Only Place It Didn't Work 55

19   The Derek Plante Goal 58

20   The Hockey Hall of Fame 61

21   Procuring a Franchise. 63

22   A Spin of the Wheel. 66

23   Breaking Down the Barriers. 68

24   Working Overtime. 71

25 The Ironman 73

26 All Tuckered Out 76

27 Win and In 78

28 LaLaLaLaLaLaLaLaFontaine 81

29 They Travel Well 83

30 The Ken Dryden Pads Caper 85

31 Perreault Hits 500 87

32 Rene Robert 89

33 Miller Time 93

34 Going Batty 95

35 Near Tragedy 97

36 The President's Cup 100

37 "Punching" Out the Leafs 103

38 Darcy Regier 105

39 The Saddest Night 107

40 The Dynamic Duo 111

41 "Now Do You Believe?" 113

42 Remember the Aud 116

43 The Trade 120

44 No Garden Party 122

45 The Year of Uncertainty 125

46 Picking Pierre 127

47 Thomas Vanek 130

48 Razor 133

49 First-Round Flopping 135

50 The Muckler-Nolan Feud 137

51 The End of the Spectrum Jinx 140

52 Mike Ramsey 142

53 Sauve's Double Shutout 145

54 "Wowie" 147

55 Hometown Heroes 149

56 Schony 152

57 Gerry Meehan 154

58 Captain Clutch 157

59 The Bowman Showcase 159

60 The Underappreciated Hall of Famer 161

61 Steady Bill 163

62 The Bottle Cap Bisons 165

63 Luuuuuuuce 167

64 The Saga of Perreault's Retirement 169

65 Mike Foligno 171

66 Sabres University 174

67 The Owners 176

68 Roger the Dodger 180

69 Wounded Knee 183

70 Larry Playfair 186

71 Attend a Party in the Plaza 188

72 A Hero's Welcome 190

73 King Kong Korab 193

74 Impact Trades 195

75 The Hardest-Working Spectacle in Hockey 198

76 The Sabres Store and the Buffalo Sports Hall of Fame 200

77 The One That Got Away 202

78 The Joker Is Wild. 205

79 Takin' It to the Streets 207

80 The Ripper 208

81 The First Game 211

82 Tom Barrasso 213

83 The Other Guy 216

84 Michael Peca's Holdout 218

85 Gretzky's Big Night 219

86 The Voices of the Sabres. 222

87 Shackie. 224

88 Les Nordiques 226

89 Support the Sabres Foundation 228

90 Scoring Frenzy 230

91 The First One Against the Great One 232

92 Floyd Smith. 233

93 Wear the Colors Proudly 235

94 An Imperfect 10, Plus One 237

95 Danny's Debut. 239

96 It Starts with the Kids 242

97 Meehan Floors the Flyers 244

98 The Voice of the Aud 245

99 Blizzard Broadcast 247

100 See Ya, Seymour. 249

Sources 253

About the Author 255

Foreword

Back when the Sabres selected me in the second round of the 1979 National Hockey League Draft, I was a 19-year-old kid from a small town in western Canada who only vaguely knew where Buffalo was, let alone what kind of place it was. But playing in the NHL was my dream, and if Buffalo was where I had to go to pursue that dream, so be it.

When you combine the time I spent in Buffalo during my playing career with the Sabres and the time I have now served as the team's head coach, it adds up to a quarter of a century. That's almost half of my life living in this great town and representing this great organization, and it has been an honor and a privilege every step of the way.

When I was inducted into the Greater Buffalo Sports Hall of Fame in 2010, I said that I was proud to call Buffalo my home because the fans in the western New York area have given me tremendous support as a player, a coach, and just as a person.

This is one of the best hockey cities in the world, a place where people love and respect the game, and they prove that to our team every time we take the ice at First Niagara Center. It means so much to us that the fans care about the Sabres the way they do. Even this past season, when things didn't go as well as we'd hoped and we didn't make the playoffs, the arena was packed every night.

Detroit likes to call itself "Hockeytown," and Toronto likes to think of itself as the Mecca of hockey. But after playing and coaching in this town for almost 25 years, I think I'm qualified to offer the opinion that those folks have nothing on Buffalonians.

Even though our franchise wasn't one of the NHL's storied Original Six, and our history encompasses only a little more than four decades, the Sabres have been one of the league's great success stories. The original owners of the team, the Knox brothers—who also happened to be the men who signed my first paychecks—were two of the classiest gentlemen you could ever meet. And with Punch Imlach building the team from scratch, the Sabres were competitive within three years of their birth, even making it to the Stanley Cup Finals in just their fifth season. By the time I came on board as the second pick of Scotty Bowman's first draft for the club, the Sabres were a perennial Cup contender.

My playing career spanned almost the entire decade of the 1980s; Buffalo is where I became a man and enjoyed my greatest successes. It would probably shock my current players to know that I scored 102 goals as a Sabre, including 20 in one season (1985–1986). It probably would *not* shock them, however, to know that I piled up more than 1,000 penalty minutes while wearing the blue and gold. I know this for sure: Sabres fans appreciated my penalty minutes more than my scoring "prowess"; that's because this is a blue-collar town, and the No. 1 attribute they're looking for in a hockey player is someone who gives an honest and full effort. I prided myself on doing just that, and that hasn't changed one bit during my time behind the bench.

This trait is something also demonstrated by writer Sal Maiorana, and that is very clear in the pages you are about to read. I know Sal because each year when he finishes covering the Buffalo Bills for the *Democrat and Chronicle* in Rochester, he gets over to cover some of our games. Although he's not a regular on the hockey beat, Sal was born and raised in Buffalo and has followed the Sabres both as a fan and now as a professional sportswriter. He has a deep knowledge of the team's history.

Sal has compiled a list of 100 things Sabres fans must know and do that covers a wide spectrum of topics and serves as a terrific and comprehensive history of our franchise. I was particularly pleased to find out that I made the cut—I came in at No. 6. Maybe he was trying to butter me up, I don't know, but I certainly thank him for the praise.

As you make your way through this book, there will be so many items that stir your memories. Sal pays tribute to the great players of the past—including Gilbert Perreault, Dominik Hasek, Rick Martin, and Rene Robert—as well as to some of our current players, including Ryan Miller and Thomas Vanek. You will celebrate as you relive the team's two trips to the Stanley Cup Finals, in 1975 and 1999, and cringe when you remember the No Goal controversy. Sal also explores the big trades that have changed the team's history, team and individual milestone achievements, the greatest wins and worst losses, and the fun activities that our fans are involved with.

This is a book that every Sabres fan who proudly wears the blue and gold—or even the black and red—has to have. I hope you enjoy it as much as I know I will.

—Lindy Ruff

Introduction

On the morning of Sunday, June 20, 1999, I was standing in the media interview room along with dozens of other reporters, unaware of the firestorm that was brewing as the Dallas Stars were parading the Stanley Cup around the ice surface at a rapidly emptying and heartbroken Marine Midland Arena.

Yes, it was morning—around 1:45 or so—and my deadline at the Rochester *Democrat and Chronicle* had long since passed. Game 6 of the Finals between the Sabres and the Stars, which had begun a little after 8:00 on the evening of June 19, had extended late into a third overtime period before Dallas' Brett Hull scored against Buffalo's Dominik Hasek to end what was then the second-longest game in Stanley Cup Finals history.

Little did we know as we stood in that room waiting for Sabres coach Lindy Ruff to enter and convey his supreme disappointment over the loss that Ruff would eventually come bursting in there not sad, but downright livid with guns-a-blazing, spewing venom over the grave injustice that the NHL had dealt his team. When he did, most of us were thinking something along the lines of, "What's he talking about?"

You see, as soon as Hull scored the goal that ended Buffalo's second trip to the Finals, we all scurried to the press elevator to get down to the locker room, and no one knew that a titanic controversy was about to erupt. Based on video replay, the goal should not have counted because Hull's skate was in the crease before the puck slithered past Hasek—a clear violation of the rules at that time.

However, by the time the NHL officials had taken a good, long look at the replays, the Cup was already on the ice, the Stars were in full celebration, and the Sabres were back in their silent dressing room peeling off their equipment.

The league had made an egregious error by not keeping both teams on the ice and the Cup in storage until a proper video review had been conducted. And once all hell broke loose, there was no way the league's hierarchy was going to overturn the original call on the ice and bring everyone back out to play. Instead, they hastily put out a lame statement trying to explain the validity of the play, although no one outside of Dallas—if anyone down there was even paying attention—bought it. More than a decade later, NHL commissioner Gary Bettman is still vilified mercilessly by Sabres fans who have never forgotten that night.

There is no doubt that that event was one of the worst in Sabres history, but it was also one of the most fascinating nights of my nearly three-decade-long career as a sportswriter—right up there with covering the four Super Bowl losses of the other pro franchise in town, the Buffalo Bills.

In *100 Things Sabres Fans Should Know & Do Before They Die,* I hope I have provided a thorough representation of the history of Buffalo's beloved Sabres. I believe the 100 players, games, incidents, and recommendations that I have included here will give you a true sense of the franchise and what it has meant to the fans of Buffalo.

Yes, the No Goal fiasco quite likely ranks as the low point in the team's story, along with the Adelphia Communications scandal involving former owner and now jailbird John Rigas, which nearly led to the ruination of the franchise. But in these pages, you will see that the positive far outweighs the negative, and the journey you are about to experience as you turn the pages or swipe across your iPad, Kindle, or Nook e-reader will conjure up wonderful memories of the 40-plus years that the Sabres have been captivating their rabid fan base.

From the very beginning, when brothers Seymour and Northrup Knox were granted an expansion franchise for the 1970–1971 season, the Sabres struck a chord with western New York. Not surprisingly given Buffalo's proximity to hockey-mad Canada, the sport had been thriving here in the form of the American Hockey League's

Buffalo Bisons for decades. But while fans streamed through the turnstiles at Memorial Auditorium to watch the guys with the Bottle Cap logos emblazoned across their chests, the town was ripe for a major league team.

The Bills, an original American Football League franchise that began play in 1960, were about to hit the big-time in 1970 when the AFL merged with the powerful and established National Football League. Buffalo's hockey fans were longing for an opportunity to break into the big leagues, as well. When that dream came true, western New York and southern Ontario responded with glee—you couldn't find tickets for games, so instantly popular and beloved were the Sabres.

Bombastic Punch Imlach, who had coached the Toronto Maple Leafs to four Stanley Cups in the 1960s before being unceremoniously fired in 1969, was the Knoxes' choice to be the builder of their team, as well as its first coach, and Imlach delivered a playoff-worthy club within three years. The great Gilbert Perreault was Imlach's first draft pick, and over the next few years he added players such as Rick Martin, Rene Robert, Roger Crozier, Jim Schoenfeld, Craig Ramsay, Don Luce, Jim Lorentz, Jerry Korab, and Danny Gare. Before Sabres fans had even blinked, their team was playing for the Stanley Cup in the spring of 1975.

Many of the players I have listed above are featured in this book, and I hope you will enjoy reconnecting with these former Sabres stalwarts, as well as relish the opportunity to learn more about some of the recent players I have chosen to write about (including Dominik Hasek, Pat LaFontaine, Alexander Mogilny, Ryan Miller, and Thomas Vanek).

As for the highlight games, there have been so many remarkable nights that narrowing my focus was a difficult task. But in the end, I think I've produced the proper balance of thrills and chills. Countering the No Goal fiasco was the afternoon the Sabres lambasted the hated Russians, quite possibly Imlach's most shining moment (even though it was just an exhibition game). There's the Brad Park

Game 7 overtime dagger in the 1983 playoffs against Boston, but there's also the "May Day, May Day, May Day" retribution 10 years later, when Brad May's overtime goal completed a four-game sweep of the Bruins and ended a first-round playoff jinx for the Sabres. And surely you will smile when you read about Derek Plante's goal against Ottawa in 1997; the Dave Hannan goal in 1994 that ended the Sabres' longest game ever, a four-overtime playoff marathon against New Jersey; and the second-round thriller against the New York Rangers in 2007 in which Chris Drury tied Game 5 with 7.7 seconds left and Maxim Afinogenov then won it in overtime.

I have included entries pertaining to many of the most famous incidents in Sabres lore, such as the Scotty Bowman trade of the wildly popular Jim Schoenfeld and Gare in 1981; Perreault's momentous 500th career goal; the 2009 night when the Sabres beat San Jose in dramatic fashion, providing a sliver of relief to a grieving community following the crash of Continental Flight 3407 in Clarence Center; the 1981 game in which the Sabres scored nine goals in one period against the Maple Leafs; the first Winter Classic, held at Ralph Wilson Stadium in 2008; the measuring of Montreal goalie Ken Dryden's leg pads during the 1973 playoffs; and so many more.

Lastly, I have included numerous activities that, as the title of the book suggests, Sabres fans should try, such as visiting the Hockey Hall of Fame in Toronto, where several men with ties to the Sabres are enshrined; participating in some of the community events that benefit the Buffalo Sabres Foundation, such as the Aces and Blades Gala, the Corporate Hockey Challenge, and the Street HockeyFest; and taking a trip to watch the Sabres on the road.

The Knoxes brought the NHL to Buffalo, and now billionaire Terry Pegula is keeping the franchise right where it belongs with pockets that are as deep as his passion for the sport, the team, and the fans who support it.

To Sabres fans everywhere, enjoy the memories.

1 Gilbert Perreault— The Original Sabre

Elvis Presley shook his hips. Frank Sinatra crooned. Bruce Springsteen sang his working class anthems. Barnum and Bailey pitched their big tops. Olympic gold medalists Peggy Fleming and Dorothy Hamill performed their figure skating artistry and basketball Hall of Famers Bob McAdoo, Bob Lanier, and Calvin Murphy buried jump shots at Memorial Auditorium. But for those who saw Gilbert Perreault play night after night for more than 16 years as a member of the Buffalo Sabres, he was possibly the greatest act to ever perform in the old downtown arena.

Perreault was the original Sabre, the very first player drafted in 1970 when the NHL granted Buffalo an expansion franchise. From the moment he jumped over the boards, you got the feeling that something remarkable might happen—a sentiment that was shared by his teammates, opponents, and fans alike.

"Gilbert Perreault, when he went behind the net and took that puck, we stood up on the bench half the time, this guy was so thrilling," said Craig Ramsay, Perreault's teammate for 14 years and his coach for about two weeks in November of 1986.

It would begin with Perreault wheeling through the Sabres zone, gathering speed with every mighty stride as his skates cut into the ice like miniature chain saws. It was usually in the neutral zone where he'd meet his first resistance. At that point the level of excitement jumped a few notches and fans' rear ends crept closer to the edge of their seats as he maneuvered his way through the opposition like a skier negotiating a slalom course.

With the first wave of defenders drowning in his wake, Perreault would cross the enemy blue line with the puck seemingly glued to his stick, his hair blowing in a gusty breeze of his own creation, and the muscles of those watching got tense with anticipation. One defenseman would try to make a play, and Perreault would zoom past him the way Jimmie Johnson dusts his NASCAR pursuers. As another defender approached, Perreault would corkscrew him into the ice, and the fans would rise to their feet, thinking the same thing as the panicked goaltender: he had no chance. A deke to the left, another to the right, maybe a third just for the hell of it, and when the carnage was over, the puck was in the net, Perreault was being hugged by his teammates, the fans' eyes were bulging from their sockets, and you couldn't wait to get home and watch the replay on the 11:00 news.

"To this day, there isn't anybody that I talk about—even Bobby Orr, with the great speed he had—there's nobody who gave me more trouble than Gilbert," said Denis Potvin, former Islander defenseman and Perreault's fellow Hockey Hall of Famer. "He was an outstanding athlete and with that wide stride and the way he handled the puck, he was the toughest one-on-one player I ever had to deal with."

The late Rick Martin, Perreault's longtime linemate in what was known as the French Connection (the Perreault, Martin, and Rene Robert line), admitted there were times when he was guilty of getting caught up watching Perreault work his magic. "He'd come down and make a move and you'd say, 'How the hell did he do that?'" Martin said. "The toughest part about playing with Gilbert is that you had to guard against just standing there watching him. But you had to keep in motion and make sure you were in position because eventually he'd decide that he was tired enough and now he was going to make a play."

Perreault was born in Victoriaville, Quebec, the town where Victoriaville hockey sticks are made, and he had one of those sticks

Hall of Famer Gilbert Perreault—the "Original Sabre"—readies his stick during a game against the Bruins at Boston Garden in the 1970s. Rene Robert (14) backs him up. Photo courtesy of Getty Images

in his hands at a very early age. He was a child prodigy; in fact, by the time he joined the Montreal Junior Canadiens, he was a can't-miss NHL prospect. During his last season as a junior, 1969–1970,

Perreault was named MVP of the Ontario Hockey Association with 51 goals and 70 assists for 121 points in 54 games. Combined with his output of 37–60–97 in 54 games the year before, that added up to 88–130–218 in 108 games.

When a carnival-style wheel spin gave Buffalo the first pick in the 1970 NHL Draft, Perreault was set in place as the franchise cornerstone. "I wanted Gilbert Perreault as I had never wanted a hockey player before," Punch Imlach once said. "The hair just stood up on my neck at what he could do. He was a superstar in the making, the man the Buffalo franchise could be built around."

Perreault was the NHL's rookie of the year when he scored a then-record 38 goals; he also led the Sabres to the playoffs in just their third year of existence and into the Stanley Cup Finals in their fifth year. By the time he retired, he had recorded 512 goals and 814 assists for 1,326 points, seventh-most in league history at the time.

Perreault played in All-Star Games and Canada Cup tournaments, was inducted into the Sabres Hall of Fame, had his No. 11 retired by the team, and received the ultimate individual honor in 1990: enshrinement into the Hockey Hall of Fame.

But all the accolades do not make up for the one thing Perreault lacks, the only thing he ever wanted for himself, the Sabres, and their loyal fans. "My vision was to win the Cup," he said. "I won on every team I was on from the pee wees to bantam to midget to junior. I won two Memorial cups as a junior, and the only thing I didn't win was the Stanley Cup. That was the only sad part—that in Buffalo we didn't win the Cup.

"Through the '70s we were building up to it, so we thought we would be back even when we didn't win in 1975. I really thought we would be there for the next four or five years after that and we'd win one or two, but it didn't happen. I don't know why. We had a lot of good teams, we were close, maybe a player or two players away from winning. You look back at a long career and there's no Cup, and that's something that's missing."

2 The Dominator

The beautiful thing about hindsight is that it's always a crystal-clear 20/20. But seriously, did the Chicago Blackhawks really need much foresight when it came to evaluating Dominik Hasek's future in the National Hockey League?

True, when Hasek and fellow rookie goaltender Ed Belfour were both on the Chicago roster in 1990–1991, Belfour earned the No. 1 job in training camp, and it did turn out to be a wise choice by coach Mike Keenan. Belfour won the Vezina Trophy (for best goaltender) and the Calder Trophy (for NHL rookie of the year) that season, and followed it up the next year—with Hasek as his primary backup and seeing action in 20 games—by guiding the Blackhawks into the Stanley Cup Finals for the first time in nearly 20 years.

Still, in his brief playing time during that second season, Hasek proved that he was a sure-fire NHL talent, and further cemented his status with a solid performance in relief of Belfour in Game 4 of the Finals against Pittsburgh (even though Chicago ended up losing the game and the series that night).

Which brings us back to foresight: what were the Blackhawks thinking a few months later when they decided Jimmy Waite would work out just fine as Belfour's backup, and that it would therefore be a good idea to trade Hasek to the Sabres for goalie Stephane Beauregard?

Whatever Chicago's reasons were, Sabres fans are just happy the Blackhawks felt Hasek was replaceable. This trade, put together by general manager Gerry Meehan, was the greatest trade in Sabres history, bar none.

Beauregard was a middling player who'd spent parts of three seasons with the Winnipeg Jets before coming to the Sabres in June 1992 in exchange for winger Christian Ruutu. Beauregard never even went to training camp with Buffalo because the trade for Hasek went through in August. And get this: Beauregard was only in Chicago for three days before being shipped off to Winnipeg in exchange for—drum roll please—Ruutu. You can't make this stuff up.

So, if you want to say that in the end, the Sabres basically traded Ruutu for Hasek, that's fine. It was *still* the greatest trade in franchise history.

During his nine years in Buffalo, Hasek was widely considered to be the greatest goaltender in the NHL—and, really, the whole world. He won the Vezina Trophy six times and captured the Hart Trophy—presented to the NHL's most valuable player—in back-to-back seasons. That achievement was particularly impressive because he was the first goalie to win the Hart since Jacques Plante 35 years earlier; in fact, he's still the only goalie to win it twice. He also backstopped his native Czechoslovakia to the gold medal in the 1998 Winter Olympics, and lifted a mediocre 1999 Sabres team to the Stanley Cup Finals.

"He really changed the style and influence of what goaltenders do," Wayne Gretzky once said of the man who became known as "the Dominator." "It used to be that that guy was just in the net. He [Hasek] changed all that. He made himself a part of a hockey club and a hockey team's success. He's a unique athlete, one of the best goaltenders to ever play the game."

Hasek had what many described as a "slinky" for a spine, and was able to contort his body into unthinkable positions to make saves. "I was born with very flexible legs," he told author Randy Schultz. "I can remember when I was nine or 10 years old, I could do almost a 180-degree split. And even as I got older, I didn't really lose much of that flexibility."

Hasek said he never truly learned how to play the goalie position properly as a youth in Czechoslovakia, which is how he came by his unique style. Playing tennis helped to quicken his hands and reflexes, while playing soccer developed his leg strength. Along with his unusual, Gumby-like body, the other keys to his brilliance were his positioning and the unpredictability of his reactions when shooters approached, which threw them off. Watching Hasek when he was playing for the Detroit Red Wings, all-time Wings great and Hockey Hall of Famer Gordie Howe once remarked, "He looks like he's guessing, but he guesses right a lot."

"They say I am unorthodox, I flop around the ice like some kind of fish," Hasek once said. "I say who cares, as long as I stop the puck?"

By the time Hasek was 16, he was playing at the first-division level in his homeland. He made the Czech national team at 18, and by 21 he had earned a place as a starter. He ultimately won five Czech goaltender of the year awards and three Czech player of the year awards.

Although he was drafted by the Blackhawks in 1983 when he was 18, Hasek was unable to leave his home due to the potential trouble a defection to the United States would have created for his parents, brother, and sister in their Communist homeland. But when Communism crumbled in 1990, Hasek was able to leave and, following two frustrating years serving as Belfour's caddie and then another year backing up Grant Fuhr in Buffalo, he burst into stardom during the 1993–1994 season. He won his first Vezina Trophy and became the first goaltender since Bernie Parent of the Flyers in 1973–1974 to post a goals-against average below 2.00—his 1.95 mark and .930 save percentage led the NHL.

Hasek would go on to lead the league in save percentage for six years in a row. His 2.11 GAA in 1994–1995 was No. 1, and on four occasions he was tops in shutouts, including a Sabres-record 13 in 1997–1998. He owns eight of the nine best single-season save

Sabres goalie Dominik Hasek blocks a shot in the Rapid Fire SuperSkills competition during the All-Star weekend on January 17, 1997, in San Jose, California. Hasek won the event in 1996.

percentage marks in Sabres history, the top six goals-against averages, and is the team's career goaltending leader in GAA (2.20), shutouts (55), minutes played (28,664), and games (491).

Throughout his tenure in Buffalo, Hasek was, to say the least, enigmatic. He was prone to fits of anger, which were rooted mainly in his desire to be perfect. He also endured a trying period during

1997 when he and coach Ted Nolan were at odds, and Hasek was accused of quitting on the team during the playoffs that year, citing a sprained knee. When *Buffalo News* columnist Jim Kelley questioned Hasek's commitment, Hasek angrily confronted the writer and ripped his shirt during a brief scuffle—an incident that Hasek has regretted ever since.

At the same time, Hasek could be philanthropic with his time and money, most notably when he spent $1 million to found Hasek's Heroes, a youth hockey program for inner-city kids in Buffalo that is still thriving long after his 2001 departure from the Sabres.

Hasek went to Detroit in 2002 and won a Stanley Cup in his first season with the Red Wings. After retiring and sitting out 2003, he returned to the NHL and played for four more years (with the Red Wings and the Ottawa Senators), then for a year in the Russian league at the age of 46, before finally retiring once and for all in 2011.

"He's the Wayne Gretzky of his position," said former Sabres coach and general manager John Muckler. Hasek's crowning achievement will be his forthcoming induction into the Hockey Hall of Fame when he becomes eligible in 2014.

The Dominator Era Begins

Before Dominik Hasek came to the Sabres in a trade from Chicago, there wasn't a whole lot to know about him except for the fact that he was a native of Czechoslovakia who had a rather unorthodox goaltending style.

Hasek left the Czech Republic national team to play for the Blackhawks, but with Ed Belfour firmly entrenched in goal, there was no room for Hasek, who spent much of his first year in North America playing in the minor leagues.

But when Belfour was sidelined by a hamstring injury, Hasek was recalled in March 1991. In only his second NHL start, at the Aud against the Sabres, Hasek made 29 saves and earned his first career victory as Chicago topped Buffalo 5–3.

"I have waited for this game almost six months," Hasek said that evening.

In that same game, Sabres center and future Hockey Hall of Famer Dale Hawerchuk registered his 1,000th NHL point on a second-period goal against Hasek.

3 Welcome to the Stanley Cup Finals

On the bus ride back from Toronto following a 1974–1975 pre-season loss to the Maple Leafs, new Sabres coach Floyd Smith was incensed by the way his team had played—and he didn't much care that the game meant nothing in the standings. Smith was Buffalo's original captain in 1970, and then took over as coach from Joe Crozier.

"If I had some other way of getting home, I wouldn't ride on the bus with them," Smith spat, sounding every bit like general manager Punch Imlach, who was never afraid to share his criticisms. "I saw things out there I couldn't believe of NHL players making the kind of money these guys are making. I don't mind losing, but you have to give an effort."

Thankfully, there weren't too many nights when Smith felt like that during what was to become a magnificent season. The once-laughable expansionist Sabres took the NHL by storm in only their fifth year of existence, advancing all the way to the Stanley Cup Finals.

"I think we surprised a lot of people that year," said Jim Lorentz, "but I don't think we surprised ourselves. We knew we were pretty good. The team we lost to was a great team, probably the toughest in the game. Every game was like a war, it really was. But we were young; we didn't really know what we were getting into. We thought we had the beginning of a dynasty and, well, that never happened."

The Sabres finished with 113 points, tying Montreal and Philadelphia for first overall in the NHL. In what was the first year of the NHL's new four-division format, the playoffs had been expanded from eight to 12 teams and the four division winners—Buffalo, Montreal, Philadelphia, and Vancouver—all received first-round byes. "We had a ball in that week off," Craig Ramsay recalled. "Smitty did a good job of keeping us loose."

Upon their return to action, the Sabres rolled Chicago out in five games, setting the stage for a showdown with the Canadiens. In what is still one of the most memorable series in team history, the Sabres eliminated the mighty Canadiens—who would begin a run of four straight Stanley Cup championships the following year—in six games to advance to the Finals against the defending-champion Flyers.

Following a 6–6 tie in their final regular season game against Philadelphia in February 1975, Smith had said, "We'll beat the Flyers when we have to." Well, the Sabres did. Twice. But twice would not be enough.

The Sabres were faced with two obstacles in this series: the Broad Street Bullies and the building where they played, the venue known as the Spectrum. The Flyers were a tremendously tough and skilled team, and Buffalo had never won a game in Philadelphia's raucous arena.

That didn't change in the first two games: the Flyers won 4–1 and 2–1 as their goaltender, Bernie Parent, began a series-long trend of frustrating the highest-scoring team in the NHL.

The Sabres believed they had a chance to strike in the first game because the Flyers were tired; they had blown a 3–0 semifinal series lead to the Islanders and had to push hard for a Game 7 victory in order to advance. And at first it seemed the Sabres were right: through two periods, Philadelphia managed only 10 shots on Buffalo goalie Gerry Desjardins. But the Sabres couldn't beat Parent. It all fell apart for Buffalo during the third period as the Flyers scored three goals in a span of less than 10 minutes.

In Game 2, Parent faced only 19 shots, stopping 18, while Bobby Clarke broke a third-period tie with a power-play goal. "We played two pretty good games here," said Don Luce after the game. "With any breaks at all, we win one, maybe two. There's no reason we should feel we can't beat them."

Despite being down 2–0, the Sabres felt good about their chances coming back to the Aud, and their confidence proved justified as they pulled out 5–4 and 4–2 victories to even the series.

Game 3 was a night that will live in Sabres' lore forever—the famous fog game, in which Rene Robert scored 18:29 into overtime on a shot that Parent couldn't see through the soupy air. "It's almost impossible to score from that angle," Robert said of his shot from the right boards—except on that night, when the temperature outside soared to 90°, turning the Aud, a building not equipped with air conditioning, into a sauna.

The Sabres fell behind 2–0 in the first 3:09, and Desjardins, battling confidence issues, pulled himself from the game between periods, allowing Roger Crozier to take over. "After the second goal against me, I thought it was a grand time to get the hell out of there," Desjardins said. "I asked to leave at the end of the period. I knew if I stayed in, everything would have gone down the drain. After all, we were only down one goal. The guys were working so hard, they could win the game—so why not put in Roger? I couldn't stop a football. I was a second slow on every shot."

Goals by Rick Martin and Danny Gare 17 seconds apart later in the first period thrust the Sabres back into it, and then Bill Hajt's goal on a rebound in the third tied the score and forced the overtime.

Two nights later there was more fog and more Sabres good fortune as they rebounded from an early goal against Desjardins and went on to the series-tying victory. "I was fighting the puck, but I felt I had to work my way out of it," said Desjardins, who allowed only one other goal and made 23 saves. "This tending goal is a rough job, you know. I think if I had to do it all over again, I wouldn't be a goaltender."

Down 2–1 in the second, Gilbert Perreault tied the game on a power play, Buffalo's first in 17 chances in the series, and then Lorentz scored what proved to be the winner later in the second.

Heading back to Philadelphia with the momentum of a victory inspiring them, the Sabres were poised to end their 15-game winless streak in the Spectrum. But thanks to another poor performance by Desjardins—"Right now, I hate this game," he said—it didn't happen. Dave Schultz, fighter extraordinaire, scored two goals, which was one more than Buffalo managed against Parent in a 5–1 loss. "I was just lucky, really," said Schultz. "I just played the way I always do. Believe me, I'm better at fighting than scoring goals."

Smith benched Desjardins for Game 6 and went with Crozier. While Crozier played well, he couldn't match Parent's 32-save shutout in Philadelphia's Cup-clinching 2–0 victory. "I was shaking my head on every shot," defenseman Jocelyn Guevremont said of Parent's mastery of the Sabres. "I think we outplayed them the whole game. It was like that the whole series."

When it was over, the fans gave their team a thundering ovation following the traditional handshake line, chanting "thank you, Sabres," just as they had in 1973. And then they applauded the hated Flyers for their victory as the repeat champions paraded the Stanley Cup around the ice at the Aud. "That was a tremendous show of class by the Buffalo fans," said Philadelphia's Bill Clement.

4 No Goal

Brett Hull's skate was in the crease. He didn't deny it on the night of June 19, 1999, when he scored one of the most controversial goals in NHL playoff history, and he doesn't deny it today.

Hull's skate was in the crease when he scored the goal that clinched the Stanley Cup for the Dallas Stars in the third overtime of Game 6. He knew it, NHL commissioner Gary Bettman knew it, and all of Buffalo certainly knew it.

But in the end, it didn't matter. Because with the Dallas Stars already smoking cigars, spraying champagne, and drinking beer from Lord Stanley's chalice in the visitors locker room at Marine Midland Arena, there was no way the NHL was going to reverse the decision that allowed the goal to stand even though video replay clearly proved it was an illegal play per the NHL rules that were in place at that time.

"I saw it, and it looked like he did," Dallas' Mike Modano said that night amidst the bedlam of the Stars' celebration. "But what can you do, drag us back out there and play?"

"What's done is done," chimed in Dallas captain Guy Carbonneau.

But it will never be "done" in Buffalo, at least not until the Sabres finally win the Cup for that elusive first time. For a town that has endured so much sporting heartbreak, the No Goal controversy stands side-by-side with the Buffalo Bills' last-second loss in Super Bowl XXV, when kicker Scott Norwood missed a potentially championship-winning 47-yard field goal.

Created in an effort to help clear traffic in the goal crease in order to allow goaltenders a fair opportunity to do their job while also reducing the risk of injury, the in-the-crease rule had been a topic of heated debate for two years, mainly because too many goals were being disallowed—more than 100 in the 1998–1999 season alone.

There should have been one more added to the list.

"If there's a guy in the crease before the puck goes in there, the goal doesn't count. It has happened all season long," said defenseman Jay McKee. "We're not whining; that's the rule. To have it end that way is devastating for us."

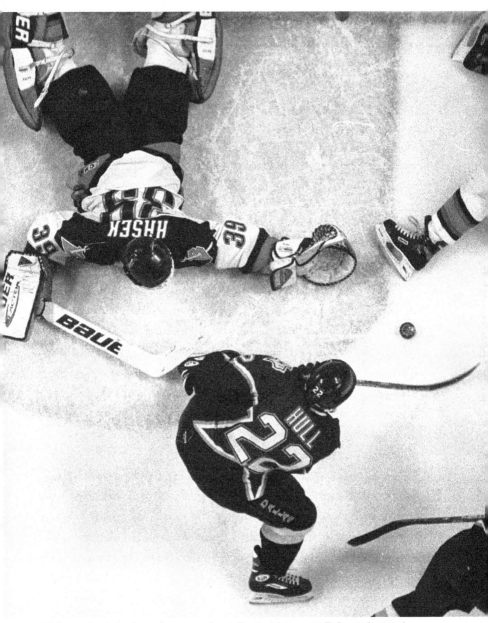

With one skate clearly in the crease, the Dallas Stars' Brett Hull shoots the Stanley Cup–winning goal past sprawling Sabres goalie Dominik Hasek in the third overtime period of Game 6 of the Stanley Cup Finals in Buffalo on June 20, 1999.

Rule 78 (b) stated: "Unless the puck is in the goal crease area, a player of the attacking side may not enter nor stand in the goal crease. If a player has entered the crease prior to the puck and subsequently the puck should enter the net while such conditions prevail, the apparent goal shall not be allowed."

In this case, Hull took a shot from just outside the crease, which Dominik Hasek stopped. The puck came back out of the crease, but Hull's skate remained inside the powder blue–painted area when he regained control of the puck and fired it into the net past a sprawling Hasek.

It should have been a no-brainer: no goal. Instead, no one from the NHL used any brains.

"It was our worst nightmare," said Sabres coach Lindy Ruff. "Somebody should have called from upstairs and said, 'This is not a goal.' All I wanted was a review. I wanted Bettman to answer the question of why this wasn't reviewed. He turned his back on me. It was almost as if he knew the goal was tainted. You can't explain the feeling."

Bryan Lewis, the NHL's director of officials, said the play was reviewed up in the replay booth and that it was determined that Hull had continuous possession of the puck and thus was allowed to have a skate in the crease.

"The debate here seems to be did he or did he not have possession and control," Lewis said. "Our word from upstairs in our view was that yes he did, he played the puck from his foot to his stick, shot, and scored. The other component of the debate is does the puck change [possession] as a result of hitting the goalie on the glove. Our rules are very clear in terms of completion of play. A puck that rebounds off the goalie, the goalpost, or an opposing player is not deemed to be a change of possession, and therefore Hull would be deemed to be in possession and control of the puck and allowed to shoot and score a goal even though the one foot was in the crease in advance of the puck."

But no matter what Lewis said, it was clear that that wasn't what happened. There were two separate possessions, in between which Hull's skate entered the crease illegally.

No goal.

No goal.

No goal.

Yet, in the end, there was no mercy for the Sabres.

"I believe everybody will remember this as the Stanley Cup that was never won in 1999," said Joe Juneau. "The goal was not a legal goal. I think because it was a goal that gave them the Stanley Cup, everybody jumped on the ice and they were afraid to make the call."

May Day

A surge of bravado coursed through the Sabres locker room on April 24, 1993, as they waited anxiously to skate back onto the Memorial Auditorium ice for the start of overtime.

Someone shouted that he was going to score the game-winning goal against the hated Boston Bruins. Then someone else refuted that claim, saying no, *he* was going to score the winner. And then someone else chimed in, and someone else, and someone else.

"A lot of guys were saying, 'I got it, I got it, I want to beat these guys,'" defenseman Doug Bodger said.

Sure, it was the confidence of youth, but it was also a case of a young Sabres team sensing the moment and understanding what was at stake as they tried to complete a stunning four-game sweep of the Bruins in the first round of the NHL playoffs. This was not going to be just any goal. Whoever scored this goal would reserve a permanent and prominent place for himself in hero worship, forever to be known as the man who not only completed a delicious sweep of the Bruins, but also exorcised the dastardly demons of playoffs past for the Sabres.

Not surprisingly, second-year Sabre Brad May wasn't making any predictions. And if he had dared to stand up and pound his chest, proclaiming himself ready to score the goal that would end Buffalo's mysterious and miserable run of first-round playoff disappointment (which dated back to 1984), his teammates probably would have looked at him en masse and said, "Yeah, right."

You see, May hadn't exactly been on a tear of late. He had gone the final 26 regular season games without a goal, and now, three games and three periods into this impossible-to-figure series in which Buffalo held a stunning three games to none lead, his drought dragged on. Never mind scoring: May had managed only one shot on goal all series. One shot.

"Hey, I had to come around sometime," May later said.

What a time to come around. At 4:48 of the overtime, May sliced his way through center ice, took a pass from Pat LaFontaine, outmaneuvered future Hall of Fame defenseman Ray Bourque, and threw a beautiful deke on goaltender Andy Moog before wristing the puck into the net to bring an unforgettably dramatic conclusion to the game, the series, and the first-round floundering.

Buffalo had started horribly. Goalie Grant Fuhr gave up four first-period goals and then exited with a hip injury, bringing Dominik Hasek into the game. Hasek gave up one goal in the second period, leaving Buffalo trailing 5–2, but Donald Audette answered moments later. Then midway through the third, Alexander Mogilny and Dale Hawerchuk scored 53 seconds apart.

Hasek preserved the tie with two big saves early in the OT, and then in a flash it was over. Keith Carney slid the puck up to LaFontaine, who was knocked down but maintained control, sweeping the puck in May's direction while still on his knees. May found himself one-on-one with Bourque—one of the best to ever play the game—but Bourque just wasn't up to the challenge that night.

"I saw [Bourque] coming out of the corner of my eye," May recalled. "It's something that 99 times out of 100 isn't going to work, especially against Ray Bourque. He probably didn't expect [the move] from someone like myself."

The Aud erupted into an ear-splitting cacophony of celebration. Brooms were flung onto the ice signifying the sweep and Sabres sticks and gloves flew like confetti as the team buried May under a pile of humanity. Up in the press box, broadcaster Rick Jeanneret was spontaneously screaming, "May Day, May Day, May Day"— one of the great calls not only in team history, but hockey history.

Lindy

The circumstances surrounding Lindy Ruff's return to Buffalo as the Sabres' head coach in 1997 could not have been more challenging— unless he had been coming in to run a talentless team coming off a last-place finish in the standings (which he wasn't).

Ted Nolan, a wildly popular coach among the fan base and certainly among the players (with the notable exception of goalie Dominik Hasek), had just led the Sabres to a surprising Northeast Division title and a first-round playoff series victory over Ottawa in the final year of his original Buffalo contract.

When Nolan's archnemesis—general manager John Muckler— was fired shortly after the Sabres were eliminated by Philadelphia, it seemed a sure bet that Nolan would stay on as coach moving forward. Instead, new GM Darcy Regier decided to offer Nolan a mere one-year deal. Nolan took a pass, leaving Regier searching for a coach. That search landed almost immediately on Ruff, a former Sabres player and captain who'd already enjoyed some success in the NHL as an assistant coach in Florida.

Although Ruff had been a fan favorite during his days as a player, the perceived wrongdoing done to Nolan did not sit well, and several players openly questioned the team's direction. Winger Dixon Ward, for one, said, "He's got a heck of a lot to lose and not a lot to gain."

Ruff made it clear at his introductory press conference that he knew what he was up against:

> I'm very excited about coming back to Buffalo—coming back to my [adopted] hometown. The team here in Buffalo reeks of what I was as a player, and that's hard work, determination, character, and emotion. I'm really looking forward to taking over and building from where they were at last year. Losing will not be acceptable in this city. The first message I gave them was, what they did last year was special. How hard they played for Ted Nolan is something nobody can take away from them. Their feelings for Ted, their loyalty, is something I can't take away from them. But at the end of the day, I hope they have respect for me.

On his way to becoming the all-time winningest coach in Sabres history, Ruff earned that respect almost from the start.

Mike Ramsey was the first player drafted for the Sabres by Scotty Bowman in 1979, and Ruff was the second, picked No. 32 overall. He made the team straight out of training camp and played the next 10 seasons without ever spending a day in the minors. At various points during his career, he was both a winger and a defenseman, and he was always among the grittiest players on the roster. His hard-working, hard-hitting style made him a beloved member of the club.

With his game beginning to wane with age, Ruff was dealt to the Rangers in March 1989 for a fifth-round draft pick that wound up becoming Richard Smehlik, a player Ruff would go on to coach in

Sabres' coach Lindy Ruff talks to associate coach Don Lever (back) during Game 4 of first-round playoff action against the Ottawa Senators at Marine Midland Arena, on April, 27, 1999, in Buffalo.

Buffalo for five years. Ruff finished his 691-game NHL career with 105 goals, 300 points, and 1,264 penalty minutes.

During his last two seasons as a player (one with Rochester in the AHL and the last with San Diego in the IHL), Ruff seemed to focus on getting a head start on his coaching career more than he did on actually contributing to either team on the ice. When he retired in 1993, one of his old coaches in Buffalo, Roger Neilson, offered Ruff a job as an assistant with the expansion Florida Panthers.

Within three years the Panthers were in the Stanley Cup Finals—although Doug Maclean had taken over for Neilson—and Ruff's work there led Regier to bring him to Buffalo despite the fact that he'd never had any head-coaching experience.

In 2010 Ruff became the first NHL coach in history to coach 1,000 games with the team that gave him his first job. He was still the head man in Buffalo through the end of the 2011–2012 season, making him the longest-tenured coach in the league by far. By the end of 2012 he was ranked in the top 15 all-time NHL coaches.

Ruff's longtime assistant, James Patrick, once explained what separates Ruff from so many other coaches:

> I think he analyzes the game way more than people could even comprehend or guess. I think it starts with that, his passion for the game, and I think he's a very good communicator. He can motivate, he can teach, and he has a strong enough bark when it's needed to get a message across. He's very well-rounded. I think his biggest attribute is that he knows the game so well and he's been able to adapt to the changes through the years, as well as adapt game to game or even shift to shift. He was a captain because he was a natural leader, and he does the same thing as a coach—he's a natural leader. He makes the tough decisions and leads by example. He sets the tone that the team has to take out every day, and that comes from his leadership skills.

7 Flying Frenchmen

Rick Martin didn't expect to be playing on the same line as Gilbert Perreault—Buffalo's first-round pick from the previous year who had gone on to win the NHL's Rookie of the Year award by scoring a rookie-record 38 goals—when he joined the Sabres as a rookie first-round draft choice. After all, they had also played on separate lines when he and Perreault were teammates for a few years in junior hockey with the great Montreal Junior Canadiens.

But when the Sabres arrived in St. Catharines, Ontario, to begin practicing for the 1971–1972 season, coach Punch Imlach was dismayed to see that Perreault had let his conditioning slip during the summer.

"Gilbert came to camp about 20 pounds overweight, and Punch put me with him and told me to 'Make him skate,'" Martin said. "That's how we first got together."

While Perreault did indeed get back into shape trying to keep up with Martin, it soon became obvious that they were also a perfect fit for one another: Perreault was a brilliant playmaker and Martin was a skilled shooter and scorer. With Perreault's gift for weaving through the defense, drawing attention, and then deftly passing the puck off to one of his wingers, the two men's styles were tailor-made for each other. And who better to dish to than Martin, whose shot could have burnt a hole through the net? Once these two hooked up, you had to wonder what Junior Canadiens coach Roger Bedard had been thinking back when he kept them separated.

Perreault and Martin were terrific for most of 1971–1972; Martin even broke Perreault's one-year-old record for rookie goal-scoring, with 44. But as perfect a tandem as they were, there was one thing missing: a worthy right winger to complete the line. And that piece fell into place in March 1972 when Imlach sent the popular but clearly over-the-hill Eddie Shack to Pittsburgh for Rene Robert.

"Robert was the guy I wanted for that wing," said coach Joe Crozier, who played a key role in the acquisition. "It was all discussed ahead of time that it was very important we had a guy in that spot. I knew Rene a long time from the American league, and he was a piece of the puzzle. He had a lot of talent, a lot of experience as far as reading plays. I knew what he could do, what type of person he was, so we went and got him."

Retired Sabres linemates (from left) Rene Robert, Rick Martin, and Gilbert Perreault—the "French Connection"—congratulate each other as their jerseys are raised together on November 15, 1995, at the Auditorium.

And from then until the end of the 1978–1979 season, Perreault, Martin, and Robert formed the greatest line in team history, as well as one of the greatest in NHL history.

"I had always played center, but they were looking for a right winger to play with Perreault and Martin," Robert said. "Joe Crozier told me, 'All we want you to do is the backchecking for Perreault and Martin and somehow be the garbage collector.'" But it was obvious that Robert was going to be much more than that. He was the missing link on a line that the Sabres could build their team around.

"Punch had always said, 'Concentrate on filling the net. I'm going to find you guys a right winger, just be patient,'" Martin said. "Most of the time he had guys who were there to check. He'd tell them, 'Make sure you're the guy back, these guys [Perreault and Martin] will go on offense.' When Rene came with the team, they kind of told him the same thing, but the problem was that Rene was a great offensive player. It just meshed instantly. It was like we had played together forever."

When pucks began consistently filling nets, the need for a nickname naturally grew. Fortunately, this didn't require a lot of thought. The Gene Hackman movie *The French Connection* was in theaters at that time, and with all three men hailing from French Canada, it was only too perfect: the French Connection.

"Rene was an underrated player; he had a lot of talent, good speed, and a great shot, and so did Rico," said Perreault. "What more can you ask for as a center? It was easy to make plays for those guys. I was more of a tap dancer. Rico had that great shot and great release, and Rene was a smart player who had a great view of the game."

The 1999 Finals

When the Sabres advanced to the Stanley Cup Finals in just their fifth year of existence, the hockey world was surprised only by the rapidity of that achievement. They may have only been five years old, but they were a magnificent team. It was no fluke that Buffalo squared off against Philadelphia for the championship in 1975.

When the Sabres made it back to the Finals in 1999 for their second and still only other appearance, there was a completely different dynamic at work. Hockey observers were stunned because no one—not even some of the players on the team—saw it coming.

"Five or six years ago when we had a team with guys like [Dale] Hawerchuk, [Alexander] Mogilny, [Pat] LaFontaine, and [Grant] Fuhr in the net, we said, 'Hey, we have a team that can go to the Finals and win it,'" veteran tough guy Rob Ray said on the eve of

Buffalo's Stanley Cup series against Dallas. "But we underachieved a lot of the time and never even came close. When they started to rebuild the team, we were thinking, 'This is going to take a long time.' [John] Muckler came in here and brought in a lot of young guys, and I hoped I was going to be around when it happened. But I really didn't think I was going to be around for the time it was going to take."

Well, here the 30-year-old Ray was, in the locker room at Toronto's Air Canada Centre celebrating a five-game blowout of the Leafs in the Eastern Conference Finals. That victory sent the Sabres on to the championship round against the heavily favored Stars with possession of the coveted Cup on the line.

The Sabres finished fourth in the Northeast Division with a mere 91 points, seventh-best in the conference, and they were underdogs in every round of the playoffs. Although Hasek won the Vezina Trophy and helped the Sabres rank second in the NHL in goals allowed, there was so little firepower on offense (Miroslav Satan had 40 goals and 66 points to lead the Sabres in both categories) that it seemed impossible that Buffalo would be able to outscore Ottawa in the first round even if Hasek was his typically unbeatable self. After all, this was a team that scored only 207 goals, third-fewest in team history (not counting the strike-shortened 1994–1995 season).

The Sabres swept the Senators in four straight by a combined score of 12–6. The key victory came in Game 2, when Satan scored in double overtime to give the Sabres a commanding two-game lead from which the Senators never recovered.

In the second round, Boston goalie Byron Dafoe proclaimed that he'd be able to match Hasek save for save after he'd held Carolina to 10 goals in a six-game series victory. Hasek wasn't great in this series, but he was better than Dafoe, and the Sabres eliminated the Bruins in six games to set up a much-anticipated showdown with neighboring Toronto (the first and still only time they have met in the postseason).

There was lots of hype coming out of Toronto, but in the end the Sabres ground out a five-game victory even though Hasek couldn't play the first two games due to a nagging groin injury. Backup Dwayne Roloson gave up five goals in a Game 2 loss, while Hasek gave up only six goals in the final three games as the Sabres dominated the Leafs, sending their fans into a frenzy.

"I'm telling you right now, I don't remember this much hype and hullabaloo when the Sabres went to the final with Philadelphia," broadcaster Rick Jeanneret said. "It was good, but this has everybody attracted. I haven't been pumped like this in years. I've talked to people who don't know one end of a stick from the other who are excited about it."

The excitement level soared even higher when Buffalo got off to a great start. Jason Woolley—one of only six Sabres who had previously played in a Stanley Cup Finals game—scored 15:30 into overtime to deliver a 3–2 series-opening victory in Dallas.

The Stars pulled even in Game 2 when Brett Hull beat Hasek with 2:50 left in regulation to break a 2–2 tie. The Stars went on to a 4–2 victory that set the stage for a raucous welcome home for the Sabres at Marine Midland Arena. Unfortunately, although the sellout crowd nearly raised the roof during the pregame festivities, there wasn't much to cheer about thereafter. Dallas' stifling defense held the Sabres to a franchise-record low 12 shots on goal and beat Buffalo 2–1.

"They can sure make it feel like you've got a plastic bag over your head sometimes," Michael Peca said of the Stars. "Their team defense is suffocating at times, but we didn't have many second and third efforts. They were one step ahead of us in all areas of the ice."

After a two-day break, the Sabres responded in Game 4 with a solid effort as Hasek turned aside 30 shots and Geoff Sanderson and Dixon Ward found a way to beat Dallas goalie Ed Belfour for a 2–1 victory. "What I saw on the tape is something I hadn't seen throughout the whole playoffs," coach Lindy Ruff said of the lame Game 3

A Wild and Woolley Affair

While Sabres fans everywhere were tearing their hair out and cursing their bad luck, the Sabres themselves were laughing. That's right: as they plopped down in front of their locker stalls at Dallas' Reunion Arena just moments after watching the Stars' Jere Lehtinen tie Game 1 of the 1999 Stanley Cup Finals with 48.3 seconds left in regulation to force overtime, the Sabres were laughing.

"We were upbeat and confident going into the overtime," said Michael Peca. "We knew we had the game where we wanted it after the third period. We knew we were going to win."

They were right.

At the 15:30 mark of a breathtaking extra period, defenseman Jason Woolley jumped into an opening in the high slot with the puck deep in the Dallas end, took a centering pass from Curtis Brown, and wristed a low shot past Stars' goalie Ed Belfour to give Buffalo a 3–2 victory and a great start in the franchise's second appearance in the Finals.

"Scoring a goal like this is one of the dreams," Woolley said. "The real big dream is still three wins away. That's the one I really want." Alas, that dream did not come true.

performance. "For whatever reason, we didn't have it; we got beat in every aspect of the game, and that wasn't going to happen again. I thought most of the game was just passion and emotion. I thought we came charging out of the gates hitting-wise and emotion-wise. We let it all hang out."

Back to Dallas the teams went for the pivotal fifth game. Sabres center Curtis Brown summed the night up perfectly, saying, "They can be maddening to play against. They play a great defensive system." Dallas won 2–0 as Belfour pitched an easy-as-could-be 23-save shutout.

Now facing elimination, the Sabres were confident they would find a way to get the series back to Dallas, but their series-long—and, really, season-long—scoring drought haunted them one last time. Hasek gave up an early goal to Jere Lehtinen, Stu Barnes matched that in the second period, and then no one scored for about the next two hours. Finally, 14:51 into the third overtime, Brett Hull scored what became arguably the most controversial goal in Stanley Cup Finals history—the famous skate-in-the-crease goal that should not have counted but did—and the Stars paraded the Cup around Buffalo's ice, just as Philadelphia had done in 1975.

"I congratulate the Dallas Stars, they played well, but I'm very bitter because of what happened, to lose like that," said Hasek. "You play for two months and the video judge didn't do his job. I don't know what he was doing, he must have been sleeping. No, I can't imagine this. I didn't know he was in the crease right away, but then I saw the replay in the trainers' room and I was about to go back on the ice because I couldn't believe it."

 **Punch**

On Thursday January 8, 1970, Punch Imlach—who earlier that week had officially become a former employee of the Toronto Maple Leafs—hopped into a chintzy rental car and drove from Toronto to Buffalo for the purpose of agreeing to become the first coach and general manager of the new National Hockey League franchise that had been awarded to Buffalo.

In his book *Heaven and Hell in the NHL*, Imlach recalled that when he stopped to get gas that day, the attendant came up to the window, shook his head as he checked out Imlach's subpar vehicle, and said, "I guess things aren't quite the same now that you're not with the Leafs."

Imlach had forged a legendary career with Toronto, having guided one of the NHL's Original Six franchises to the playoffs in 10 of his 11 seasons there, and winning four Stanley Cup championships during the 1960s in the process. He was one of the most popular sports figures in Canada, let alone Toronto. But on April 6, 1969, moments after the Boston Bruins had completed an easy four-game quarterfinal playoff sweep of the Leafs, team president Stafford Smythe pulled Imlach into an office at Maple Leaf Gardens and said, "Well, that's it. You're through. I want to run the club."

Eight months later, after lawyers for Imlach and the team came to an agreement on a settlement for the remaining year left on his contract, Imlach picked up his compensation check and returned his fancy company car—a big, classy Oldsmobile that he had cherished.

As he pulled out of the gas station that day, the attendant's words burned in Imlach's ears. Whether he liked it or not, though, the symbolism was unmistakable considering the step he was about to take—going from the glamorous, tradition-rich Leafs to the infantile, sure-to-be-laughable, and as yet unnamed Buffalo team.

So once he arrived in Buffalo, Imlach agreed to the terms put forth by his new bosses, Sabres co-owners Seymour and Northrup Knox, but asked for one thing in return: he wanted a company car, "the biggest and brightest Cadillac Eldorado in town." If he didn't get it, he told them, he wasn't coming to Buffalo. The Knoxes agreed. So began Imlach's quest to not only prove that Smythe was a buffoon who had made an egregious error in firing him, but to build an exciting, winning hockey team in Buffalo. And he succeeded.

As Seymour Knox told Wayne Redshaw, one of the contributing writers for the book *Sabres—26 Seasons in Buffalo's Memorial Auditorium:*

> When we conducted meetings and interviews with the candidates we had lined up, Punch stood out like a bright light. He liked the challenge our franchise presented. He certainly had everything we wanted in a general manager: stature and credibility within hockey circles, a background of being successful,

and a business awareness that was truly a revelation to some of the members of our board. He was a guy who could do it all, and on top of that, he was brash, topical, entertaining, and exactly the kind of personality we needed to sell NHL hockey in Buffalo.

Gerry Meehan, who became one of the first Sabres when Imlach selected him in the 1970 expansion draft, agreed. "I think great stability is what comes to mind when I think of Punch," Meehan said. "He brought to the organization a reputation as a winner from Toronto, and he was a winner at the minor pro level in Quebec City. He was the steely, hard-working, aggressive, no-nonsense leader that a young team needed. I can't imagine anyone else being more perfect for this job."

As someone once said after his gall bladder surgery, "In Imlach's case, they probably removed the bladder and left the gall." But that's what made Imlach the successful hockey man that he was.

As remarkable as his tenure was in Toronto, you could argue that Imlach's stint in Buffalo was even more impressive. After all, he built the Sabres from the ground up, starting with his first overall draft pick, Gilbert Perreault. Through tremendous drafting and trading, he had the team—which had to compete in the East Division with the established Original Six teams—in the playoffs by their third season, and in the Stanley Cup Finals in year five.

Imlach coached the first season and a half before being sidelined by a heart attack that ended his coaching career. He remained on as GM until being fired in 1978, leaving an unmatched legacy in Buffalo.

"Running the Buffalo hockey club will be the toughest job in hockey," Imlach said the day he signed his first Sabres contract. "The tougher it is, the better I like it. This is a job of building from the bottom up. I've done it before and I can do it again."

10 Soviet Slaughter

The importance of Buffalo's seismic 12–6 demolition of the Soviet Union Wings in January 1976 didn't hit hulking defenseman Jerry Korab until he and his Sabres teammates skated onto the ice at the Montreal Forum the next night.

In fact, it hit him about as hard as one of the many crunching body checks he had delivered the day before at Memorial Auditorium, when the Sabres dazzled the hockey world with an epic performance that sent the mighty Russians scurrying back to their locker room in shame.

"I'll never forget going into the Forum the next night and getting a standing ovation from the Montreal fans for our victory over the Soviets," Korab recalled. "That was something to remember."

Punch Imlach remembered it for the rest of his life.

Imlach, the architect of the Buffalo franchise and its general manager at the time, went to his grave in December 1987 secure in his belief that the Sabres' victory over the Soviets was the proudest moment of his Hall of Fame hockey career. Here was a man who had coached the Toronto Maple Leafs to four Stanley Cup championships during the 1960s, then built the Sabres from the ground up as an expansion team and watched it reach the Finals in just its fifth year of existence in 1975. Yet it was this game, played on a Sunday afternoon at the sold-out and perhaps-never-louder Aud, an exhibition that meant nothing in the NHL standings, from which Imlach derived his greatest satisfaction. "It had to be one of Punch's most gratifying days in hockey," recalled Floyd Smith, the Sabres coach at that time. "I couldn't have cared less, but it was a personal thing for Punch."

Never mind that the game was played during a period in American history when relations between the United States and the former Soviet Union were dangerously frigid. The Cold War was still raging and tensions between the super powers were at a boiling point, both politically and athletically. But none of this concerned Imlach. He wasn't American—he was Canadian through and through—and while he recognized the sociological differences between the U.S. and the Soviet Union, to him this game wasn't about that. As Smith said, this was personal to Imlach because as a proud Canadian, he was infuriated by the ever-growing worldwide perception that the Soviets were surpassing Canada as hockey's premier superpower. Hockey was Canada's game, and Imlach hated everything about the Soviet hockey juggernaut.

So when the NHL Board of Governors agreed to host a series of eight exhibition games pitting NHL teams against two touring Soviet teams—the Red Army and the Wings—Imlach was thrilled when his Sabres were chosen along with Montreal, Philadelphia, the New York Rangers, Pittsburgh, Chicago, Boston, and the New York Islanders to represent the league.

"I remember the Soviet Wings game as if it was yesterday," Korab said. "Imlach told us in no uncertain terms he wanted this game—a lot. Well, he couldn't have wanted it any more than each and every player on the team, or the fans. We came onto the ice, and it had to be several minutes before it quieted down. They couldn't even introduce the players. We were just shaking, we were so excited. We could almost feel the ice shake. It was like we were going to war. Right after the anthems, the noise was so loud the building reverberated."

And it didn't stop for the next two-and-a-half hours as the Sabres dismantled the Soviets.

"That game sticks in my mind, and I still get goose bumps thinking about it," said Rick Martin. "The crowd was fired up, the team was fired up, and if we would have played like that against the NHL teams, there wasn't a team that could have touched us."

Korab set the tone in the first few minutes with a big body check on Soviet star Alexander Yakushev. "I remembered how Yakushev drove Team Canada batty in the '72 [Summit] Series," Imlach said. "He would sneak along the boards to the side of the Canadian net, stand just off the post, and deflect pucks. Having him there meant our goalie had to play back in the net, and that reduced their effectiveness. We had Korab cued to watch for big Yak sneaking around the boards to get to his favorite spot. When Yakushev saw big Kong [Korab] coming, he jumped up against the boards to try to avoid the hit, and Korab caught him in the gut with his shoulder."

The crowd roared its approval, and the Soviets shriveled. Buffalo defenseman Jocelyn Guevremont scored the first goal of the game six minutes into the first period with a blast from the point, and the bloodletting was underway. Gilbert Perreault and Martin scored to make it 3–0. After a Soviet power-play goal, Martin picked off a pass Imlach had told the team to watch out for during film study, then cruised in alone to make it 4–1. "Jesus, you were right," Martin said to Imlach after the game.

The score was 4–2 at the end of the first period, 9–4 after two. In tacking on to their advantage in the third, the Sabres continued to physically pound the Wings. "It was the high point of the season for me, beating the Russians so handily, so completely," said Imlach. Martin finished with two goals and three assists, Fred Stanfield with a goal and three assists, and Danny Gare with two goals.

Red Fisher, the esteemed hockey writer for the *Montreal Gazette*, wrote of Buffalo's greeting from the fans: "It was a thunderous display of admiration for a team which had excelled. It was public, yet somehow private. It was something these 18,000 people wanted to share with the Sabres, and with them alone. It was rich and warming. It may never happen again to a team coming in to play Montreal, but those who were there to hear and witness it will never forget it."

Rico

He grew up just outside of Ottawa in the small town of Hull, where hockey was such a passion that the kids would trudge off to school each morning with their books, their lunches, *and* their hockey equipment.

"We'd bring our sticks to school and go right from there to the outdoor rinks," Rick Martin once said. "Then we'd go home, eat, do our homework, and go back out and play, because the rinks were lit at night. There were parish rinks every two or three blocks, so there was always somewhere to play."

The story is much the same in most of the other small towns there in the corridor where the Ottawa River separates Ontario from Quebec.

"We'd play every day, and there'd be 30 guys out there, 15 on each team," Martin said. "Just think of it: when there's 15 guys on your side, you're going to run into your own guys half the time. You developed some good quickness and skills in tight. That's why guys like Perreault and [Guy] Lafleur were so good with the puck; that's the way they were brought up. Usually, one guy would get the puck and just go."

Gilbert Perreault made a name for himself skating circles around the kids in Victoriaville, Quebec, and Guy Lafleur did the same in Thurso, but Martin did it a different way in Hull. He, too, was a wonderful skater, but what separated him from his peers was his shot.

Sabres left winger Rick Martin takes the ice during an NHL game in 1975. One-third of the famed "French Connection" line of the 1970s, Martin was known for having one of the hardest shots in the game. Photo courtesy of Getty Images

Oh, what a shot it was. And it was that shot, and the frequency with which it ended up in the net, that prompted Sabres general manager Punch Imlach to say Martin was "the greatest natural goal scorer I've seen."

Martin exploded on the NHL scene in 1971–1972, when he set the league record for goals by a rookie with 44, then netted 37 in his sophomore season. After that came back-to-back 52-goal seasons, and if he had scored just one more in 1975–1976, he would have joined Phil Esposito as the only players in history to that point with three straight 50-goal seasons.

"You hear about a heavy shot, but with his it was a wisp and it was by you," said Glenn "Chico" Resch, who saw more than he wanted of Martin's howitzers during his days tending net for the Islanders and the Colorado Rockies. "When goalies go into a game, they have mental checklists: who do you have to worry about? Rico was always at the top of the list.

"His shot wasn't as hard as Bobby Hull's, but he was up there for the quickness. His shot was one of those where you thought, 'If I don't get a jump on this, it's by me.' That was the big thing."

Resch's story was shared by many of the goaltenders who faced Martin during the 1970s. One of those was the obscure Lyle Carter, who played briefly for California in 1971–1972, Martin's rookie season. "Martin hit me with a shot, and I thought it had gone through my skin and stuck in my ribs," said Carter. "I felt it for a month. It can carry your glove right off your hand."

"I didn't slap pucks at walls [the way Bobby Orr said he used to when he was growing up], but I shot a lot of pucks during practice," Martin said. "I always had a natural shot, but as I started playing junior, then I really worked on it. I always had a lot of speed on it, so I started working on quickness and accuracy. I'm not going to say I didn't have a natural ability, but I also worked a lot harder on it than most guys. Every day after practice, I'd stay out there a little longer. I'd shoot more pucks in one year than some guys shoot in 10.

"When I got to the NHL, I found out right away that if you want to play at this level, it was all about quickness and reaction. The opening is only there for a second, so you're talking about trying to gain just fractions of seconds, but that was the difference between getting the shot off and getting your ass flattened."

Injuries curtailed Martin's scoring during the late 1970s, but he did enjoy one more great year when Scotty Bowman took over the team in 1979. Even though the French Connection had been dismantled when Bowman traded Rene Robert just before the start of the season, Martin scored 45 goals, and the Sabres narrowly missed a second trip to the Stanley Cup Finals.

But Martin was convinced that Bowman did not like him, and their relationship soured early in the 1980–1981 season. Martin suffered a knee injury in an altercation with Washington goalie Mike Palmateer, and Martin always insisted that Bowman did not believe he was seriously injured. With Martin only able to play sporadically over the next three months, Bowman worked hard to find a trade partner—and that team wound up being Los Angeles. Bowman

50-Goal Scorers

There have been only six occasions in which a Sabres sniper scored at least 50 goals in a season, and Rick Martin had the distinction of being the first to do so.

Martin scored 52 goals in 1973–1974, even though his playmaking center and French Connection linemate, Gilbert Perreault, missed a third of the season with a broken leg.

Martin then scored 52 again the following year when the Sabres advanced to the Stanley Cup Finals. The hard-shooting left winger just missed making it three years in a row when he scored 49 in 1975–1976.

Danny Gare is the only other Sabre to have two 50-goal seasons; he scored a hat trick in the final game of the 1975–1976 season to get to 50, and then had 56 in 1979–1980.

The only other players who have eclipsed the magical mark are Alexander Mogilny, who owns the single-season team-record with 76 goals in 1992–1993, and Pat LaFontaine, who scored 53 on his way to a team-record 148 points during that same season.

shipped Martin and Don Luce to the Kings, bringing an unsatisfying end to a magnificent, decade-long term in Buffalo during which Martin scored 382 goals and 695 points.

Martin played only four games for the Kings before retiring, and he later named the Sabres, several doctors, a Buffalo hospital, and Bowman in a $10-million malpractice lawsuit that was ultimately settled out of court in Martin's favor about 10 years later.

Despite that bad blood, Martin eventually returned to the Sabres family, had his No. 7 retired by the team, and became an ambassador for the franchise. He was a frequent visitor to HSBC Arena, and was a popular participant in charity golf tournaments and Sabres functions until he passed away due to a heart attack in March 2011.

Breakfast, Anyone?

In 1981 the Winnipeg Jets used the No. 1 overall pick to select Dale Hawerchuk. When it was their turn to make a selection in the 10th round with the 196th overall pick, the Pittsburgh Penguins took a gritty winger by the name of Dave Hannan.

A quick look at the two men's résumés would indicate that their draft positions were pretty much on the mark. Hawerchuk went on to score 518 goals and 1,409 points and is enshrined in the Hockey Hall of Fame, while Hannan and his 114 goals and 305 points will only be a visitor to the museum in downtown Toronto.

However, in the early morning hours of April 28, 1994, during the fourth overtime period in Game 6 of Buffalo's first-round playoff series against New Jersey (which had started on April 27), it wasn't Hawerchuk who scored one of the most memorable goals in team history. It was Hannan, whose backhander beat Devils goalie

Martin Brodeur, ending the longest game any Sabres team has ever played.

"I've always been a big part of a team's success in a small way," said Hannan, alluding to the fact that he was the type of player who did the little things that are so vital while rarely pulling off the big things—like scoring overtime goals in the playoffs. "And that's what makes me feel good, because I've always been consistent, and the respect of my teammates is what I enjoy. That is what you look for in the game."

He sure earned a measure of respect that night, not to mention hearty thank yous all around from his exhausted teammates after he ended what was then the sixth-longest game in NHL history: a six-hour, 12-minute marathon that ended at 1:52 in the morning.

Of course the real hero of the night was Dominik Hasek, who stopped all 70 shots New Jersey fired at him, including 39 in the overtime periods, in what was a pressure-packed elimination game for the Sabres.

"Hasek played the best game I've ever seen a goaltender play," said New Jersey's Bobby Carpenter. Added Brodeur, who stopped the first 49 shots he saw before Hannan finally beat him: "We had so many chances, but [Hasek] came up big. It was unbelievable."

With Wednesday night morphing into Thursday morning and zeroes filling the scoreboard, it seemed as if the teams would play forever. The Aud began to thin out. "I thought they were great hanging in here that long," Sabres defenseman Randy Moller said of the fans who stayed. "And they were still yelling and screaming at the end. Maybe they passed out amphetamines or something."

Even the players made light of the situation. Sabres winger Randy Wood recalled, "Going out for the seventh period, guys in the locker room were saying, 'This is unbelievable. Somebody score a goal. We've got to go home, we're going to have a huge baby-sitting bill.'"

Easy as 1-2-3

Although a great goaltender, Ed Belfour was always considered a bit of a loose cannon—and that was clearly evident on the night of March 22, 1992, when he was tending net for the Chicago Blackhawks.

In a game at Chicago Stadium, the Sabres peppered Belfour for five second-period goals, including three in a span of 39 seconds, the fastest three-goal spurt in Sabres history. Pat LaFontaine, Wayne Presley, and Donald Audette produced the historic trio of goals. Shortly thereafter, Belfour's anger exploded.

He left his crease to go into the corner to check LaFontaine, prompting Sabres tough guy Rob Ray to retaliate. That touched off a brawl, and by the time Buffalo's easy 6–2 victory was complete, the teams had combined for 207 penalty minutes.

With Belfour clearly off his game—and maybe his rocker—Blackhawks coach Mike Keenan yanked him for the third period and sent in Chicago's backup, a guy named Dominik Hasek. Five months later, the Sabres acquired Hasek in a trade for goalie Stephane Beauregard and a fourth-round pick (which turned out to be Eric Daze).

As for the Sabres fastest two goals, that happened on October 17, 1974, when Don Luce and Lee Fogolin scored four seconds apart (it was Fogolin's first NHL goal).

That it was Hannan, the 10th-round draft choice, who scored the goal, probably shouldn't have been a surprise—there's been a long list of unlikely overtime goal-scorers throughout Stanley Cup playoff history.

"It's funny, they say in overtime games in the playoffs, it's the grinders who always score the goal," Hannan said. "Our line [Hannan, Wayne Presley, and Jason Dawe] had a lot of chances to score that night. A couple of times, Wayne and I came down on two-on-ones. I didn't want to shoot, so I passed it over to him and let him take the shot because he's the scorer on our line. He would come back to the bench [after not scoring] and say, 'Just shoot the puck. If you get a chance, just shoot the puck.'"

So Hannan took his linemate's advice and scored the goal that made his name a permanent part of NHL lore. "My first thoughts were, 'We're going to Game 7.' Then I was so tired, I wanted to lie down right there," Hannan said.

13 The Winter Classic

The game itself that New Years Day of 2008 was a snooze: a choppy, sloppy bore-a-thon that was plagued by constant stoppages of play to repair the makeshift ice surface built in the middle of the football field at Ralph Wilson Stadium.

But if you asked anyone in the crowd of 71,217 who had come to watch the Winter Classic if they cared one bit, they would have screamed "no" and then pelted you with a snowball for having interrupted their tailgate party to ask the question.

When the Sabres played host to the Pittsburgh Penguins at the home of their NFL brethren, the Buffalo Bills, it wasn't just a hockey game. It was an event, one of the biggest ever staged in western New York. "I don't think they can equal it," Sabres broadcaster Rick Jeanneret said, speaking of the NHL. "I know they're going to have one every year, or two every year, whatever they've got to do. I just don't think they can capture what we had at that football stadium on that afternoon."

There had already been an outdoor game played between Montreal and Edmonton back in 2003 in Alberta, Canada, and more than 57,000 Canadians didn't seem to mind frigid temperatures that dipped below zero. The night was spectacular.

Following the 2004–2005 NHL lockout, when the struggling league began exploring the possibility of creating an annual outdoor game—if for no other reason than to create some buzz in the

United States—it considered several cities. Buffalo was the obvious choice. After all, which American city, at least based on reputation, was better-suited to hosting the Winter Classic than wintry Buffalo? Not to mention that scheduling wouldn't be an issue. Ralph Wilson Stadium would surely be vacant by then because the building's moribund tenants, the Bills, hadn't played a home playoff game since 1996—or any type of playoff game since January 2000. (Through 2011, they still hadn't.)

As for Buffalo's opponent, the league chose the Penguins for two obvious reasons: the presence of the iconic Sidney Crosby, the NHL's best player and most marketable commodity, and the proximity of Pittsburgh to Orchard Park—close enough for thousands of Pittsburghers to make the trip north for the game.

Criticize the NHL for any number of things—and it usually deserves it—but the league knocked this one out of the proverbial park. The Ralph was a magnificent venue, and every available ticket

The Sabres play the Pittsburgh Penguins during the second period of the NHL Winter Classic outdoor hockey game at Ralph Wilson Stadium in Orchard Park, New York, on New Year's Day in 2008.

was purchased, including thousands by Penguins fans. Merchandise sales reportedly reached $1 million. Snow fell intermittently, which made the scene remarkably picturesque and unique. And of course Crosby lived up to his superstar billing, scoring the walk-off goal in a shootout to give the Penguins a 2–1 victory that hardly put a damper on the day.

"The atmosphere and excitement, I don't think you can beat that," Crosby said. "It's something to look back and say we had a lot of great memories being a part of it."

Easy for him to say, playing on the winning team. But Adam Mair of the losing Sabres felt the same way. "It was a great stage for the National Hockey League to get an event like this and send it across the United States and Canada," Mair said. "I think they got what they were expecting. You couldn't have scripted it any better. You had the best player in the world going against arguably one of the best goaltenders [Ryan Miller] in the world at the end. It was great."

With snow falling pretty steadily in the first period, the ice was treacherous and the game had to be stopped for both repairs and to sweep off the accumulating snow. "It's too bad it snowed so hard because you couldn't do much with the puck out there," Sabres left wing Jochen Hecht said. "All we could do most of the time was dump it in and chase it. There was no room for nice plays, so that was the only bad thing about it."

Colby Armstrong scored 21 seconds into the game by banging home a rebound after Miller had stopped Crosby. But from there the Sabres carried the play until Brian Campbell scored the tying goal early in the second off a pass from Tim Connolly.

Through a scoreless third period, Buffalo continued to dominate, but ex-Sabres goalie Ty Conklin, playing for injured Pittsburgh regular Marc-Andre Fleury, never cracked. In the shootout, Ales Kotalik scored for the Sabres, but then Miller allowed a goal to Kris Letang, setting the stage for Crosby to break the tie.

Oh, What a Night

The night of January 27, 1991, will live in infamy in Buffalo. That was the evening that Bills placekicker Scott Norwood was wide right on a 47-yard field-goal attempt, allowing the New York Giants to defeat the Bills 20–19 in Super Bowl XXV.

It is a defeat that Buffalo fandom has never forgotten; more than two decades later, it still stands as the city's most crushing pro sports moment.

That was an altogether lost weekend for Buffalo's primary pro sports franchises; the Sabres also came up empty, dropping a 5–4 decision at the Aud to Calgary after losing 4–1 in Montreal the night before. Those two losses kick-started what became a six-game losing streak as the Sabres failed to provide any comfort to a wounded region in the immediate aftermath of the Super Bowl loss.

The other three times the Bills played in—and lost—Super Bowl games, the Sabres won only once: on January 26, 1992, when the Bills dropped Super Bowl XXVI 37–24 to Washington. The Sabres defeated Winnipeg that night, 5–2. On January 31, 1993, the Bills were embarrassed by Dallas in Super Bowl XXVII, 52–17, and the Sabres lost 5–4 in overtime at Edmonton. And on January 30, 1994, the Bills lost 30–13 to Dallas in Super Bowl XXVIII, while the Sabres fell 3–2 at the Aud to Florida.

"It was great for hockey and great for the city of Buffalo," Sabres center Connolly said. "Unfortunately, we didn't come out with the win."

This was one day that Sabres fans didn't mind losing.

14 Thank You, Sabres

From the moment the Sabres came into existence prior to the 1970–1971 season, they established an immediate and undeniable connection to the city, something neither the Buffalo Bills nor the Buffalo Braves had at their births.

When the Bills began play in the fledgling American Football League in 1960, they drew only mediocre crowds to War Memorial Stadium. It wasn't until 1963, when they began to show signs of becoming a winner—and the AFL was starting to be taken seriously—that the fans took notice.

As for the Braves, they simply had the misfortune of being born and joining the National Basketball Association the same year the Sabres became a National Hockey League franchise. From the very beginning the Sabres outdrew the Braves at the Aud, and with the exception of a few years during the mid-1970s, the Braves struggled both on the court and at the gate, ultimately lasting only eight seasons in Buffalo before moving to San Diego.

Even during their first two seasons, when victories were few and far between, the fans showed remarkable support for the Sabres. And when the team rewarded that loyalty with a stunning performance in 1972–1973, earning a Stanley Cup playoff berth in just their third season, that support soared to an unprecedented level.

On the night of April 12, 1973, as the powerful Montreal Canadiens were finishing off a six-game first-round series victory over the Sabres, the fans let it be known what this team meant to them.

It started in the upper balcony, the orange-colored seats where fans were afforded a panoramic view of the ice surface at the expense of a nose bleed. "Thank You, Sabres," they chanted, as the final minute of that magical season ticked away on the big royal blue scoreboard that hovered over the center-ice faceoff circle. Like lava pouring from a volcano, the chant slid down to the blue seats, and then to the reds. "Thank You, Sabres. Thank You, Sabres," they sang in unison, the decibel level increasing with each verse until the folks in the upper and lower golds had joined the chorus—and then it couldn't get any louder.

"Thank You, Sabres. Thank You, Sabres. Thank You, Sabres." Over and over it reverberated throughout the arena, a passionate, appreciative, and heart-warming salute that puddled the eyes of those who were being thanked—Gilbert Perreault, Rick Martin, Rene Robert, Roger Crozier, Jim Schoenfeld, Tim Horton, Craig Ramsay, Don Luce, Gerry Meehan, and the rest of the Sabres.

It did not matter that the Sabres were about to be eliminated by the eventual champion Canadiens. All that mattered was that this young, energetic hockey team had given the citizens of Buffalo—people in desperate need of an escape from the harsh realities of a failing economy, horrid weather, and the pitiful Bills—a reason to smile, a reason to put their troubles aside.

"I'll never forget it," said Robert, emotion gripping his voice as he recalled that night. "I've never experienced anything like that in my life. Here we are, getting beat out in the playoffs, and the fans are cheering, 'Thank You, Sabres.' This is something that I'll always remember. This is an experience that someone has to have somewhere down the road. It brings tears to your eyes."

Martin interrupted this outpouring of gratitude when he scored with 12 seconds remaining to bring the final score to 4–2. But soon after the fans had finished celebrating the last goal of the season, they picked up the chant again, serenading their beloved Sabres throughout the traditional postgame handshakes.

"It was kind of the signature of the Buffalo people," said Schoenfeld. "They identified very strongly with their athletes and their teams, and if you gave them an honest day's effort, that's all they asked for. Everybody would like to be associated with a championship team and everybody wants to identify with a winner, but these people went beyond that. If you gave them everything you have, that was enough to satisfy them, and they felt that season that we had given everything we had, and this was their way of showing their appreciation for that effort."

15 The Defection of Mogilny

In the spring of 1988, Don Luce, the Sabres' director of player personnel, attended the world junior hockey championships in Moscow and was mesmerized by a 19-year-old Russian rocket named Alexander Mogilny.

Mogilny had become the youngest Soviet Union player to win an Olympic gold medal when he helped the Central Red Army to victory at the Calgary Games a few months earlier. Now he was back with the Soviet junior team, dominating play and earning the tournament's designation as best forward.

"He may have been the best player in the world at that time, that was my feeling when I saw him," Luce recalled.

When Luce returned to America to continue planning for the Sabres 1988 amateur draft, he and general manager Gerry Meehan discussed the possibility of using their extra fifth-round draft choice to acquire Mogilny.

"At that time no Russian player had come out, so it was a gamble, no question. But we had an extra fifth-round pick," Luce said. Meehan agreed it was worth it, even though the chances were remote that the Soviet Union would allow Mogilny to come west and play in the NHL.

In January 1989 Luce and Buffalo's director of scouting, Rudy Migay, traveled to Anchorage, Alaska, to watch the world junior championships once again, and they made it a point to meet with Mogilny and make sure he knew that the Sabres had drafted him.

"We ran into Alex in the hallway of the hotel he was staying at," Luce said. "He spoke broken English, and I didn't even know if he understood what I was saying, but I gave him my business card. I told him we had drafted him the previous June, and if he wanted to talk, to give me a call."

That call, made by a friend of Mogilny's, came as Luce was sitting in his office at the Aud on Tuesday, May 2, 1989. After being assured it wasn't some hoax, and that indeed Mogilny was in Stockholm, Sweden, with the Russian national team and was planning to defect, Luce ran down to Meehan's office and told his boss what was going on. Meehan then requested and received permission from team owners Seymour and Northrup Knox to pursue the matter. What transpired over the next 72 hours was straight out of a James Bond movie.

"We had to visit the U.S. embassy, which Gerry did, because we didn't want to take Alex in until we had everything in place," said Luce. "And we were going from hotel to hotel, checking out of one in the morning to go to another one at night to make sure we weren't being trailed. We were told to be very careful, and I guess looking back it was more dangerous than we thought it was at the time. It was kind of like, you do it, but you don't realize what could really happen. This had never been attempted before, so what Alex did took an unbelievable amount of courage. It was a scary time for him, as well as Gerry and myself."

Though excited about the prospect of luring Mogilny to America, Meehan proceeded cautiously. "I had never met Alex, never seen him, so I wasn't convinced that we had the real thing until I got Don in the same room as Alex and Don confirmed that he was the guy," Meehan said. "We went to the hotel where Alex's friend was registered, and sitting on the sofa were two individuals with Alex between them. I asked Don if that was Alex Mogilny. He said, 'That's him,' and I said, 'Let's get to work.'"

Meehan's expertise in immigration law greatly facilitated the process. When the legalities were finalized, Luce and Meehan plotted their final strategy: getting to the airport and getting the hell out of Stockholm with the player who they felt could turn the Sabres franchise around.

"We didn't know what was going to happen, we just knew we had to be secretive," Luce said. "We ended up leaving the rental car in the hotel basement when we left to go to the airport and took a cab. We didn't know if we were being followed. Our flight wasn't until the afternoon, but we left before dawn so we'd get to the airport by 6:00 or 7:00 in the morning, because once you're in the airport, you're kind of shut off from the public."

Said Meehan, "Once we passed passport control, there was a sense of relief. There had been a suggestion that Alex had been kidnapped, and what we were concerned about when we got to the airport early in the morning was whether we would be identified by anybody who was looking for Mogilny as a kidnap victim, or anybody at passport control who might have been advised to be on the lookout for Alex."

Once inside the terminal, Luce and Meehan learned how narrow an escape they had pulled off.

"Alex had his friend with him who could speak English, and he bought a paper and it had a trail of some of the hotels we had been at," Luce said. "The Russian team had left Sweden, and Alex wasn't with them, so there were two or three days where they didn't know where he was. I guess the media found this out, so they must have figured Buffalo owned his rights, and they probably checked the hotel registers to see if Gerry was in town, and he was. It was quite a trip, one I'll never forget."

16 Drury and Briere Bolt

On the afternoon of July 1, 2007, the Sabres did not lose a game, nor did a member of their extended family pass away. But there isn't much doubt that it was one of the saddest days in the team's four-plus decades of existence.

When the NHL's free agency signing period began, it took barely minutes for the Philadelphia Flyers and the New York Rangers to deliver a pair of daggers to the collective hearts of Sabres fans—not to mention to a Buffalo team that was considered one of the up-and-comers in the league, with back-to-back appearances in the Eastern Conference Finals.

Unable to come to contract terms with cocaptains Chris Drury and Danny Briere, the team lost both players, who bolted Buffalo for big-money deals. Drury went back home to the tristate area to play for the team he followed as a kid—the Rangers—for five years at $35.25 million. Meanwhile, Briere jumped all over an astounding eight-year, $52-million deal offered him by the Flyers.

Just like that, two players who'd scored a combined 69 goals and 164 points in 2006–2007 were gone: Drury, the heart and soul of the team, and Briere, it's most talented offensive player. Given their skill, their leadership, and their popularity with the fans, it was a dark, dark summer day in Buffalo. In fact, even several years later, angry fans still think of those departures as the reason why the Sabres failed to make the playoffs in 2007–2008 and were knocked out in the first round each of the following two seasons.

The circumstances surrounding the departure of both players were maddening; it appeared that both Drury and Briere hoping to return to the team, but management didn't do enough to make it happen.

In Drury's case, it became public knowledge that his agent and Sabres general manager Darcy Regier had come to an agreement at the start of the season on what was believed to be a four-year deal worth $21.5 million. But Regier never officially offered the proposal for signing. "We had conversations with Chris in particular in the fall, and unfortunately weren't able to come to a deal," Regier said during a press conference. "Things evolved, things changed."

When that deal fell through, Drury decided to bag negotiations during the season, waiting until the off-season when they could see what the market would bear. "When it got so close to free agency, the potential to maybe see what the Rangers wanted and if they were interested—come noon Sunday when they were—I knew that it was somewhere that I wanted to go and to kind of fulfill a lifelong dream," Drury told the *Buffalo News*. "I thought showing a little more urgency certainly would have helped the situation, if in fact [the Sabres] did want me back."

Sabres managing partner Larry Quinn even admitted, "I think we probably failed somewhere. Chris Drury, to me, is the epitome of a great hockey player and a great person. I really wanted him to continue here. We weren't able to do that."

As for Briere, Regier said he knew during the 2006–2007 season that it was going to be very difficult to retain Briere because he would command the type of contract that the small-market Sabres could not match. Sure enough, that's what happened when the Flyers burst through the door.

"We're going to be less competitive without Danny Briere and Chris Drury," Regier said that day with a look of anguish and concern splashed across his face. "But the sky's not falling. This is a good hockey club. We'll be good. We'll figure out a way—somehow, some way—to be better. But people shouldn't give up on these young men. They shouldn't give up on the coaching staff. They shouldn't give up on the community. The sky's not falling."

Maybe not, but it sure felt that way that day, a day that will live in Sabres infamy.

17 Continental Flight 3407

For much of the day, the Sabres' management team considered postponing the game scheduled for that Friday night in February 2009 at HSBC Arena against the San Jose Sharks. And the NHL was fully on board with that decision if that's what the Sabres wanted to do.

But after much debate, the organization decided that the one way it could help a grieving community was to play the game and give fans at the arena, as well as those at home watching on television, two-plus hours to forget the sorrow of what had taken place the night before.

Less than 24 hours earlier, Continental Flight 3407—a regional plane that had originated in Newark, New Jersey—fell from the sky above Clarence Center, an area where several members of the Sabres organization lived, and crashed into a home, killing one person on the ground and all 50 people aboard. The flight had been only minutes away from landing at the Greater Buffalo Niagara Falls International Airport.

"I think that people want to be with other people in times like this," Sabres president Larry Quinn told a gathering of reporters after the first intermission of the game. "I think the arena and the games here are really our town hall. It's the only place in town where people from different strata of society get together. People that aren't here are probably gathered in their family rooms watching the game with family, so I think it does have a nice community purpose to it."

This was one night when perhaps the result of the game wasn't really paramount. But there was no doubt, given the reaction inside the arena, that when Jason Pominville tipped in Craig Rivet's shot from the point with 3.9 seconds left to force overtime, the score meant something. And then when Derek Roy gave the Sabres the lead in the shootout after a scoreless overtime, and Ryan Miller stopped San Jose's last attempt by Milan Michalek, the building erupted in thankful glee. The Sabres' 6–5 victory had provided the community with a vital shot in the arm.

"It's been a real tough day for all of Buffalo," Rivet said. "If it can somewhat ease the pain that's going to happen, I hope it helped."

A few of the players lived less than a mile from the crash site, and actually heard the plane coming and the horrifying sound of the crash.

"I was in my bed, and I heard it and thought it sounded really weird, really close to us," said defenseman Teppo Numminen. "Then I heard a little poof afterward, and I was thinking, 'That doesn't sound good, doesn't sound right.' So I looked out of my window, and I saw the red sky, and I knew something was wrong."

Coach Lindy Ruff didn't hear the plane come down, but he heard the sound of emergency vehicle sirens filling the air. "I heard the sirens and watched [TV] 'til 1:30 in the morning," Ruff said. "It was incredible, surreal at times. You think maybe it's just something small [and then] ending up as big as it was. This is bigger than sports, it's a lot bigger. I know we have to play a game, but something this big touches way too many people."

The investigation into the crash—the first in the United States since 2006—went on for months, but the sense of loss will never go away for those who lost family members, many of whom were from the Buffalo area. But for one night, a hockey game helped some folks take their mind off the tragedy.

"We're happy that we can be a bit of a distraction, but hockey is just a small part of life," goalie Ryan Miller said. "We just hope we add to the people's feeling of community and feeling of pride for being from Buffalo."

18 The Only Place It Didn't Work

When news broke that Scotty Bowman had been hired to become the new general manager of the Sabres, team captain Danny Gare happened to be leaving town to return to his home in British Columbia for the summer after having spent the previous few days in a hospital recuperating from mononucleosis.

When Gare walked into a Buffalo bank to withdraw money for the trip, the teller recognized him and said, "Did you hear the news? Scotty Bowman is going to be the new general manager."

Gare's reaction, when questioned by reporters: "I didn't believe her. I didn't think they would ever get him, but it's great news."

And that's what everyone thought, most notably the team owners, Seymour and Northrup Knox, who managed to pry Bowman away from the dynastic Montreal Canadiens, where he'd just won four consecutive Stanley Cups as the head coach. "We feel we have obtained one of the top hockey men in the business in Scotty Bowman, and we are very hopeful of his winning a Stanley Cup for Buffalo," a smiling Seymour said that June 1979 day when Bowman was officially introduced as the top man.

Bowman—who had also won the Cup with Montreal in 1973, as well as having led the St. Louis Blues to three straight appearances in the Finals when he coached there in the late 1960s—was supposed to be the man who could finally get a talent-laden but sometimes underachieving Sabres team to the promised land. When he rode into Buffalo with all that Bowman bluster, it should have been the start of a glorious new era in Sabres history. But the Bowman years wound up terribly disappointing, a frustrating and fruitless pursuit of the elusive prize.

In addition to his five Cups in Montreal, Bowman would win four more (one with Pittsburgh in 1992 and three with Detroit in 1997, 1998, and 2002, the last with ex-Sabre Dominik Hasek as his goalie) after he was fired by the Knoxes in 1986, giving him an all-time record nine. But in the seven-plus years he ran the Sabres operation, the team won only three playoff series, and his last Buffalo team finished with the fewest points in the league for the first and only time in its history.

A Bad Time for a Slump

On November 17, 1984, Sabres coach Scotty Bowman was on the precipice of NHL history. With 689 career victories, he was just one behind all-time leader Dick Irvin when he brought the Sabres down to Washington to go after the record-tying win.

If you were in Las Vegas and were looking for a sure-thing wager, this might have been it. To this point in his career—covering his time with both Buffalo and Montreal—Bowman had coached against the Capitals 45 times and had never lost. Never.

This was the night that remarkable streak came to an end—Washington beat Buffalo 3–2. Little did Bowman know that this defeat was an ominous sign of a miserable month to come. From there, the Sabres went on an eight-game winless streak; it wasn't until December 8 when Bowman finally pulled even with Irvin when the Sabres defeated Boston 3–1. Four more winless games followed before Bowman passed Irvin on December 19 when the Sabres whipped Chicago 6–3.

That victory improved the then 51-year-old Bowman's record to 691–285–202. By the time he coached his final game for Detroit in 2002, Bowman's record was 1,244–573–314, plus 10 shootout losses. In the postseason he was 223–130 and won nine Stanley Cups—although unfortunately for Sabres fans, none of those Cups were won in Buffalo.

Bowman's time in Buffalo was marked by upheaval. He began his tenure as coach/GM in 1979–1980 and guided that team to the semifinals, where they lost to the eventual champion Islanders. The next year he was determined to concentrate on his GM duties, so he hired Roger Neilson as coach. But Neilson lasted only a year before Bowman went back behind the bench at the start of 1981–1982. Two months into that season, Bowman turned the coaching reins over to assistant Jimmy Roberts, one of his former Canadien star players. But then Bowman took back the job later that season and continued to coach until the end of 1985. Jim Schoenfeld was next, but Bowman relieved him less than three months into the 1985–1986 season and coached into the start of 1986–1987, when he was fired.

Bowman's vision when he arrived in Buffalo was to remake the roster with young stars as he weeded out many of the players left over from the 1970s. Those who left included mainstays such as Gare, Schoenfeld, Rick Martin, Rene Robert, and Jerry Korab. Bowman replaced them with a stockpile of first-round draft picks that he used on players like Mike Ramsey, Steve Patrick, Phil Housley, Tom Barrasso, Paul Cyr, Dave Andreychuk, and Adam Creighton.

"Because of previous occurrences with Scotty, there were two guys who said, 'The minute he comes here, we're gone,'" Martin said. "That was Korab and Robert. They were the first to go, and I said, 'I'm on the list; I'm not far behind.'"

It was a bold and ambitious rebuild, and the majority of those draft choices did actually enjoy solid careers with the Sabres. But the chemistry was always just a bit off, partly because of the often-nervous atmosphere that permeated the locker room due to Bowman's iron-fisted style.

His years with St. Louis and Montreal resulted in an amazing record of 529–193–150 in the regular season, 96–54 in the playoffs; in Pittsburgh and Detroit he was 509–247–104–10 in the regular season, 109–58 in the postseason. He also earned nine Cups and four other trips to the Finals. But the Buffalo years yielded no Cups, no Finals appearances, just one trip to a conference final, and a record of 210–134–60 in the regular season, 18–18 in the playoffs.

His former goalie in Montreal, fellow Hall of Famer Ken Dryden, may have described Bowman best when he said, "He is complex, confusing, misunderstood, unclear in every way but one: he is a brilliant coach."

It just didn't always seem like that in Buffalo.

19 The Derek Plante Goal

Although the scene on the ice was wonderful—with his young Buffalo Sabres teammates giddily celebrating one of the franchise's greatest victories—veteran defenseman Garry Galley knew the best was yet to come.

So after spending a few minutes partaking in the revelry that followed the never-to-be-forgotten Derek Plante overtime goal that decided Game 7 of Buffalo's 1997 first-round playoff series against the Ottawa Senators at Marine Midland Arena, Galley scrambled back to the locker room and grabbed a prime seat for the show.

"I watched everyone come in," he said. "I was one of the first guys in the room. I saw Teddy [Nolan, the head coach], Paul [Theriault, assistant coach], Donny [Lever, assistant coach], and all of the players. I really got a jolt out of watching those guys come in with their smiles. I knew what they were feeling, because I had been there before. To see these guys have that kind of smile on their faces after seeing so many long faces through this series over a lot of things, I think it was nice. You cannot teach it. For them to feel it and be a part of it is something that will help this organization take a real step forward."

Ottawa Senators goalie Ron Tugnutt reacts after allowing the winning goal by Sabres center Derek Plante in a 3–2 overtime victory for Buffalo in Game 7 of the first round of the 1997 playoffs.

Galley will never forget those priceless Kodak moments, those snapshots of gap-toothed Sabres kids like Plante and Michael Peca and Matthew Barnaby and Steve Shields bouncing into the locker room in the aftermath of the pulsating 3–2 victory that brought an end to a tumultuous and fabulously exciting NHL Eastern Conference quarterfinal series.

And none of the 18,595 patrons in the building that night will ever forget the sight of Plante's hot slap shot burning a hole through Ottawa goalie Ron Tugnutt's glove, the puck seemingly moving in slow motion as it floated into the net. Tugnutt was unable to reach behind himself to keep it out, resulting in the loudest roar heard in Buffalo since *New York Daily News* columnist Mike Lupica tagged the Buffalo Bills as "the serial killers of the Super Bowl" a few years earlier.

"What do I feel?" Plante said. "Relief. It's over and we're finally going on. There's been so much talk about how we haven't been able to get past the first round. We did it."

This was the Sabres' first ever Game 7 appearance at home, and it remains their only Game 7 victory.

Plante was the undeniable hero of the contest, but the Sabres might never have reached overtime if not for the play of unsung goalie Steve Shields. The young goaltender was making his fourth consecutive start in the series because superstar Dominik Hasek had suffered a season-ending knee injury early in Game 3 at Ottawa. "This is about as gutsy an effort as you're going to see," Dixon Ward said of Shields. "He just came out of nowhere. Nobody gave him much of a chance to contribute. When Dominik went down, a lot of people said, 'Uh-oh, trouble.' But he absolutely rose to the occasion. He is our series MVP."

The Senators were leading 2–1 in the third when Buffalo caught a huge break. When Plante won a faceoff from Alexei Yashin to the left of Tugnutt, the puck popped into the air, then floated right over Tugnutt's shoulder and into the net at 6:29. "I was actually trying to go to the net and was going to try to chip it by him and try to pass to [Michal] Grosek going to the net," Plante said. "Yashin realized it and he flung it harder than I did right into the net."

The Sabres carried play the rest of the period and brought the momentum into the overtime, but Ottawa had the better chances— Shields had to make two difficult saves to keep the Sabres alive.

Owning Ottawa

When the Ottawa Senators entered the NHL in 1992, their roster was littered with players who probably couldn't have made a quarter of the other team's lineups around the league. The Senators were among the worst first-year teams in the history of the league, and the Sabres certainly had a hand in their inaugural-season record of 10–70–4.

In the first game played between the two teams—who would later become fierce Northeast Division rivals—Buffalo rolled to a laughable 12–3 victory as Pat LaFontaine had two goals and three assists despite playing barely half the game before being ejected for committing a high-sticking major penalty.

That first year Buffalo went 5–1–1 against Ottawa and outscored the Senators a combined 35–15; by the time Ottawa had completed its fourth season, Buffalo owned a record of 17–3–2 against them and had outscored the team from Canada's capital city 99–42.

Things finally began to turn for Ottawa in 1996–1997; after losing the first four games to Buffalo, the Senators won the final two, earned their first playoff berth in franchise history, and extended the Sabres to seven games in a first-round series before losing.

Then Plante turned a rather innocent-looking play into a seismic occurrence when he knocked down a clearing attempt by Ottawa defenseman Steve Duchesne and unleashed the wicked drive that Tugnutt couldn't handle.

"As soon as he shot it, I kind of felt like it was going in," Nolan said. "To see the way it did go in, it kind of went in slow motion."

20 The Hockey Hall of Fame

For those who live in western New York, fascinating sports history is just a day trip away. The Baseball Hall of Fame is located about four hours away from Buffalo in Cooperstown, New York; the Basketball

Hall of Fame is about a six-hour ride in Springfield, Massachusetts; the Boxing Hall of Fame is three hours away in Canastota, New York; and the Pro Football Hall of Fame is located in Canton, Ohio, about seven hours away. But of course the closest of all is the Hockey Hall of Fame, which is just 90 minutes across the Canadian border in Toronto.

The Hockey Hall of Fame has long been a popular destination for Buffalo hockey fans, primarily because of its proximity, but also because of the passion that Buffalonians have for the game and its history. Fans often make the pilgrimage as part of an overnight stay in Toronto—Canada's largest city offers tourists a thriving entertainment center with great restaurants, concerts, and Broadway shows along with Major League Baseball's Blue Jays and the NBA Raptors.

The Hockey Hall of Fame—which is located on Yonge Street within walking distance of the home of the Maple Leafs, Air Canada Centre—has undergone a major overhaul to bring it up to date with today's multimedia technologies. Visitors can also see the Stanley Cup on display, as well as all the other major individual trophies and NHL awards.

As for the Sabres organization, it is well-represented in terms of Hall of Fame inductees. There are 18 men enshrined who had ties to the Sabres.

Topping the list is Gilbert Perreault, the original and greatest Sabre, who was inducted in 1990. Seven other Hall of Fame players spent part of their careers wearing the Sabres uniform: Tim Horton (inducted in 1977), Dale Hawerchuk (2001), Clark Gillies (2002), Grant Fuhr (2003), Pat LaFontaine (2003), Dick Duff (2006), and Doug Gilmour (2011).

The original principal owner of the Sabres, Seymour H. Knox III, earned his induction in 1993. As for front-office personnel, Punch Imlach, Buffalo's first coach and general manager, was inducted in 1984; Marcel Pronovost, who coached the Sabres briefly, was inducted in 1978 for his prowess as a player; and Scotty Bowman, the winningest coach in NHL history, was enshrined in 1991.

A distinguished list of media members who hailed from Buffalo and covered the team have also been inducted into the Hall, including newspaper reporters Charlie Barton (1985), Dick Johnston (1986), Jack Gatecliff (1995), and Jim Kelley (2004), and broadcasters Ted Darling (1994) and Rick Jeanneret (2012).

21 Procuring a Franchise

For nearly half a century, the NHL got on fine with only its original six franchises in Toronto, Montreal, Boston, New York, Detroit, and Chicago. The league was in major markets, its product was beloved, and those venues were packed to capacity just about every night.

But expansion had become a trend in the other major league sports, and the NHL realized it needed to bring its game to new regions in order to remain viable. In 1965 a plan was put forth to double the size of the league to 12 franchises. This got Fred Hunt to thinking that Buffalo would be an ideal place for the NHL to put down a stake.

Hunt was the general manager of Buffalo's AHL team, the Bisons, at the time. The club had been in operation for 25 years and had almost always drawn well at Memorial Auditorium. Buffalo also had a professional football team in the fledgling American Football League that would soon be part of a merger with the established National Football League. It seemed as if the time was right for the city to go major league in hockey, too.

One day Hunt was playing golf with a friend and hockey fanatic, Dr. George Collins. Hunt told Collins about the NHL expansion, and that the NHL had mandated that any prospective franchise

Why the *Sabres*?

Originality was foremost on the list of prerequisites established by Sabres owners Seymour and Northrup Knox when it came time to naming their new NHL franchise.

Buffalo's minor league AHL team had been named the Bisons, as was the city's triple-A baseball team—obvious derivatives of the city's namesake. Even the name of the town's pro football team, which had begun playing in the fledgling American Football League in 1960 and would join the National Football League in 1970, was a play on the Buffalo name, as they were called the Bills, a nod to that old cowboy, Buffalo Bill.

So the Knoxes put it to western New York's hockey fans to choose the nickname via a mail-in contest. This drew an overwhelming response; more than 13,000 entries were submitted, providing more than 1,000 possibilities.

Among the proposed names: the Flying Zeppelins, the Streaks, the Buzzing Bees, the Comets, the Mugwumps, and the Herd. In the end, the Knoxes chose the Sabres, which had been sent in by four people. Chuck Burr, the team's first public relations director, announced in a press release that "a sabre is renowned as a clean, sharp, decisive, and penetrating weapon on offense, as well as a strong parrying weapon on defense."

Once "Sabres" was officially chosen, a lottery was conducted among the four people who had suggested the name to determine who would receive the prize—two season tickets for the inaugural season. The winner turned out to be Robert Sonnelitter Jr. of Williamsville.

would need local revenue. Hunt then asked if Collins knew anyone who might be interested in putting a Buffalo bid together. Collins certainly did—brothers Seymour H. III and Northrup Knox.

Soon the Niagara Frontier Hockey Corporation was born. But there were substantial obstacles that would have to be overcome before the NHL would even consider Buffalo as one of its new locations. The Knoxes would need to negotiate a fair purchase price of the Bisons, then get other investors on board to finance the new expansion team. And they would need to convince the city to expand the Aud's capacity from 10,000 to at least 15,000, renovate it to NHL standards, and work out a lease that would be equitable to both the team and the city. "We tackled and solved these and other problems one by one," Seymour said.

So off to New York City the Knoxes went to present their bid to the expansion committee, one of 15 applications hailing from 10 different cities. "At the time of the initial franchise application, we were informed that we were the best-financed, prepared, and well-liked group among all the applicants," Seymour wrote in his book *Anatomy of a Franchise*. "Paradoxically, the league granted franchises to Los Angeles, Minnesota, Oakland, Philadelphia, Pittsburgh, and St. Louis, while shutting the door to us."

Though disappointed, the Knoxes were not deterred, and they kept all their options open. The first one that presented hope was the impending failure of the Oakland franchise. The team was in financial peril almost from the time it began playing, mainly due to lack of interest in the Bay Area.

The Knoxes decided to purchase a stake in the Oakland club with the intention of moving it to Buffalo. The NHL thanked the Knoxes, then told them they had to keep the team in Oakland because the league needed to establish itself on the West Coast. The Knoxes were in the NHL—just not in Buffalo.

At this point a compromise was reached. If the Knoxes continued to fund the team in Oakland, the league would consider a second expansion, perhaps as early as the 1970–1971 season. On January 20, 1969, the league approved the addition of two more teams. While the Knoxes now had their foot in the door, there was much more work to be done.

First, they had to find a buyer for the Oakland team—which they did in Trans-National Communications (who would later change the name of the team to the California Golden Seals). Then they needed more capital to pay the inflated expansion rate of $6 million. Finally, they needed to take care of all the original details that had been tied to their original bid involving the Aud and the city. Incredibly, in less than a year's time, the Knoxes made it all happen. On December 2, 1969, the NHL announced that its next two teams—bringing the league roster to 14—would be located in Buffalo and Vancouver.

22 A Spin of the Wheel

Former Canadiens great Bernie "Boom Boom" Geoffrion was working as a scout in between head coaching gigs in 1969 when he saw Gilbert Perreault during a trip back to his old stomping grounds in Montreal.

From high above the ice surface in the press box at the Forum, it didn't take long while watching Perreault play for the Junior Canadiens for Geoffrion to conclude that "you could start a franchise around a prospect like that." And that's exactly what Buffalo's Punch Imlach did thanks to one very fortuitous spin of a wheel.

On the afternoon of June 9, 1970, the ballroom of the Queen Elizabeth Hotel in Montreal was filled to capacity. There was a carnival-like atmosphere in the room—not surprising when the object of everyone's attention was a big, numbered wheel, "The kind you'd see on the midway," Imlach said.

That wheel was going to determine whether Buffalo or Vancouver would get the first selection in the NHL Entry Draft being held two days later—in other words, which team was going to win the right to pick Perreault, the perfect cornerstone to start an expansion team.

"I wore out my knees praying that I would win first choice in the amateur draft," Imlach wrote in his book *Heaven and Hell in the NHL*. "I wanted Gilbert Perreault as I had never wanted a hockey player before."

The wheel was numbered 1 through 13, with 7 being neutral and cause for a do-over. Imlach won a coin toss for the right to pick which set of numbers he preferred on the wheel, and he took the high digits, 8–13, leaving 1–6 for Vancouver GM Bud Poile.

NHL president Clarence Campbell then stepped up to conduct two spins of the wheel, the first to determine which team would have the initial choice in the Expansion Draft, the second spin—the Perreault spin—to determine who would have the first pick in the Entry Draft.

Around and around the wheel went, and when it stopped, it was on the No. 8. Imlach would have the first pick in the Expansion Draft—a victory, but considering the table scraps that would be available, a hollow one at that. Around and around the wheel spun a second time, and when it stopped, it looked like it was on the No. 1. At least that's what Campbell thought.

"Number one!" Campbell bellowed, touching off a raucous celebration by the Canucks contingent. "Vancouver wins first choice in the amateur draft."

Oops.

"The Sabre Dance"

When the Sabres settled on their moniker, it wasn't too hard to decide what the team's theme song would be.

"The Sabre Dance," written by Armenian composer Aram Khachaturian in 1942, is a movement in the final act of the ballet *Gayane* and depicts a whirling Armenian war dance in which the dancers display their skill with sabers. It was perfect for the fledgling hockey team.

The rapid pace of the song has lent "The Sabre Dance" to many other uses, as well. It has long been a popular concert band piece. It was also used as accompaniment by travelling circuses and on television variety shows such as *The Ed Sullivan Show* when novelty acts such as plate spinners appeared. More recently, the tune has been heard on episodes of *The Simpsons*, *The Big Bang Theory*, *Two and a Half Men*, and *Late Night with Conan O'Brien*.

The hand on the wheel had partially obliterated one of the 1s on the board and, in actuality, the winning number was 11. Imlach and the Sabres group leaped out of their seats to make this point, yelling, "Eleven, eleven!"

Campbell took another look and quickly corrected himself: "There has been a mistake [although he didn't say it had been his mistake]. The winning number is 11."

The Sabres picked Perreault. Appropriately enough, he donned a No. 11 sweater with the team, and went on to wear it for 16½ years in Buffalo before retiring early in the 1986–1987 season with 512 goals and 814 assists for 1,326 points. Vancouver took Dale Tallon second, who wound up scoring 98 goals and 238 assists for 336 points.

23 Breaking Down the Barriers

When you stand 6'2", weigh a little more than 200 pounds, and enjoy smashing your opponents into the boards, you get a reputation for being a tough guy.

Jim Schoenfeld was tough—no doubt about that—but he was never really comfortable being the team enforcer during his days as one of the Sabres' most accomplished and respected players.

"I don't think I ever really had a reputation of being a tough guy in junior," Schoenfeld said. "I don't think I was a player who went out of the way to look for a fight. Once in a while you have to fight, and if you do well, people might think that's something you might be suited for."

The people who were in the usual sellout crowd at the Aud on December 13, 1972, certainly got the impression that Schoenfeld was a fighter, and a pretty good one at that. In one of the most

The Sabres' Jim Schoenfeld (6) and the Penguins' Brian Spencer (22) race for the puck behind the net in second-period action in Buffalo on November 14, 1977.

memorable scenes—and games—in team history, Schoenfeld engaged in a wild brawl with Boston tough guy Wayne Cashman. The fight took on legendary status when both players went crashing through the doors to the Zamboni entrance and continued their mêlée on the concrete as the Aud rocked with glee.

"It gets magnified because the Zamboni doors flew open," Schoenfeld remembered. "If the doors don't fly open, then it's just another night, a hockey game with a couple of scraps. The fact that the doors flew open adds a definite signature to the night, but to me it was nothing more than two hungry teams battling hard."

Oh, it was much more than that. The big, bad Bruins, led by Bobby Orr and Phil Esposito, were the defending Stanley Cup

No Brotherly Love

On the night of April 7, 1997, the Sabres were in Hartford trying to wrap up their first Northeast Division title; they failed to do so, however, as the Whalers prevailed 4–2.

One Sabre suffered another defeat that night: Rookie center Wayne Primeau, playing against his brother, Keith, dropped the gloves and fought his older sibling for the first time—at least in an NHL game. Keith got the better of him.

"We're a close-knit family, but we're both the type of guys who like to win and will do whatever it takes to win," Wayne Primeau said at the time.

"It doesn't matter who it is," said Keith, who also scored a goal in the game. "He was scuffling with our goaltender [Sean Burke], and I had to do something. There was some hesitancy, yes. I knew who it was. That's blood, man. I was real disappointed it happened."

Wayne ultimately got the last laugh that year. The Sabres clinched the division a few nights later, and Keith's Whalers missed out on qualifying for the playoffs.

champions. They came to Buffalo riding a 12-game unbeaten streak. The Sabres, league doormats for their first two years in the NHL, had been the hockey story of the year for the first two months of the season. After winning only 16 games in 1971–1972, Buffalo had already won 14 and was battling the Bruins, the Canadiens, and the Rangers for superiority in the established East Division.

Even though the Sabres hadn't lost in 15 home games, the Bruins were unimpressed; they were intent on flexing their muscle, maintaining their reputation as the league's meanest and most physical team, and putting the upstart Sabres in their place. Schoenfeld, however, would have none of it. He squared off in separate bouts with Orr, Carol Vadnais, and then Cashman, and his inspired teammates—after falling behind 2–0—rallied to blow out the Bruins, 7–3, as Gilbert Perreault scored twice and his French Connection linemate Rene Robert came up with three assists.

Nearly 40 years have passed, and Schoenfeld still gets asked about that night. "Too much was made of that fight," he said. "It certainly didn't change my career, nor did it change Wayne Cashman's career. Wayne was a player I had a great deal of respect for as a kid watching him with the Bruins and then playing against him, and that respect probably grew after the fight. It wouldn't have mattered to Wayne if he would have spanked me in that fight, and it wouldn't have mattered to me if I would have spanked him. It was just part of the game. This was just one of those nights where we happened to be playing the Bruins and our team really pulled together and we won the hockey game."

24 Working Overtime

It has been said—at least by hockey fans—that there's nothing more exciting than overtime in the playoffs. Apparently Rene Robert didn't feel the same way, because he had a penchant for ending overtime games, usually in favor of the Sabres.

Robert scored the game-winner in three of the first four games in which the Sabres had to go beyond 60 minutes during the postseason—twice against the Montreal Canadiens and once against the Philadelphia Flyers.

The first time it happened—in Game 5 of Buffalo's first appearance in the playoffs, in 1973 against the Canadiens—defenseman Larry Hillman recalled seeing the play unfold and thinking, "I can't think of a better guy to have busting in like that. Rene is one of the surest shots on our team." Which is why he was the right wing on the famed French Connection, and why his No. 14 is retired and hanging from the rafters at what is now called First Niagara Center, right there alongside Gilbert Perreault's No. 11 and Rick Martin's No. 7.

In that first overtime game against Montreal, the Sabres entered the series as overwhelming underdogs to a Canadiens team that would ultimately win the Stanley Cup. Montreal won the first three games, but Buffalo averted a sweep with a win on their home ice. The teams flew back to Montreal for a fifth game that no one thought the Sabres could win given that they were 0–8–3 all-time to that point in the Forum.

Despite those low expectations, Perreault set up goals by Martin and Robert 1:08 apart in the second period to give the Sabres a 2–1 lead. After Guy Lapointe scored in the third to force overtime, Perreault and Robert combined on the winner 9:18 into the extra period.

"The play developed in Rick's corner," Robert remembered. "One of the defensemen pinched in, and Gilbert was able to get loose, and by the time he got loose, I had beaten [Serge] Savard on the far side. When Gilbert saw me, he gave me a hard pass, and I knew once I got the puck, nobody could catch me. I knew what I wanted to do; I was just hoping I could do it. I saw the opening, I had about a foot and a half to shoot at [on Ken Dryden's stick side], and I knew from past experiences if you faked him high, he had a tendency of twitching and pulling up, so what I did was shoot the puck along the ice and he just had no chance. It was an absolutely perfect shot."

Two years later, Robert beat the Canadiens again, this time in Game 5 of the semifinals at the Aud. Buffalo had won the first two games of the series, then absorbed back-to-back 7–0 and 8–2 wallopings at the Forum and were trailing 4–3 with the third period ticking down in the pivotal fifth game. It looked as though the Canadiens were primed to seize control of the series, but then Craig Ramsay scored on a power play with 5:25 left, and Robert struck 5:58 into overtime to win the game. Buffalo then closed out the series with a gritty 4–3 win in Montreal to advance to the Stanley Cup Finals for one of only two times in franchise history.

Robert's last overtime winner was the most memorable of all in the bizarre third game of the 1975 Stanley Cup Finals, when fog enveloped the ice for most of the third period and overtime at the steamy Aud. "It was like playing in a graveyard," said Jerry Korab following Buffalo's first victory in the Finals.

Philadelphia had won the first two games at the Spectrum, so Buffalo was desperate to protect its home ice. It wasn't looking good early when the Flyers jumped to a quick 2–0 lead, but the Sabres battled back and pulled even when an unlikely offensive source, defenseman Bill Hajt, swatted in a rebound after Bernie Parent had stopped Martin.

That left it up to the likeliest source of offense in these overtime situations, Robert, to give Buffalo the victory. His low shot from an impossible angle along the right boards got past Parent, who barely saw it through the soupy fog.

"I didn't see Perreault's pass [in the neutral zone], and I saw Robert's shot too late to come out and stop it," said Parent. "I'm surprised the overtime took so long; it was hard to see the puck from the red line. If three men came down and made a good pass from the red line, you couldn't see the puck. But it was the same thing for [Sabres goalie Roger Crozier]."

The Ironman

Every day growing up in Rexdale (a suburb of Toronto), Craig Ramsay was still asleep when his father, Bill, went to work at Bell Telephone. He'd leave the home before 6:00 in the morning and wouldn't return until after 6:00 at night. And then he'd do it again the next day. A husband and father of three, Bill Ramsay had responsibilities that he did not take lightly. He had a job to do, so he did it—every day.

There was a consistency to Bill Ramsay, as well as toughness, a desire to work, and the knowledge that in order to be respected, you have to earn it. He passed every one of those attributes on to his only son, Craig.

"I never saw my dad miss a day of work," Ramsay said of his father, who passed away in 1993.

And very rarely did Bill ever see his son miss a day of work.

From March 27, 1973, to February 10, 1983, Craig played in 776 consecutive games for the Sabres, a streak that ranks as the fourth-longest in NHL history. It was a streak that was defined by consistency, toughness, desire, and respect. It was defined by Bill Ramsay.

"You can't grow up and watch that without thinking, 'Geez, that's the way you're supposed to do it,'" Craig said when recalling the memory of his father punching that daily time clock. "My father was a hard worker. And I think that rubbed off on me. I always felt that if you get paid to play hockey, you go play. And if I could play, then I was going to play."

Of course Cal Ripken's consecutive Major League Baseball games streak is a monumental feat that stands alone in the annals of sport. But Ramsay's streak, as well as the three in the NHL that are longer (Doug Jarvis with 964, Garry Unger with 914, and Steve Larmer with 884), have to be considered somewhat miraculous when you consider the often violent nature of hockey.

"I was lucky," Ramsay said, "and you have to be with something like that. In some cases, I'd get a flu and I couldn't play, but we'd happen to have that day off, and the next day I'd be OK. I always thought if I had a day, I could play no matter what the injury was. I would never play a game if I didn't think I could help the team, but in those days you didn't carry a lot of extra players. Today, there are some nights where a coach might say, 'Take a night off and be ready for the next game.' In our case, we didn't have a lot of extra players."

But Ramsay's career was about so much more than just his streak. He was one of the best defensive forwards to ever play in the NHL, but he was also talented enough to score 252 goals and 420 assists for 672 points, stats that still rank fifth, third, and fourth, respectively in team history. What's more, his 1,070 games ranks second behind Gilbert Perreault and his 27 short-handed goals are the team record.

Not bad for a 5'10", 170-pound guy who wasn't a very fast skater, wasn't a great shooter, and wasn't an intimidating body checker. All Ramsay did was play good, steady hockey every night. Punch Imlach summed it up best when he once said of "the Rammer," "We had plenty of personal differences, but I have never had any doubts about his hockey ability."

"When I finally signed, we had a picture taken at the rink, and Punch asked me, 'When are you going to get a haircut?'" said Ramsay, who was a second-round pick in 1971. "I said, 'Gee, I just did.' It wasn't the best of starts. He was a tough guy, there's no question about it. There was always a feeling of apprehension and uncertainty when Punch was around."

Ramsay began his first pro season in Cincinnati, but was recalled after only 19 games and never played in the minors again. He was paired with Don Luce on the team's checking line, beginning a nearly 10-year playing relationship that benefited both men.

"Craig was an extremely intelligent player," said Luce. "He wasn't big, he didn't have all the skills of some other players, but he was incredibly gifted at the hockey sense of the game. What a pleasure he was to play with."

One of Ramsay's greatest strengths was penalty killing; in fact, he was among the best in the NHL at the art:

First of all, I wanted to do it, I loved it. It was a great challenge to go out there and be that guy. The team is shorthanded, you need somebody to step up, and I wanted to be that guy. We were aggressive about it, more aggressive than most any team at that time other than maybe Boston. We tried to score goals; we looked at it as an offensive situation for us. We didn't get a chance to play on power plays or in any great offensive situations, so Donnie and I looked at penalty-killing as a chance to really go for it, and that's why we scored shorthanded goals [52 combined]. We gambled, took some chances.

In his 14th and final season in the NHL, Ramsay was awarded the Selke Trophy, presented annually to the league's best defensive forward, and helped the Sabres finish No. 1 in the NHL in penalty-killing efficiency (82.4 percent). Yet while he was clearly still a productive player, he wanted to retire in order to concentrate on coaching.

Ramsay assisted Jim Schoenfeld and Scotty Bowman, then took over as head coach for one month after Bowman's departure in 1986 before being replaced by Ted Sator. Ramsay worked in Buffalo's front office until 1993, but after 22 years in the organization, he knew he wanted to get back behind a bench. He has held various jobs in the NHL since, including serving as an assistant in Tampa Bay when the Lightning won the Stanley Cup.

26 All Tuckered Out

A few minutes had gone by since John Tucker's overtime goal ended one of the most exciting and—from Boston's point of view—most controversial playoff games in Sabres history.

A boisterous sellout crowd at Memorial Auditorium was still on its feet celebrating Buffalo's dramatic 6–5 victory over the hated Bruins, refusing to leave the building until their newest hero, John Tucker, came out for a curtain call.

Tucker should have skated back onto the ice and performed six victory laps—one for each goal he scored during a wild two-games-in-two-nights weekend that saw the Sabres beat Boston twice to tie their best-of-seven Adams Division semifinal series at two games each.

Instead, the modest Tucker—unwilling to hog the spotlight despite obviously deserving it—dragged linemate Pierre Turgeon out with him for a quick salute to the crowd before scurrying back into the locker room, where he proceeded to downplay his magnificent performance.

It is understandable that in the heat of a bitterly fought play-off series, Tucker could not fully appreciate the magnitude of his accomplishment. But upon further reflection years later, it struck Tucker that scoring six goals and three assists in the span of about 27 hours in the NHL playoffs was the highlight of his career.

"It was my biggest thrill in hockey," said Tucker, who played 12 NHL seasons with Buffalo, Washington, the Islanders, and Tampa Bay. "It was unbelievable how people were into it, how loud everything was and the emotion that was going through everyone. I just kept getting the puck to the net and it kept going in off of guys. It was uncanny."

It was also completely unexpected. Tucker came to the Sabres as a second-round draft choice in 1983 and scored 101 goals during his first five years with the team. Not bad, but Wayne Gretzky certainly wasn't concerned about relinquishing his annual stranglehold on the NHL scoring title.

And during the first two games of this rugged series, when the penalty boxes were sometimes more heavily populated than the team benches, Tucker hadn't scored a point. In fact, he had managed only one shot on goal as Buffalo was pummeled at Boston Garden 7–3 and 4–1.

The Sabres, back in the playoffs for the first time since 1985 and just one year removed from finishing dead last in the NHL standings in 1986–1987, were desperate when they returned to the Aud for Games 3 and 4.

But thanks to Tucker, they got right back into the series. Tucker had a stunning Game 3 performance, scoring four goals—including one on a penalty shot, a first in Sabres playoff history—in Buffalo's fight-filled 6–2 romp. The four goals were a team playoff record, as well as just one shy of tying the NHL mark set by the legendary Maurice "Rocket" Richard. The next night Tucker was at it again, assisting on three goals and scoring two—including the winner in overtime, which had been set up by what the Bruins felt was a dubious tripping penalty on Glen Wesley.

Tucker's winner 24 seconds into the power play caromed off Boston defenseman Gord Kluzak and goalie Reggie Lemelin before entering the net. The entire Boston organization then erupted in anger, spewing venom at referee Kerry Fraser.

Goalie Daren Puppa, who had allowed Boston to tie the game with 1:33 left in regulation, recalled thinking, "The only thing a goalie thinks about in overtime is 'no more' and 'I hope our guys get one.'" Not surprisingly on this weekend and this night, Tucker got the one.

"I really didn't put all that much on it and it kind of got lost in the crowd," said Tucker. "I wasn't even sure it went in at first, it took so long. I never knew until the light went on."

27 Win and In

If anyone ever questions how much power Punch Imlach wielded during his time as the general manager of the Sabres, all they need to do is refer to the night of April 1, 1973.

The Sabres were locked in a battle with Detroit to secure the final playoff berth in the East Division, and the race came down to the last night of the season. If Buffalo could defeat St. Louis at the

Aud, it was in, regardless of what the Red Wings did in New York against the Rangers. However, a Buffalo loss *and* a Detroit victory meant the Sabres would be eliminated.

Sunday night games at the Aud normally started at 7:05, but Imlach changed the starting time of the game with St. Louis to 8:35 when he learned that, due to an afternoon NBA contest at Madison Square Garden, Detroit's game there against the Rangers wasn't slated to begin until 8:30. Imlach reasoned that late-game strategy might hinge on what was happening in New York, so the NHL and the Blues agreed to the switch. Punch was a tough man to say no to, and in this case he had a legitimate reason.

While the delay was certainly a masterful stroke of genius by Imlach, it wasn't exactly good for his already-nervous players to have to sit around for an extra hour and a half before the most important game of their lives—particularly goaltender Roger Crozier, who was jittery before every game he played no matter what was on the line.

"Roger was a very nervous goalie the day of a game," Gerry Meehan recalled. "I felt bad for him in that regard because he would get so agitated before the game. I guess it was his way of getting ready to play. I just assumed that was one of the quirks of being a goalie, and that goalies were a different type of player who had different ways of preparing for a game."

On this night, Crozier and the Sabres weren't the only ones feeling pressure. It had been a magnificent season for the Sabres, leaping into playoff contention in just their third year of existence. There was a palpable pall of trepidation hanging in the air at the Aud as the fans nervously filed in, wondering if all the fun would be ruined during the next 60 minutes of hockey.

The mood certainly didn't brighten when Wayne Merrick scored for the Blues just 1:54 into the game. Long before smart phones and the Internet came along, the only way fans there at the game could track the Red Wings score was by getting scoreboard updates in the arena—and the first one offered some hope as the Rangers jumped out to a 2–0 lead on the Red Wings, bringing a tremendous roar from the crowd.

The Sabres, however, had said all along that they didn't want to back into the playoffs, and at 15:35 of the first period they began their quest to burst through the front door when Gilbert Perreault tied the game with a backhander off a rebound of a shot by Rick Martin.

Then, within a span of 3:45 in the second period, the Sabres took control. Larry Mickey swatted in his own rebound for the go-ahead goal and Jim Lorentz took a pass from Meehan and beat St. Louis goalie Jacques Caron from a tough angle to make it 3–1.

From that moment on, the Sabres played confidently, dominating the Blues, who had already secured the fourth playoff spot in the West Division and really had nothing to play for anyway. The Red Wings ultimately battled back to tie New York, but it became a moot point; St. Louis was unable to break through on Crozier and Buffalo's sturdy defense.

When the horn sounded to end the game, the fans went wild while the players streamed onto the ice and buried Roger Crozier in a sea of humanity. Coach Joe Crozier led his boys into the dressing room, where he presented them with six bottles of champagne that he had been saving for a few months just for this occasion.

"It was like a balloon that was busting and all that pressure was gone," Joe Crozier said, remembering the feeling of finally clinching the playoff berth. "We had worked so hard, and now we were the first expansion team from the East Division to go into the playoffs."

28 LaLaLaLaLaLaLaFontaine

It is reasonably safe to say that no professional athlete in Buffalo sports history has ever had a greater impact on his team and the community in a shorter period of time than Pat LaFontaine.

"It's pretty vivid in my mind when he first came here," said LaFontaine's former teammate, Grant Ledyard. "Patty has an aura about him. We used to complain that he was everybody's best friend, but nobody was really close to him. That speaks volumes for him because he spread himself pretty thin. Everybody wanted a piece of him, but he was great with everybody. You saw the magic that happened between he and Alex [Mogilny], and I was lucky to be part of that."

LaFontaine arrived in Buffalo via a trade from the New York Islanders early in the 1991–1992 season; however, due to a knee injury and several concussions, he spent an inordinate amount of time in street clothes. But his one injury-free season, 1992–1993, was quite enough to cement his legacy. He finished second in the NHL in scoring behind Pittsburgh's Mario Lemieux with a team-record 148 points, the most ever scored by an American-born player, with many of the assists coming on goals by Mogilny (who scored a team-record 76).

During every other year that LaFontaine was a member of the Sabres, he missed huge chunks of playing time because of injuries. Combining the 1993–1994, 1994–1995, and 1996–1997 seasons, he played a total of only 51 games. And in 1997, when the Sabres refused to let him play because of his head injuries, they traded him—and his hefty salary—to the New York Rangers. His lone

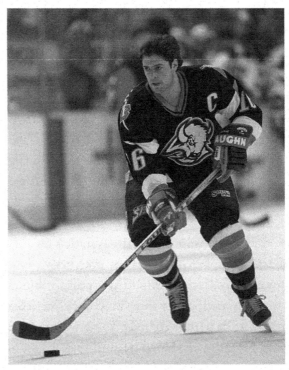

Sabres captain Pat LaFontaine handles the puck while wearing the team's new uniform during practice on April 11, 1996, at the Memorial Auditorium. Though his time in Buffalo was marred by injuries, in 1992–1993 he set a team record for points with 148, the most ever by an American-born player in the NHL.

season with the Rangers was cut short by another concussion, and that's when he decided to retire for good.

Despite the brevity of his playing career with the Sabres—he played only one full season during the six years he skated for Buffalo—LaFontaine was such a dynamic talent that the organization chose to retire his No. 16 sweater. He was also elected to the Sabres Hall of Fame. At the time of his retirement, LaFontaine ranked second all-time to Joey Mullen in goals scored by an American (468) and third in points (1,013) behind Mullen and ex-Sabre Phil Housley. He was ultimately inducted into the Hockey Hall of Fame, as well as the United States Hockey Hall of Fame, and *Sports Illustrated* named him the greatest American player.

Though he spent his first eight NHL seasons with the Islanders and played in the Stanley Cup Finals with them in 1984, he has often said that his time in Buffalo was actually his most rewarding.

"I learned a lot as a player playing with some great players on the New York Islanders, obviously going to the Stanley Cup Finals my first year," he said. "I learned a lot and was able to take that with me to Buffalo, and the prime years were spent right there in Buffalo. Those teams and wins and goals and assists are so special, but I also look at the off-ice, and I learned so much from so many special people."

LaFontaine was the Sabres captain for several years. He was also the public face of the team in the community, serving as a spokesperson for the United Way and on the board of trustees for Children's Hospital, as well as spending much of his free time visiting children at area hospitals.

"They said it would be a big thrill for them to meet a Buffalo Sabre," he recalled, "so I went there and tried to put a smile on their face, and developed some friendships and special relationships. Their courage and inspiration had a profound effect on me. Some special children I had met through the United Way and Children's Hospital inspired me through their courage [when he was battling post-concussion syndrome]. To this day, they still inspire me. We talk about heroes, but people like that show us what courage and perseverance are all about."

"Pat brought a singular focus onto the ice," longtime Sabres broadcaster Rick Jeanneret said, "but his legacy extended beyond the ice."

They Travel Well

When the Sabres rolled their way to back-to-back appearances in the Eastern Conference Finals during the 2005–2006 and 2006–2007 seasons, it seemed as though wherever they played on the road, there were scores of Sabres fans there to cheer them on.

You hear it all the time with college football teams who "travel well"—meaning their fans follow them all over the country (most notably to warm-weather bowl-game sites) to provide support. If there's any team in the NHL that "travels well," it's the Sabres.

Sadly, part of this is due to Buffalo's sagging economy. The city just does not retain its young people—kids who grew up in Buffalo go off to college and usually don't come back unless they're visiting family for the holidays. Job opportunities dwindle more every year in Buffalo, so the town's population continues to decrease as people leave for places where they can earn a living.

But all those Buffalo transplants around the country don't lose interest in their hometown hockey team just because they've moved away. Since so many Buffalonians are scattered around the country, and because hockey is a passion that is bred into the people of western New York, it stands to reason that when the Sabres come to town, those transplanted Buffalonians go to the game to cheer on their team.

The warm-weather NHL franchises always get a boost when the Sabres pay a visit. Countless people have moved from Buffalo to places like Tampa Bay; Miami; Phoenix; Raleigh, North Carolina;

Road Trip with the Road Crew

For Sabres fans who do hit the road to follow the team, one great option is to join the Sabres Road Crew.

As the team's website explains, the Road Crew is an interactive online community where fans can connect with each other to discuss everything from the previous night's game to where they can gather in other cities to watch Sabres' games on television or in the opposing team's arena.

Part of the Road Crew's allure is the "Tour Stop" parties that are planned for selected road games each season. Usually held the night before a game, these parties are a great way to meet new friends who love the Sabres. On some occasions, coach Lindy Ruff, general manager Darcy Regier, and broadcasters Rick Jeanneret, Harry Neale, Rob Ray, and Kevin Sylvester have made appearances to talk to fans.

Anaheim; Dallas; and Los Angeles. And those cities also represent ideal places for Buffalonians to take a vacation that could easily include a Sabres away game. Obviously, Florida is also a popular "snowbird" destination for retired northerners, so that brings additional Sabres fans into the Miami and Tampa Bay venues.

For Sabres fans who still reside in the area, Buffalo's proximity to so many other NHL cities makes it possible for folks to hop into their cars and do an overnighter in places like New York, New Jersey, Pittsburgh, Philadelphia, Montreal, Ottawa, Columbus, and Detroit.

Although Toronto is the NHL franchise that's closest to Buffalo, since every ticket at Air Canada Centre is spoken for—and the ones that aren't cost hundreds of dollars—that's actually the least popular road destination for Sabres fans.

30 The Ken Dryden Pads Caper

Former Sabres public relations director Paul Wieland was renowned for his often ingenious practical jokes. But during the 1973 playoffs against the heavily favored Montreal Canadiens, he had an idea that gave the Sabres a much-needed competitive advantage that turned out to be no laughing matter.

Wieland was a former goaltender, so he knew a little about the tools of the trade. Late in the regular season, he had a hunch that Montreal goalie Ken Dryden's leg pads were wider than the NHL-mandated 10 inches. Wieland told team management, but coach Joe Crozier and general manager Punch Imlach decided to sit on the information until the teams met in the playoffs.

Prior to the start of Game 3 at the Aud, with the Sabres already trailing two games to none in the series, Imlach instructed Wieland to sneak into the visiting dressing room and measure Dryden's pads to confirm his suspicion. Sure enough, the pads were too wide.

"In the Aud you could get into the other dressing room with a key, so we sent him [Wieland] in there, and he told us they were too wide," Crozier remembered.

The penalty for illegal goalie pads was a two-minute minor to be assessed at the start of the next period. Crozier and Imlach agreed to use the loophole to their advantage in a tie game near the end of regulation so the Canadiens would have to start the overtime period shorthanded. That scenario did not present itself in Game 3, which Buffalo lost, or Game 4, which it won.

But with 29 seconds to go in Game 5, the score tied at 2–2, and overtime looming, the time was right. Crozier called referee Bruce Hood over to the Buffalo bench to make the unusual request to have Dryden's leg pads measured. Had the Sabres waited until the end of regulation to ask, the penalty would not have been assessed until the start of a potential second overtime period. After time ran out, Hood put a tape measure on the pads and reluctantly slapped Montreal with a penalty.

"When Joe called the pads on Dryden, that was great because I thought Bowman's head was going to explode," Rick Martin recalled with a laugh. "Whatever hair he had on his head, he was pulling them out, and Joe just stood there smiling. That was just beautiful. We were laughing our asses off."

Bowman immediately asked for a measurement of Roger Crozier's pads, but because he hadn't done so during the third period, that measurement couldn't be taken until the intermission after the first overtime. Therefore, any potential Montreal power play would not occur until the start of the second overtime. Now Bowman was really aggravated, and he continued to rant at Hood to no avail.

Hood was actually sympathetic toward Bowman, and at one point threatened to call an even-up penalty on the Sabres because he felt that their tactic had been underhanded. But the referee eventually realized that a rule was a rule, and he was there to enforce it whether he agreed or not.

The Sabres' plan almost had a storybook conclusion when, on the ensuing power play, Jim Lorentz came within inches of ending the game. But his shot clanged off the goal post, and Montreal was able to ward off any further threats and killed the penalty. In a way, it was probably appropriate that the Sabres didn't score on that power play, since there is no question many people would have considered the victory to be "tainted" if they had.

The game continued on for another seven minutes before Rene Robert really gave Bowman a reason to scowl, taking a pass from Gilbert Perreault and whistling a shot past Dryden for the game-winning goal.

Perreault Hits 500

Mike Foligno was sitting in front of his television on the evening of March 8, 1986, when the phone rang. On the other end was Larry Playfair, who had been his Buffalo Sabres teammate until two months prior, when Scotty Bowman traded Playfair to Los Angeles.

"He said, 'Be sure you assist on Bert's goal,'" Foligno recalled. "I told him, 'I can't promise you anything, but I'll try.'"

"Bert" was Gilbert Perreault, of course, and the "goal" would be Perreault's milestone 500th, which he was one shy of when Playfair made his long-distance call.

The next night, Foligno—who had recently been reunited as Perreault's linemate by Bowman—outworked New Jersey defenseman Joe Cirella to gain control of a loose puck behind the Devils' net midway through the second period. Foligno then fed a pass out front to Perreault, who was cruising in unguarded from the right slot. When the puck arrived, Perreault didn't bother trying to receive it and make a move; he simply snapped a quick one-timer to the lower right corner. New Jersey goaltender Alain Chevrier never had a chance.

At that moment, as the historic 500th goal came to rest in the back of the net—making Perreault only the 12th player in NHL history to reach that lofty plateau—the roof nearly lifted off Memorial Auditorium. The sellout crowd of 16,433 was wildly celebrating what still stands as the single-greatest individual achievement in Sabres history. But their glee couldn't compare with Foligno's.

Foligno, who used to jump into the air after scoring his own goals, jumped into Perreault's arms and bear-hugged him so tightly he nearly squeezed the breath out of his teammate. He then helped lift the Sabres captain and icon into the air and carried him around the ice.

"He gave me a moment to remember for the rest of my life," Foligno said that night after the Sabres punctuated the feat by winning the game 4–3. "There are things we have trouble recalling as we get older, but I'll never forget this. I know it's something I will recall many times."

The Sabres endured a difficult 1985–1986 season. Former Sabre Jim Schoenfeld made his NHL coaching debut, but lasted only 43 games because an impatient Bowman, unhappy with the team's .500 record, fired him and took over coaching duties himself. The Sabres didn't respond, ultimately finishing last in the old Adams Division and missing the playoffs. Perreault's 500th goal served as the high point of the season.

He was 36 by then, and his great speed and stickhandling ability had begun to wane. He started his 16th NHL season fairly well, with 13 goals in the first 32 games, but the rigors of the schedule began to wear on him. He had had only four goals in the previous two months when the Devils came to the Aud for a Sunday night game. One of those four goals had come two nights earlier against Hartford, bringing him to the cusp of 500 and prompting Playfair to call Foligno.

Just moments before Perreault scored, Chevrier had robbed him with a terrific kick save on a point blank shot. But no goalie could have stopped Perreault's next shot. "I heard Bert yelling," Foligno said in describing the play. "I knew I had to get it out quick, but I had to go to the other side of the net because I was already behind it. Then I sent it out front and he made no mistake."

"You don't think about it; it was so quick, I just shot it," Perreault explained. "I saw Mike had a good chance to get it out in front of the net and I just put it in. It was a good play by Mike."

In typical low-key Perreault fashion, when asked what scoring 500 goals meant to him, he deadpanned, "I guess that means I had a pretty good career, eh."

Before Foligno released Perreault from his bear hug, the rest of the Sabres streamed onto the ice to offer their congratulations. "I saw them coming and said, 'Hey, what's this? Isn't there supposed to be a rule against this?'" Perreault said.

"We had to do it up right," Foligno said. "I don't know how many guys have scored 500 goals, but I know it's not many. It's a great feeling for myself, I'm thrilled, and I know I speak for the other players on the team when I say I'm proud to have played with Gilbert Perreault."

Rene Robert

When Rene Robert was acquired in a trade from Pittsburgh late in the 1971–1972 season, he was completely sure that he wanted to come to Buffalo—and he was just as sure that he didn't want

Rene Robert, shown in 1978 action, was acquired through a trade with Pittsburgh in 1972 and became the final piece of the "French Connection" line of Gilbert Perreault and Rick Martin. The trade was one of the most one-sided in NHL history.

to leave when he was traded to Colorado prior to the start of the 1979–1980 season.

A gifted offensive player since his days in junior, where he once scored 69 goals and 143 points in one season, Robert was growing stagnant in Pittsburgh coach Red Kelly's system. His career, which consisted of numerous minor league stops and brief NHL stints with Toronto and the Penguins, was going nowhere when Sabres general manager Punch Imlach—still recovering from the heart attack he had suffered a few months earlier—told assistant GM Fred Hunt to call Kelly with a trade proposal.

In what became one of the most lopsided trades in NHL history, Kelly agreed to take the aging Eddie Shack and some cash in exchange for Robert, who went on to become one of the cornerstones on which the Sabres were built. Teaming with Gilbert Perreault and Rick Martin to form the dynamic French Connection line, Robert's slick skating, pinpoint passing, sharp shooting, and gritty determination had the sellout crowds at the Aud rocking with excitement for more than seven years.

"We went and got him and put him on that line with Perreault and Martin," said coach Joe Crozier. "He was the guy I wanted for that wing."

Robert was thrilled to get out of Pittsburgh, and with good reason: after scoring seven goals in 49 games there, he had six in only 12 with Buffalo to close 1971–1972.

"I kind of sensed something, because at the time the Sabres were a young team, they had only been in the league two years, so they had nowhere else to go but up," Robert said, recalling his excitement about coming to Buffalo. "And to come in and play with Perreault and Martin, who I had played against in junior, I knew there was a lot of potential."

With Robert on the right wing, the line clicked immediately. He was the perfect complement to Perreault's playmaking and Martin's cannon shot. Robert could make plays, he could shoot, and he could stay high and get back to play defense if the opposition broke up a rush and started the other way.

"Rene had won scoring championships with Three Rivers and he was always a great offensive player," said Martin. "When they put him on the line, he could read where I was going and I could read where he was going. I actually got the puck more from him than I did from Gilbert, so for me it was great to get him on the line; now I had two people to get the puck to me."

During his time in Buffalo, Robert scored 222 goals and 330 assists for 552 points, figures that still rank in the Sabres top 10 in their respective categories. His 22 playoff goals rank behind only Perreault, Martin, and Danny Gare, and only Gare could match Robert's flair for the dramatic, as each scored three overtime winners.

Robert scored a team-high 40 goals and finished second to Perreault in points (83) during his first full season with the Sabres (1972–1973). With Perreault missing two months of 1973–1974, Robert slumped to 21 goals and 65 points. But he helped lead the charge to the Stanley Cup Finals in 1974–1975 by becoming the first Sabre to amass 100 points, including another 40 goals.

That was his statistical high point, but he was still second, second, third, and fourth in scoring on the team during his last four years in Buffalo.

But none of that mattered in 1979, when Scotty Bowman took over the team. Bowman saw a 31-year-old player who had dipped to 62 points in 1978–1979, and he felt it was time to send Robert on his way when the Colorado Rockies offered defenseman John Van Boxmeer in return. Robert was so angered by the trade that he refused to take part in Sabres functions during Bowman's tenure with the team.

Said Robert:

I loved it here and I never wanted to leave Buffalo. This was my home and the best years of my life were spent in Buffalo. But that was beyond me, I couldn't control my destiny.

The only reason he traded me is because he never saw eye-to-eye with me, yet we didn't even know each other aside from All-Star Games or when I played in the Canada Cup. We built a franchise from scratch here, and some pretty good hockey players came through this organization, and to let one guy ruin everything that was built in the first 10 years, it was hard to swallow. That's the grudge that I carry.

If he had left that team alone for one year, just said, "I'll leave my feelings aside and let the players play for one year and then I'll evaluate things at the end of the year," we would have won the Stanley Cup. Instead, he went the other way. He wanted to prove a point that he was the boss, so he got rid of me. He wanted to build his own team and prove to the organization that he could do it on his own, and he ruined the franchise.

33 Miller Time

If Dean Miller had had his way, his son Ryan would have been scoring goals in the NHL rather than preventing them. But Dean was never going to get his way, at least not in a dispute with his intelligent, headstrong, and supremely talented son—not even when Ryan was only eight years old.

The Miller clan hailed from Michigan, but Dean had to move his family out to northern California due to his job at Symantec, the computer virus protection giant, when Ryan was in grammar school. They only lived on the West Coast for a few years before moving back to Michigan, but one of the key moments in Ryan's life occurred in a rundown hockey rink in the basement of a Santa Clara shopping mall.

Ryan, who had always wanted to be a goaltender, was fed up with his father's refusal to let him try the position. So during a Mite game, Ryan turned to Dean, who was the coach of his team, and said he wasn't going to take his regular shift on the ice as a forward until Dean agreed to let him play goalie in the next game. Aggravated, but sort of helpless at the moment, Dean told Ryan if he scored three goals, he'd let him play goalie in the next game. Ryan scored twice on his first shift and finished with four goals to lead his team to a victory.

So in the next game, there he was, standing between the pipes and starting a journey that has taken him to fame and fortune as one of the NHL's best puck stoppers, the Sabres' all-time leader in goaltender victories, and a silver medal in the 2010 Winter Olympics.

"I refused to play hockey until I could play goalie," Miller told the *San Jose Mercury News* in 2003 when he returned to the area as the Sabres' backup goaltender for a game against the San Jose Sharks. "He was not at all eager for me to switch. He wanted me to be a good skater and he wanted me to be a forward. He was kind of biased as a forward; goalies are always the weird ones, kind of the outcasts. But he has a lot more respect for the position now that he's had to watch me grow with it."

The Miller name is legendary in Michigan, as 10 of them have played college hockey at Michigan State, including Dean and his father, Butch. Ryan is one of five who have gone on to play in the NHL, the others being his younger brother, Drew, who won a Stanley Cup with Anaheim in 2007, and his cousins Kelly, Kip, and Kevin Miller. But Ryan is the only goaltender of the group, and he happens to be considered the greatest in Spartans history.

Miller won the Hobey Baker Award as the nation's best college player in 2001, and was a finalist in 2002. He also set an NCAA career record with 26 shutouts, and posted a 73–18–12 record. And before he accomplished any of that, he'd already been the Sabres fifth-round pick in the 1999 NHL Entry Draft. With his résumé becoming more impressive each year, Sabres fans—looking for a goaltender to replace the great Dominik Hasek, who had departed from Buffalo after the 2001 season—grew excited about Ryan's arrival.

Despite his great promise, it took a while for Ryan to have an impact with the Sabres. He spent almost all of three seasons with Rochester in the AHL (including 2004–2005, when the NHL was shut down and he won the AHL's goalie of the year award) before he was finally ready to become the Sabres' No. 1 goalie in 2005. Over the next two seasons he won 70 games, including a single-season team-record 40 in 2006–2007, and helped guide the Sabres into the

Eastern Conference Finals both years. He then broke his own mark with 41 victories in 2009–2010.

Ryan became an international star thanks to his performance in the Olympics, where he went 5–0–1 with a 1.35 GAA and .946 save percentage during the United States' run to the gold medal game, which they lost to Canada on Sidney Crosby's overtime goal.

"We're always kind of pinching ourselves to see if it's a dream or not, but it's not a surprise to be honest with you," Dean Miller told the *Buffalo News*. "He had a plan early in life, and he's been marching to that plan. I've always told him, 'Always forward, never straight,' and he's always moving forward."

Going Batty

On the night of May 20, 1975, Memorial Auditorium was a very spooky place; defenseman Jerry Korab even remarked that it was like "playing in a graveyard."

It was Game 3 of the Stanley Cup Finals against the Philadelphia Flyers, and the Sabres were at home for the first time in the series, already down two games to none. A heat wave was rolling through the western New York region; it should have been about 60° outside, but it was actually 90°.

That was great for the folks who had endured a typical Buffalo winter and then the usual rain and cloudiness of the spring; they were in Nirvana, frolicking around in shorts and T-shirts. It was not great, however, for the ice surface in an arena that was not equipped with air conditioning *and* had a nonexistent ventilation system.

The combination of the cold ice and the warm air created a fog inside the building that had a huge effect on the play. Given the conditions, which looked like something out of a vampire movie, it wasn't all that surprising that a bat actually made an appearance and became a nuisance.

That is until Jim Lorentz put an end to it.

"It was dive-bombing the crowd and a couple times it got near the ice and I remember Bernie [Parent, the Flyers goaltender] taking a couple swings at it with his goalie stick and missing," Lorentz told former Sabres PR director Paul Wieland for his book *Then Perreault Said to Rico...The Best Buffalo Sabres Stories Ever Told.*

Eventually, the bat made the mistake of flying into Lorentz's stick range; when he had the chance, Lorentz didn't miss.

"I was waiting for a faceoff in the Flyers zone," he said. "I looked down the ice toward our net and I saw the bat coming toward me. At this time, deep in the game, the bat didn't have much energy. It was flying in a straight line and flying high enough that I was able to get at it. I just reached up with my stick and swatted it out of the air and it fell to the ice."

The fans, at least those who could see what had happened through the soupy mist, roared with delight, and there was some good-natured laughing amongst the players on the ice. But the dead critter now needed to be removed from the ice, and nobody was stepping up to volunteer.

"I remember all the players standing around looking at it," said Lorentz. "The officials wouldn't touch it either. Then [Flyers winger] Rick MacLeish came over, took his glove off, and picked it up and buried it in the penalty box."

That didn't exactly endear MacLeish to the men who worked in the penalty box, but there wasn't anywhere to dump the roadkill.

And Lorentz hadn't exactly endeared himself to animal lovers, who pitched a fit when they heard what he had done. There were estimates that hundreds of people called the *Hockey Night in Canada* broadcast demanding that Lorentz be arrested for cruelty to animals. He also received letters from people too numerous to count wondering if he felt more like a man for having killed a defenseless animal.

Lorentz told Wieland, "I've often said I'd like to take all these people who objected, put them in a room, and let a bat loose and see what they'd do."

35 Near Tragedy

Less than a half hour after thinking he was going to die right on the ice at Memorial Auditorium, Clint Malarchuk was in the back of an ambulance on the way to Buffalo General Hospital joking with the doctors and paramedics who were caring for him. "Can you have me back for the third period?" Malarchuk asked, eliciting laughter from the medical personnel.

But no one—least of all Malarchuk—had been laughing when the goaltender was bent over in the crease with blood pouring out of his severed jugular vein on the night of March 22, 1989. He had been clipped by an errant skate during the first period of a game against the St. Louis Blues.

"When I saw the blood, I flipped my mask off," Malarchuk recalled. "It was incredible. As my heart would beat, it would squirt. I thought I was dying then, I really did. I knew it was my jugular vein and that I didn't have long to live. They said it was the jugular vein and I was scared. I didn't know how much time I had or if they could fix it."

Malarchuk had just joined the Sabres via a trade a few weeks earlier. The club needed goaltending help because regular starter Daren Puppa had been sidelined by a broken arm and Jacques Cloutier was wearing down due to all the ice time he was logging. General manager Gerry Meehan acquired Malarchuk from Washington for the stretch run and the playoffs in exchange for defenseman Calle Johansson. He was making his sixth start as a Sabre when the Blues came into the Aud.

Steve Tuttle and Buffalo defenseman Uwe Krupp battled to make a play early in the game after St. Louis' Rick Meagher sent the puck toward the front of the net. As the players crashed into Malarchuk, Tuttle's skate caught the goaltender on the neck, opening a six-inch gash.

Blood immediately began to pour from Malarchuk's throat as many in the crowd of about 14,000 screamed in horror, several even passing out due to the stomach-churning sight. The ice below Malarchuk was completely red in a matter of seconds. Fortunately, Sabres trainer Jim Pizzutelli was able to reach Malarchuk quickly to cover the wound with a towel and stanch the bleeding.

Luckily, Malarchuk was wounded near the players' locker room door. A stretcher was called for, but with the doorway right behind the net, Malarchuk said, "No way!" He insisted on skating off the ice as Pizzutelli kept the now blood-soaked towel pressed firmly against his neck.

"I didn't go into any real shock," Malarchuk said the next day after he'd been released from the hospital. "I think maybe if I had any shock, it was this morning. I'm not going off on a stretcher, I never will. The day I go off on a stretcher, they're going to have to make funeral arrangements. I'm proud of the fact that I got off the ice on my own power."

The sight of Malarchuk in that type of distress left an indelible impression on everyone there, particularly some of his teammates. "When he took his mask off, it was pretty shocking and disruptive," said John Tucker. "I had never seen anything like that in hockey. It was a helpless feeling to be standing there and not know what to do. I had to skate away."

Cloutier replaced Malarchuk in the game, which Buffalo went on to lose 2–1, and while arena workers were able to scrape most of the blood off the ice, it was still visible. "The only time I wasn't thinking about it was when they had the puck," Cloutier said. "All the time when we had the puck or the play was dead, it was on my mind."

Malarchuk underwent surgery that night to repair the wound, and two days later, wearing street clothes, he was back at the Aud to watch his team play Vancouver. He was introduced to the crowd during a break in the action and was given a two-minute standing ovation.

Malarchuk missed only five games before making a relief appearance in the season finale 10 days later. He also saw action in Buffalo's first-round playoff loss to Boston, and would go on to play three more seasons with the Sabres before finishing his playing career in the minor leagues.

And Then It Happened Again

As if the frightening Clint Malarchuk incident wasn't enough for Buffalo hockey fans, a similarly bloody, life-threatening situation happened about two decades later at HSBC Arena.

On February 10, 2008, Richard Zednik, a Florida Panthers winger, was inadvertently clipped in the neck by one of his teammates' skates. The incident happened in one of the corners on the bench side of the ice surface, and Zednik knew exactly what was happening. He immediately skated to the bench, leaving a stomach-churning trail of blood in his wake as the crowd gasped in horror.

"The worst that went through my mind is, 'Somebody better get him help, or else...' I don't even want to say it," said Zednik's teammate, Stephen Weiss. "Just his face coming off was something you don't want to see. I don't know how to explain it, but it was a scary look. It looked like he was very scared."

Medical personnel stanched the bleeding at the arena, and Zednik was transported to Buffalo General Hospital, where he underwent surgery to repair the wound, then spent a few days recuperating before being allowed to return to Florida.

36 The President's Cup

It was a cruel twist of fate that sent the Sabres to Raleigh, North Carolina, for their 2006–2007 season opener at the RBC Center, home of the defending Stanley Cup champion Carolina Hurricanes.

Barely four months earlier, that same venue had been the scene of one of the most gut-wrenching playoff disappointments in team history when Carolina defeated a depleted Sabres squad in the seventh game of the Eastern Conference Finals on a night when four of Buffalo's top six defensemen were sidelined by injury or illness.

The gritty Sabres had entered the third period with a 2–1 lead before all that adversity finally caught up with Lindy Ruff's team and the Hurricanes scored the game's final three goals to send the Sabres—a team virtually no one thought would even make the playoffs in the first season after the NHL lockout—home for the season.

And now here the Sabres were, starting what would become a magnificent journey through the 2006–2007 season, right back in Carolina—with the Hurricanes raising their Stanley Cup championship banner for the Sabres to see. But the Sabres were fine with it.

"It's never easy playing a season opener in somebody else's building, because they get motivated with their crowd," Danny Briere said. "But this is a little different because we have some motivation on our side, too. We have something to prove there, so I'm excited about starting there. And hopefully it's gonna give us a taste that if we give it our all this year, that's a place we want to be, raising the banner next year."

The Sabres won that night in Carolina. They won the next nine games, too, for a team-record 10–0 start. Over the course of the season they wound up winning a franchise-record 53 games for 113 points, ranking No. 1 in the NHL.

Unfortunately, the President's Cup trophy was the only one Buffalo took home—just as in 2005–2006, the Sabres lost in the conference finals, this time to Ottawa. "It's tough to swallow, and we feel like we let the fans and the city down," said Briere, "especially after the way the season played out. I really thought it was our year, but we weren't able to get it going against the Senators."

It was a bitter disappointment, indeed, but what a ride that team had taken its loyal followers on. Briere scored 95 points—the highest Sabre total since Pat LaFontaine (148), Alexander Mogilny (127), and Dale Hawerchuk (96) were scorching nets in 1992–1993. Thomas Vanek's 43 goals were the most since LaFontaine (53) and Mogilny (76) in 1992–1993. And goalie Ryan Miller earned a team-record 40 victories, three more than Dominik Hasek's best single-year total.

If ever the Sabres were going to finally win their first Stanley Cup, this should have been the season. All the pieces seemed to be fitting neatly into place. But once the playoffs began, there were signs that maybe it wasn't going to happen.

In the first round, the New York Islanders gave the Sabres fits despite the one-sided four-games-to-one final. New York earned a split of the first two games in Buffalo, and the Sabres won the final three games by a total of only four goals. In the second round, the New York Rangers lost the first two games in Buffalo, then won a pair of 2–1 games at Madison Square Garden to pull even. The pivotal fifth game looked lost for Buffalo, but furthering the notion that maybe this was their year, Chris Drury scored with 7.7 seconds remaining in regulation to tie the score. Maxim Afinogenov won it in overtime, and then Buffalo closed the series out with a 5–4 win back in Manhattan.

Waiting for the Sabres in the conference finals was Ottawa, the same team Buffalo had shockingly eliminated in five games the previous year. Payback turned out to be a bitch for the Sabres. Ottawa won the first three games, including a double-overtime victory in Game 2. After the Sabres avoided the sweep by winning

And the Award Goes to...

The 1996–1997 Sabres squad was one of the franchise's most beloved and celebrated teams. They certainly earned their nickname, "the hardest working team in the NHL." This group of low-profile players (with the notable exception of superstar goalie Dominik Hasek) outworked more talented teams on a nightly basis, winning the Northeast Division and then a first-round playoff series against Ottawa.

At the annual NHL awards banquet, the Sabres were rewarded for their efforts. Hasek became the first Sabre to win the league MVP Hart Trophy, as well as the first goalie to win it in 35 years. Not surprisingly, he also won the Vezina Trophy as top goalie. Center Michael Peca took home the Selke Trophy as the league's top defensive forward, and Ted Nolan won the Jack Adams Award as coach of the year.

Here is a list of the Sabres' many NHL award winners:

- Presidents' Cup trophy (most points): Team award, 2006–2007
- Hart Trophy (league MVP): Dominik Hasek, 1997, 1998
- Calder Trophy (rookie of the year): Gilbert Perreault, 1971; Tom Barrasso, 1984; Tyler Myers, 2010
- Vezina Trophy (best goaltender): Bob Sauve and Don Edwards, 1980; Tom Barrasso, 1984; Dominik Hasek, 1994, 1995, 1997, 1998, 1999, 2001; Ryan Miller, 2010
- Lady Byng Trophy (most gentlemanly player): Gilbert Perreault, 1973
- Frank J. Selke Trophy (top defensive forward): Craig Ramsay, 1985; Michael Peca, 1997
- William M. Jennings Trophy (fewest goals allowed): Tom Barrasso and Bob Sauve, 1985; Dominik Hasek and Grant Fuhr, 1994; Dominik Hasek, 2001
- Lester B. Pearson Award (most outstanding player, now named for Ted Lindsay): Dominik Hasek, 1997, 1998
- Jack Adams Award (coach of the year): Ted Nolan, 1997; Lindy Ruff, 2006
- Bill Masterton Trophy (perseverance and sportsmanship): Don Luce, 1975; Pat LaFontaine, 1995
- King Clancy Trophy (leadership and community): Rob Ray, 1999
- NHL Foundation Award (community): Rob Ray, 1999; Ryan Miller, 2010

in Ottawa, the Senators closed it out in remarkably appropriate fashion.

Jason Pominville had scored an overtime goal in Game 5 in Ottawa the previous year to win the series, and the player he had skated around to do it was Daniel Alfredsson. A year later at HSBC Arena, Alfredsson exacted sweet revenge by scoring the winning goal in overtime to produce a matching five-game wipeout.

"There's a lot of disappointment right now," said Ruff. "We put a lot of work in throughout the year, and we had a lot to be proud of, and there isn't going to be a grave feeling of letting everybody down. The fan support has been absolutely tremendous and the expectations were sky high, and that room was as quiet as quiet can be. It's a great group of guys."

Sadly, less than two months later, both Drury and Briere bolted via free agency. The Sabres haven't come close to matching the success of 2006–2007 since.

"Punching" Out the Leafs

The reporters milling about at the Mount Royal Hotel in Toronto on the night the 1970 amateur draft ended posed a question to Maple Leafs general manager Stafford Smythe: "How do you think Buffalo will do against your Leafs this first year?" Smythe replied, "They won't win a game."

He was almost right. By season's end, Toronto had won five of the six matchups against the expansion Sabres—but the Leafs did actually lose the two teams' very first meeting. That contest marked Punch Imlach's return to Toronto, his first game there since Smythe had fired him in 1969, and it was the one game he wanted to win more than any other on the 78-game first-year docket.

It would be three short years before the Sabres won the right to participate in the NHL playoffs, and only five years before they were playing for the Stanley Cup. But this game at Maple Leaf Gardens had all the trappings of a postseason showdown—because Imlach made it that way.

"We knew that this game might be as close to a playoff game that we would play all year, so that's the way we tried to play it," said Gilbert Perreault.

By the time the stunning 7–2 Buffalo victory was complete, Imlach looked as if he'd just won the lottery. "That has to be one of my biggest thrills in hockey," Imlach said. "I'd rank it with a Stanley Cup win, or maybe with that big game we won at Detroit in the last game of the season to make the playoffs my first season with the Leafs. The players knew what this game meant to me."

Bitter over his dismissal in Toronto and eager to whip his former employers with the team he had built from scratch, Imlach treated this trip to Toronto as if it was Game 7 of the Cup Finals. He recalled thinking the day before the game, "It's 6:00, exactly 24 hours before we walk into the dressing room at the Garden." Two hours later, while having dinner with his chief scout, John Andersen, he looked at his watch and said, "Exactly 24 hours and they'll be dropping the puck."

The night did not start well, as Roger Crozier allowed an early power-play goal to Toronto's Garry Monahan. But Don Marshall and Phil Goyette—who had just rejoined the Sabres after leaving training camp, intent on retiring after getting a look at what a mishmash group they'd be playing with—then took the ice for their first shift as Sabres on a power play, and Marshall tied the game by flipping a rebound past Leafs goalie Bruce Gamble.

Gerry Meehan and Toronto's Mike Walton traded goals early in the second period. But from then on it was all Buffalo. The recently acquired Larry Keenan scored twice to make it 4–2 by the end of the second, Meehan netted his second of the night, and then two more fresh recruits just grabbed off the scrap heap by Imlach—Steve Atkinson and Paul Andrea—wrapped up the rout.

Greeted by a standing ovation when he took his spot behind the Buffalo bench at the start of the game, Punch was amazed to hear the Toronto crowd chanting his name by the end of the fascinating night.

"I lived in Toronto all my life until this year," Sabres ticket manager Bobby Hewiston told the *Buffalo News* that night, "and I never saw a Maple Leaf Gardens crowd like this one. They cheered Buffalo as much as they did Toronto."

A few days after the game, Imlach paid $420 for advertising space in the *Toronto Telegram* to thank the fans of Toronto for the way he was treated during his return to the Garden. His ad read: "To great hockey fans: Thanks for an unforgettable reception."

38 Darcy Regier

When Darcy Regier arrived in Buffalo during the summer of 1997 to take the reins of a franchise in disarray, it wasn't long before he realized things were going to be different for him than they had been back when he was with the Islanders.

"I remember when I first came here, and somebody gave me the finger when I was driving down the road," Regier told the *Buffalo News* during an interview in 2006. "I thought at first that it was my driving. Then I realized that my driving was fine."

In Buffalo, people take their hockey—and their hockey GMs—seriously. This had not been quite the case back when he was just the assistant general manager of the listless New York Islanders, a team with a flagging fan base that probably couldn't have identified the behind-the-scenes Regier if he was had been walking out of the team's Long Island practice facility in broad daylight.

But in Buffalo, a small town immersed in a passionate love affair with hockey and the Sabres, everyone knew who Regier was the moment he took over for the fired John Muckler in June 1997. And he was none too popular in his first few weeks on the job.

Regier's tenure in Buffalo began amidst tremendous discord, and the first key decision he made remains one of the most controversial of his career, even 15 years later. He decided to offer wildly popular coach Ted Nolan a one-year contract because he wasn't sure if he and Nolan could coexist. When Nolan declined—which Regier knew he would—the new GM hired Lindy Ruff as his first (and, through 2012, only) coach.

Regier, who grew up in a small town in Saskatchewan, the son of Mennonites, played hockey as a youth and ultimately played 26 games in the NHL, 11 of which came with the Islanders during their run of Stanley Cup dominance during the early 1980s. He went to work for Islanders GM Bill Torrey upon retiring, and thought he was the heir apparent to the top job when Torrey left to manage the Florida Panthers.

Mike Milbury was hired instead, then proceeded to hand Regier a pink slip. That's why Regier was available when Sabres president Larry Quinn brought him to Buffalo to right a ship that was sinking under the weight of colossal chaos. Regier got the Sabres pointed in the right direction during his very first year, and his first two seasons together with Ruff resulted in Buffalo advancing to the conference finals in 1998 and the Stanley Cup Finals in 1999.

The early 2000s saw the franchise in the dark period of the Adelphia Communications scandal, in which team owner John Rigas and his son, Tim, were sent to prison and the Sabres went into bankruptcy. Regier guided the organization out of the abyss and was rewarded with two more conference finals appearances on his watch.

Despite this success, Regier has never been a fan favorite because his management style has always been so painfully patient. He has never been a guy to pull the trigger on big deals, and some would say he has stuck with the core players on the team for too long.

While fans sometimes focus on negative incidents such as Nolan's departure, Pat LaFontaine's concussion-related exodus, the contentious contract dispute with Michael Peca, the loss of both Danny Briere and Chris Drury to free agency on the same July 2007 day, and the parade of recent trade-deadline duds he has acquired, Regier's tenure in Buffalo has been noteworthy.

On the day he was hired in Buffalo, Regier said, "My stamp will come over time. It will come not by my direct actions, but by actions reflected in the organization."

With the glaring exception of the lack of a championship—something that no other Sabres GM has delivered, either—Regier has steered the team through some of its most trying times. That may be the most indelible mark he will leave behind.

"He's been through a lot," said Ruff, who has stood side-by-side with Regier along the way as the longest-tenured NHL coach through 2012. "It's incredible, really. For him to deal with what he's dealt with—bankruptcy, new owners, rolling through all that stuff—there were days that I don't know how he did it. But he did it. There was stuff he didn't know how to do, but he found ways to get it done."

39 The Saddest Night

Thousands of events have taken place in front of tens of millions of fans during Memorial Auditorium's storied 56-year existence.

They have cheered the Sabres in victory, booed the opposition in defeat, and treated every other home team—be it the Braves, the Bisons, Canisius, Niagara, St. Bonaventure—and every other opponent the same. There have been concerts, conventions, circuses, Cub Scout jamborees, commencements, figure skating productions, auto shows, dog shows, exhibition tennis matches, bicycle races, and roller derbies. You name it, it has played the Aud, and in almost every instance the people who passed through the turnstiles were there to have a good time and be entertained.

But on the night of February 21, 1974, the usual sellout crowd for the Sabres game against Atlanta did not come for the entertainment. They did not come to cheer the Sabres, nor to boo the Flames. That night, which was unlike any other in the history of the Aud, they came to mourn the passing of Sabres defenseman Tim Horton, who had died in a one-car crash on the Queen Elizabeth Way just outside of St. Catharines, Ontario, in the wee hours of that cold winter morning.

"When they called me to come down and identify the body, I couldn't believe that this could ever take place," Joe Crozier, the Sabres coach at the time, recalled. "When I lost Tim Horton, damn it, I lost my heart."

There had been so much enthusiasm built during the previous year as Buffalo made its first foray into the NHL playoffs. It seemed that this young team, with its French Connection line and its solid complimentary parts, could only get better. And the 44-year-old Horton was going to be there to help assist in that process, just as he had done so marvelously in 1972–1973.

As was commonplace during the last five or so years of his career, Horton had said that he planned to retire after a playoff loss to Montreal. But once training camp got under way, he had allowed general manager Punch Imlach to talk him into playing again.

Horton told Imlach in negotiation that it was going to cost around $150,000 and a new car—a spiffy Ford Pantera that he'd had his eye on for a while. Imlach agreed to the money, but he had reservations about the car, especially when he found out it was a $17,000 sports car. Imlach later wrote in his book *Heaven and Hell in the NHL* that he was worried about Horton driving that car, and even remarked to him, "You're liable to kill yourself in that thing." Five months later, that's exactly what Horton did.

Horton had suffered a broken jaw in a Monday morning practice, and since he couldn't practice the next day, he asked Crozier if he could drive up to Toronto to take care of some business before the Sabres arrived there Wednesday to play the Leafs. Ever the gamer, Horton decided to play, broken jaw and all, and even performed well enough to be named third star in Buffalo's 4–2 loss.

Horton went to his home in Oakville, Ontario, then got up early to drive back to Buffalo. He was traveling a reported 100 miles per hour when an Ontario Provincial Police officer nabbed him on radar and drove after him in pursuit. He never caught Horton, however, because his car careened out of control at around 5:00 AM. Horton's body was ejected from the car and landed some 120 feet from the mangled auto in the median.

Police found Crozier's number in Horton's wallet, so that was who they called to come identify the body.

That night the Sabres took the ice to play a game they did not want to play, and it was amazing that they played well enough to earn a 4–4 tie.

Said Mike Robitaille, who idolized Horton (as did many of the Sabres):

> I'll never forget the first game we played after he died. It was an awful night to walk in and see his locker stall empty. You had a feeling like he was a safety net for all of us. When he walked in the dressing room, everything was OK, Timmy's here. He was the glue—just his presence, his past experience, and being the person that he was.
>
> He made the biggest impact in my life of anyone I've ever been involved with in hockey. I became an experienced player because of Tim. He was everything to me: my mentor, my

hero. I idolized him. I used to stand at the blue line during warm-ups the way Tim did. He would stand there and take his one foot and bring the heel of his skate up, so I did the same thing just because Tim did.

Jim Schoenfeld, who had been mentored by Horton since his first day as a Sabre, will never forget the mood in the Aud that night:

I thought I had a pretty good handle on things, I thought I was OK and I'd go to the rink and play. But I remember being on the ice as part of the starting lineup during the national anthem, and they had the moment of silence for Tim. It was strange, it was almost like you could feel the compound grief of everyone in the building and it was kind of overwhelming. I remember trying to play the first shift with tears coming out of my eyes and I remember finishing the shift and going to the bench and Joe Crozier came down and comforted me. The loss was not only felt then, but it's been felt ever since. Tim was not only a great mentor and hockey player and someone I looked up to that way, he was a hell of a guy.

National TV Debut

Just three days after the tragic death of beloved defenseman Tim Horton, the Sabres appeared on national television for the first time.

The date was February 24, 1974, and Buffalo played host to the Boston Bruins on NBC's *Game of the Week*. Despite playing with heavy hearts, the Sabres beat the powerhouse Bruins for the only time that year, 3–2.

Gerry Meehan and Rene Robert scored 1:59 apart in the second to overcome an early 2–1 deficit. "The Sabres had to come up with a great game to beat us, and they did," said Boston coach Bep Guidolin.

Sabres coach Joe Crozier, who was amazed by what his team had accomplished in tying Atlanta the day Horton died, called this victory Buffalo's best game of the year. Meehan said, "It was a continuation of the Atlanta game. We carried on as we did when we went out to win that one for Tim Horton."

The Dynamic Duo

There is no question that the French Connection line is the most famous and beloved line in Buffalo Sabres history. But the trio of Gilbert Perreault, Rick Martin, and Rene Robert actually never came close to the single-season production achieved by Pat LaFontaine and Alexander Mogilny during 1992–1993.

Consider this: the French Connection was at its peak in 1974–1975, the year the Sabres advanced to the Stanley Cup Finals. The thrilling threesome combined for 131 goals and 291 points. They followed that up with their second-best year, 1975–1976, scoring 128 goals and 286 points. But in 1992–1993, LaFontaine and Mogilny combined for 129 goals and 275 points. That's right: the *two* of them had nearly identical numbers to the *three* flying Frenchmen.

LaFontaine set franchise single-season records for points (148) and assists (95) that season, and Mogilny established the new team record for goals with 76. LaFontaine also scored 53 goals that season, more than any member of the French Connection ever scored in a single season (Martin scored 52 twice). That achievement still stands as the third-highest total on the team, behind only Mogilny and Danny Gare's 56 in 1979–1980. Mogilny's 127 points that year were 14 more than Perreault scored during his best season, when he had 113 in 1975–1976.

"Alex and Patty played a huge part in the confidence of that team," said defenseman Grant Ledyard. "Dave Andreychuk had moved on that year [traded to Toronto in February], and I believe if that part hadn't left, that would have helped us move on in the playoffs [the Sabres ended their first-round drought by beating Boston, but were then swept out by Montreal]. That group was pretty special, Alex with his 76 goals and Patty with his 148 points."

That year the Sabres scored 335 goals, tied for sixth in the NHL and third-most in franchise history behind only those French Connection–led teams in 1974–1975 (354) and 1975–1976 (339).

It was as if the puck had eyes that year, and seemingly every time they were in possession, there was a sense that something good was going to happen. Randy Wood, a grinding winger, echoed Ledyard regarding the confidence the Sabres had when LaFontaine and Mogilny were operating. "The first thing you think of is we got a pretty good chance of winning," said Wood. "When you have guys going like that, it makes it easier on the rest of the team. You just throw out the grappling hook and hold on for the ride. Yee-haw!"

LaFontaine had already established himself as one of the premier players in the NHL during his days with the Islanders, scoring at least 30 goals during each of his last six seasons with New York, including 54 in 1989–1990 (when he also registered what was then his highest point total, 105). His old coach, fellow Hall of Famer Al Arbour, once said of him, "When he's really skating, all you can see is the vapor trail. Once he gets by you, the only way to get him is with a whaling gun."

A contract dispute prompted the Islanders to deal LaFontaine to Buffalo in a deal that included Pierre Turgeon, and as soon as he arrived, Mogilny's career took off. Nicknamed Alexander the Great, Mogilny had defected from his native land in 1989 at the age of 20 and had endured two mediocre seasons in Buffalo as he tried to cope with a new life, a new language, a well-publicized fear of flying, a new style of play, and worrying about the ramifications of his defection for both himself and his family.

But once he was teamed with LaFontaine, Mogilny scored 39 goals in 1991–1992 (LaFontaine had 46 in just 57 games), setting the stage for their scoring explosion the following year.

"Now Do You Believe?"

There is no question that Buffalo Sabres broadcaster Rick Jeanneret has a flair for the dramatic. It really doesn't matter whether it's three minutes into the first period or three minutes into overtime, nor whether it's a middling game in November or a Stanley Cup playoff match in June.

One of his great calls was, "Now do you believe? Now do you believe? These guys are good! Scary good!" This legendary question was asked when Jason Pominville scored in overtime of Game 5 against Ottawa in the second round of the 2006 playoffs, eliminating the favored Senators and sending the Sabres on to the Eastern Conference Finals.

Of course Sabres fans already believed before that night—in fact, the game that started them believing came about a week earlier, when Buffalo pulled off a thrilling 7–6 overtime victory in Game 1 of that series. "I don't know if it's a wise thing to run and gun with them," coach Lindy Ruff said after Chris Drury's goal 18 seconds into the overtime period ended the highest-scoring postseason game in Sabres history. "We want to run with them, but I don't think we want to gun with them."

Well, it worked out just fine that night at ScotiaBank Place.

The season had not started well for the Sabres, particularly their three early meetings with Ottawa. The Senators won every game by a cumulative score of 21–5, the last loss dropping the Sabres to 8–9. After that game, however, Buffalo went on a tear, winning 15 of 17. From then on, they battled the Senators for supremacy in the Northeast Division.

Buffalo Sabres Hall of Fame Class of 2012 inductees Rick Jeanneret (left) and Dale Hawerchuk salute the crowd before a game between the Sabres and the Winnipeg Jets in Buffalo on November 8, 2011.

Ottawa—which finished with a league-leading 314 goals—always maintained the upper hand, winning two of the next three meetings with Buffalo, but in the final two weeks the Sabres won seven of eight games, including a pair of confidence-producing victories over the Senators. Ottawa won the division with 113 points, Buffalo had 110, and both teams continued their rolls in the first round of the playoffs as the Senators took out Tampa Bay in five games and Buffalo beat Philadelphia in six.

Before the second-round series began, Senators general manager John Muckler, who had previously held that position in Buffalo, predicted, "This is probably a matchup of the fastest two teams in the league, and it really should be exciting." And Ruff had said he expected the series to be "a track meet." Yet no one could have envisioned the first game would be quite as exciting as it turned out to be.

The opener had already been an up-and-down, shinny type of game, and then it really got crazy when the teams combined for three goals in the final 1:37 of regulation. With Buffalo trailing 5–4 and playing shorthanded, things looked pretty bleak. But then Derek Roy beat Andrej Meszaros to a loose puck at the Buffalo blue line and steamed in two-on-one with Tim Connolly. Roy passed to Connolly, then converted Connolly's return pass to tie the game.

"I knew we had to go for it," Roy said. "I wanted to try to cheat a little bit. I stole the puck off the defenseman. Timmy just waited the 'D' out, got it over to me, and I had the empty net."

On that same power play, however, the Senators regained the lead when Bryan Smolinski scored his second goal of the night just 24 seconds later. But Buffalo tied it with 10.7 seconds remaining when Roy, who finished with five points, took a seemingly harmless

"These Guys Are Good, Scary Good"

As Jason Pominville steamed down the left wing, beating Ottawa's Daniel Alfredsson through the neutral zone and then making a bee line toward Senators goalie Ray Emery, Sabres fans watching on television crept to the edges of their couches and bar stools in anticipation of what was about to happen.

It was overtime in Game 5 of the Eastern Conference semifinals, and the Sabres had the favored Senators, the Northeast Division champs with a conference-leading 113 points, on the brink of elimination.

Buffalo was shorthanded because Jay McKee had taken down Alfredsson just moments earlier, and with the high-scoring Senators on the power play, there was a chance they could send the series back to Buffalo for a nerve-wracking sixth game with Ottawa—once down 3–0 in the series, now within 3–2 and owning momentum.

Instead, Pominville—who hadn't even made the Sabres roster coming out of training camp that year—grabbed a loose puck in his own end and lugged it out himself. With Alfredsson curiously skating as if he were trapped in quicksand, Pominville zipped right past him for a clean backhand that Emery couldn't handle. Just like that the Sabres were moving on to the conference finals to play Carolina for the right to advance to the Stanley Cup Finals.

It was a stunningly dramatic goal. Up in the broadcast booth, play-by-play announcer Rick Jeanneret screamed one of his typically spot-on calls: "Now do you believe? Now do you believe? These guys are good, scary good!"

shot from the point that Ottawa goalie Ray Emery mishandled. Daniel Briere corralled the rebound behind the net, centered it out front, and Connolly was able to score on a backhander.

When the teams returned for the overtime, things happened so fast that some fans were still in the concession lines when the game ended. Senators defenseman Anton Volchenkov coughed up the puck in his own zone, and Mike Grier collected the turnover. He found Drury in the left circle and fired a shot over Emery's shoulder to win it.

"The puck might have hit some water on the ice there, and Volchenkov, it just kind of died on him," Drury said. "Tough break for him. Then Mike made a great pass, and I was able to get a good shot on."

As Jeanneret implored, Sabres fans indeed started to believe that their team finally had a chance to advance to the Stanley Cup Finals and win. Sadly, they instead ran into a veteran Carolina squad in the Eastern Conference Finals. Thanks to a spate of injuries to the defensive corps, Buffalo wound up falling in seven hard-fought games to a Hurricanes team that went on to beat Edmonton to win Lord Stanley's chalice.

42 Remember the Aud

On a day during the inaugural season of Buffalo's new downtown arena, Joe Crozier—one of the team's former coaches who had since become a front-office executive—sat in a luxury suite high above the ice surface watching coach Ted Nolan put the team through a game-day morning skate. The place was glimmering in its newness, and there was no doubt that the Sabres were happy in their new digs, originally called Marine Midland Arena, later HSBC Arena, and now First Niagara Center.

But as Crozier sat back in a comfortably cushioned seat, he smiled in remembrance of his old friend, the Aud.

"The Aud had charisma," Crozier said. "It was a smaller rink and the people were closer to the ice, so you had a lot going for you in that place. There was so much enthusiasm in that building. I remember I'd come in and there would be people lined up in the lobby waiting to buy tickets. The fans were great; they really helped us. There was a hell of a difference for us playing at home with those people behind us."

Ground was broken for the Aud on Lower Terrace Street in December 1938, and when it opened on October 14, 1940, with an official dedication parade and luncheon to honor those who lost their lives in World War I, it was considered a convention center and municipal auditorium rather than a sports and entertainment arena.

But that perception quickly changed. When there wasn't a political rally, a concert, a circus, a dog show, or an auto show booked, the new building was home to the minor league Buffalo Bisons, the new American Hockey League franchise that had moved from Syracuse and became the Aud's first primary tenant. From 1940 through the end of the 1969–1970 season, the Bisons played at the Aud before folding their operation when the Sabres began playing in the NHL in October 1970.

While anyone who was anyone played at the Aud during its 56-year existence, no one was more beloved than the city's hockey teams—the bottle-cap logoed Bisons and the swashbuckling Sabres. Hockey was always the lifeblood of the building, and the coaches and players knew it every time they stepped on the ice.

"The crowds were awesome," remembered Danny Gare, who joined the Sabres in 1974–1975 and has been sporadically involved

Farewell, Old Friend

The 1995–1996 edition of the Sabres struggled on the ice, missing the playoffs, but the organization performed like a champion on the night of April 14, 1996, when they played their final game at Memorial Auditorium.

Never mind that Buffalo defeated Hartford 4–1 to improve its all-time record in its first home to 581–289–155. The closing ceremony and the heartfelt way the Sabres turned out the lights on the old barn made the team's farewell a classy, well-planned affair.

Team owner Seymour Knox III, who died a month later after a long bout with cancer, said after the final game, "I tried my best, but I think probably some [tears] snuck out. It was an emotional evening." Sadly, that was to be Knox's last game, as well.

Former Buffalo captain and coach Floyd Smith introduced former players Rene Robert, Don Luce, Rick Martin, Danny Gare, Craig Ramsay, and Larry Playfair. After the banners and retired numbers were lowered from the rafters and carried off the ice, captain Pat LaFontaine—who had scored his 40th goal of the season earlier in the night—shot one last puck into the net and skated off as the lights dimmed.

"To think of all the players that have played here and worn the jersey, and the fans that have watched the games over the years—to be the last player [on the ice] is something I'll always cherish," said LaFontaine.

with broadcasting the team's games for nearly two decades. "You look at Boston, Philly, Chicago, all tough places to play, but I would put the Aud right up in the top three or four in advantage. When we skated out on the ice, you were so pumped; they were playing that *Sabre Dance*. And the people and their proximity to the ice, they were loud and vocal and you could feel the energy. When we needed them, they would lift you."

Outside of Gilbert Perreault, no player in the history of the franchise spent more time on the Aud's ice than Craig Ramsay. Starting with the 1972–1973 season, the building was sold out for the rest of the decade, a period of 359 games, and Ramsay played in every last one—his team-record consecutive-games-played streak of 776 began that year. Ramsay seconded Gare's opinion about how important the home-ice advantage was for Buffalo.

"Teams hated playing at the Aud," Ramsay said. "There were a lot of games that were over in the first 10 minutes. We'd have teams down 3–0 in the first 10 minutes and that was it, and it was a matter for them of just keeping from getting hurt. And when we had those quick starts, the crowd would just be jumping, they loved it. Teams would come in there, and there was nowhere to go, nowhere to hide, there was no open space. The fans loved the banging from our big people, they loved our speed with our counter attack. We were an exciting team to watch, the people loved it, and we felt such a great relationship with them during those years. It was fun for all of us to be in the building."

The new arena was built at the foot of Washington Street, about two blocks away from the Aud. When the city didn't know what to do with the old building, it stood there for more than a decade after it was last used in the spring of 1996. It was finally razed in 2009. Today the lot where it stood is still an empty expanse as city planners try to figure out what to build there.

"I guess it never had the majesty of a Boston Garden or Chicago Stadium, because there really aren't any great championship banners there," George Gould, the longtime manager of the Aud, told the *Buffalo News* shortly before the lights were turned out for good. "But there are so many great memories there. There were a lot of things that went on in that building. That building was always there for us."

43 The Trade

It was a day that Larry Playfair has never forgotten, even 30 years later. The former Sabres' defenseman/tough guy is not alone. There are countless longtime Sabres fans who have never forgotten the afternoon of December 2, 1981, when Scotty Bowman performed open-heart surgery on the Buffalo roster by trading Jim Schoenfeld, Danny Gare, and Derek Smith to Detroit in exchange for Mike Foligno, Brent Peterson, and Dale McCourt—one of the biggest trades in franchise history.

"I was too young to know what the heck was going on," recalled Playfair. "But that trade, in my opinion, took the heart of our team right out. I don't know why there was a trade; I'm not smart enough to give you an answer. As a kid on the team, I'd been here two-and-a-half seasons, and these were guys like Schony [Jim Schoenfeld], who I idolized. You walked into the dressing room and there was a big void. I would say it's akin to a teenager losing his father and now you're in charge of the house. The guys that came in weren't bad guys, they were new teammates, but I remember the hole I felt, the emptiness, the 'Oh my God, what have they just done; we'll never make the playoffs now.'"

Bowman was never a heart-and-soul guy. To him hockey was a business, and he ran the Sabres like one. Never mind the fact that Schoenfeld had been a pillar on the team for a decade, a past captain who would have spilled a gallon of blood on the ice if that's what it took to get the job done. Gare, who at the time of the trade was the Sabres captain, was the same kind of player and was Buffalo's fan favorite, as well.

None of that mattered to Bowman. The Sabres were in the midst of a slump, he thought they needed a kick in the pants to get them going, and trading Schoenfeld and Gare was the price he was willing to pay.

Bowman's rationale was simple. He felt Gare and Schoenfeld were on the down sides of their careers. McCourt, the No. 1 overall pick in the 1977 draft by Detroit, still had potential even though he'd already shown that he hadn't been worthy of being the top pick. Peterson was a workmanlike player who would fill Smith's role. And Foligno, the No. 3 overall pick in the 1979 draft, was a gritty, hardnosed forward—just what the Sabres sorely needed—who could replace Gare.

Both Schoenfeld and Gare expressed surprise and bitterness about the way Bowman had treated them.

"In a way I'm kind of glad I'm going because I didn't understand a lot of things that were going on with this hockey club," Gare said. "This is a very unhappy team right now. I couldn't see myself going to the rink every day under these circumstances. I'm shocked. Hockey is a business, but I thought there should be something personal to it. I gave my best to this club at all times. I thought the organization had a little more class than this. The only thing that hurts is that one man can be so powerful. I just can't understand why he is the way he is."

Said Schoenfeld, "As great as it is here, it's almost a relief not to have to deal with Bowman anymore. I have nothing good to say about that man, and that's not because I was traded. He wants a young team, but I never saw a Stanley Cup won by a bunch of kids, or a Super Bowl, or a World Series."

In the 24 hours after the deal was consummated, the team received almost 800 calls in protest. In a memorable scene at the Buffalo airport, Schoenfeld broke down and cried while being interviewed by Channel 7 sports anchor Rick Azar, and the normally stoic Azar was visibly shaken, as well.

Both men softened their stances on Bowman as the years passed; Schoenfeld even wound up coaching the Sabres for a brief time while Bowman was the general manager.

"It's funny at the time how traumatic things seem, but then when you look back, it's nothing more than a slight inconvenience because we went on to Detroit and made some new friends there, then went to Boston, and you find the beat goes on," said Schoenfeld. "But sure, it was a big hurt when I had to leave Buffalo."

44 No Garden Party

As a youngster growing up in Toronto, Boston's Brad Park often imagined living out this exact scenario: Stanley Cup playoffs, Game 7, overtime, puck in his possession, a shooting lane opens, back goes the stick, and away goes the shot, so hard that it nearly tears a hole through the back of the net.

While raising his stick in celebration, Park would mimic the sound of the crowd going wild, paying homage to their hero. He'd soak it all in, take a bow, then go retrieve the puck and do it all over again.

"I used to fantasize about it," Park said. "In my fantasies I would play against Glenn Hall, who was a great goaltender then for the Chicago Blackhawks, and I would skate against Bobby Hull and Stan Mikita and I would beat them all. But when I finally got to the NHL I never scored the winning goal against anyone...until tonight."

Unfortunately for the Sabres, Park's fantasy became a reality on the night of the Bruins' 3–2 overtime victory at Boston Garden over Buffalo in Game 7 of a bitterly fought 1983 second-round playoff series.

Substituting for Hall, Mikita, and Hull were Buffalo's Bob Sauve, Gilbert Perreault, and Lindy Ruff. As Park raised his stick in celebration, he didn't need to mimic the crowd noise—14,685 leather-lunged Bostonians took care of that in grand style, paying homage to their hero at a decibel level that would have made a heavy metal guitarist wince. Park didn't get a chance to take a bow and soak it all in, however, because his Bruin teammates soon had him buried in a sea of gleeful humanity. Lastly, there was no need to retrieve the puck and do it all over again, because that goal ended the series and sent the Sabres despondently back to Buffalo.

"It's just so final," Buffalo defenseman Mike Ramsey said. "It was so close, and then it's over and it's so final."

Ric Seiling, who scored both Buffalo goals, just shook his head amidst the silence of the Sabres' locker room and said, "It's the shame of this series that the winner didn't skate out of here with the Stanley Cup. It was the kind of hockey you'd like to see in the Finals. We should have been playing for the Stanley Cup tonight, not just a handshake."

Buffalo had surprised the Bruins with a 7–4 victory in Game 1, and after four games the series was tied at 2–2 as Boston rolled to a 6–2 triumph in Game 4 at the Aud to regain home-ice advantage. The fifth game was a 9–0 nightmare for the Sabres. Having scored 15 goals in two games, it looked like the Bruins would go back to Buffalo and wrap it up. "Sometimes it's better to lose like that, it gets you refocused," said Craig Ramsay. "What's the difference in the final analysis—one goal or nine goals? It really doesn't matter."

And it certainly didn't seem to matter as Buffalo rallied from a 2–0 deficit in Game 6 with rookie Phil Housley scoring twice and Ruff netting the game-winner in the third period for a 5–3 series-tying victory. Seiling's two early Game 7 goals were matched by Barry Pederson and Park in the second period, and after a tension-packed scoreless third period, the game went to overtime, though only 1:52 of extra time was needed.

Pederson won a faceoff back to Park, who recalled, "When I got the puck, I looked to see what we had in front of the net. I knew

I had time, but I waited a little too long and, when I shot, Craig Ramsay got his stick on it."

While everyone on the ice except Ramsay and Park thought the puck was under Sauve, who had gone down to block the shot, the puck actually caromed right back to Park. In the instant it took for them to realize what had happened, the Sabres knew they were in big trouble.

"Everybody else seemed to be down on the ice," Buffalo's Andre Savard said. "I took a look at the puck and then saw Bobby down and I was certain the puck was underneath him. I looked around waiting for a whistle, and the next thing I see was Park winding up and shooting at an open net."

Peeters Peters Out

Although it was still a few months before the playoff series with Boston, there was plenty on the line the night of February 16, 1983, at the Aud when the Sabres played host to the Bruins. Boston came into Buffalo riding a 17-game unbeaten streak, the Sabres were on a four-game losing streak, and Bruins goalie Pete Peeters was looking to etch his name into the NHL record book.

Peeters had not lost in his last 31 decisions, and he was one game away from tying the all-time record for consecutive games for a goaltender without a loss (a record set by Boston's Gerry Cheevers during the Bruins' Stanley Cup championship season in 1971–1972).

And as the Sabres were ending Peeters' bid with a 3–1 victory, Cheevers was right there to see it—because at the time, he was Boston's head coach.

"It's a bitter disappointment that we didn't win tonight or tie, because I think a lot of our team and myself were cheering for Pete to break the record," said Cheevers, who saw Gilbert Perreault and Phil Housley beat Peeters before Brent Peterson wrapped it up with an empty-net goal . "Buffalo played very well, though, and that was it. I'm bitter that we lost. There's nobody that wanted him to break that record more than me. I told him that I was sorry that we didn't give him the effort he deserved tonight."

Winning goaltender Bob Sauve thought about Cheevers' mark and said, "I don't know if anyone will ever break that record. It's a big one, and with all the teams around the league now, I'm not sure that it can be broken."

So far, no one has.

45 The Year of Uncertainty

For at least a decade—perhaps more—Buffalo sports fans have lived in fear that the Bills—their beloved yet perpetually talent-starved National Football League franchise—will pack their belongings and move to Toronto or Los Angeles or some other NFL-barren city.

Contrarily, the Sabres have always been firmly entrenched in Buffalo, one of the NHL's rock-solid franchises ever since they made their debut in 1970.

Well, except for one year: The year of uncertainty, 2002–2003.

During the summer of 2002, when Sabres owner John Rigas and his sons, Tim and Michael, were arrested for bank, wire, and securities fraud for embezzling more than $2 billion from Adelphia Communications—the company the elder Rigas founded on a $300 investment—the Sabres' future in Buffalo was perilous to say the least.

With the Sabres owing Adelphia approximately $160 million—money Rigas took from the company to buy and run the club—the NHL had to step in to operate the bankrupt franchise after Rigas stepped down as chairman of Adelphia. While the league's primary goal was to find a new owner that would keep the team in Buffalo, there was a chance that any prospective buyers could move the team wherever they so desired.

There were several interested parties, and for several months it looked as if Buffalo businessman Mark Hamister and his New York–based partner Todd Berman would be the winning bidders. But when it became apparent that Hamister did not have the necessary financial assets for long-term viability, NHL commissioner Gary Bettman had to reject his candidacy, a crushing blow to fans who saw Hamister as someone who would certainly keep the Sabres in Buffalo.

As the search for a new owner continued, the Sabres were also enduring one of their worst seasons ever, winning only four of their first 23 games—a stretch that included a team record–tying 12-game winless streak. And without superstar goaltender Dominik Hasek, who had been traded to Detroit prior to the 2001–2002 season, the Sabres did not have a marquee player. Attendance dipped 28 percent from the previous season.

"It didn't matter where we went on the road, nobody wanted to talk about hockey," broadcaster Rick Jeanneret said. "Visiting reporters from other towns, they all wanted to talk about the bankruptcy and the future of the team. It starts wearing on guys."

Their poor play, the increasing number of empty seats, and the debt that needed to be repaid severely hampered the league's efforts to sell the team. And while there were a few other nibbles as the calendar flipped to 2003, nothing panned out.

That is until an unlikely figure re-emerged. Former team president Larry Quinn, who had in effect been forced out of the organization when the Rigas family gained full control of the team from the Knox family, entered the fray as a managing partner for Tom Golisano, a Rochester, New York, billionaire and former New York State gubernatorial candidate.

When it was clear to Bettman that Golisano—the founder of Rochester-based Paychex, then the nation's second-largest payroll-processing company—had the bankroll to not only buy the team but also sustain the operation, the deal was finalized.

"I think people should stop worrying about the Sabres in Buffalo, because our knight on a white horse came riding in," Bettman said when he announced the transfer of ownership to Golisano. "This represents an opportunity for the Sabres to move forward under strong ownership and to give the fans and this community the assurance that the franchise will be here."

One of the first things Golisano did after taking control was to send the Sabres onto the ice at HSBC Arena for their final game of the season in their old blue and gold uniforms. And when he announced a reduction in ticket prices for the 2003–2004 season, that white horse he was on was certainly riding high in western New York.

"This franchise has been here for 33 years, and it would've been very sad to say Buffalo doesn't have a hockey team anymore," said the original Sabre, Gilbert Perreault, who actually was listed as one of the team's creditors. "But now Mr. Golisano is here and it looks like it's going to be here for a long time."

Golisano owned the team from March 2003 until he sold it to current owner Terry Pegula in March 2011.

Picking Pierre

When Pierre Turgeon skated onto the Memorial Auditorium ice for the first time as a Sabre in September of 1987 to play a preseason game against Washington—and scored a goal on that initial shift—he was greeted by a banner that read "From Perreault to Turgeon...The Tradition Continues." How's that for some serious pressure for the 18-year-old French Canadian whom the Sabres had selected No. 1 overall three months earlier in the 1987 NHL Entry Draft?

Gilbert Perreault, the original Sabre, the quintessential French Canadian star, was the first player drafted by the expansion Sabres in 1970, and went on to play all 16½ of his NHL seasons with Buffalo, where he scored 512 goals and 1,326 points on his way to the Hockey Hall of Fame.

Partly because Perreault had called it a career during the previous season, the Sabres finished dead last in the NHL, giving them the opportunity to select Turgeon—widely regarded as a can't-miss prospect—as their No. 1.

The symmetry was unmistakable. With the departure of the only other player Buffalo had ever drafted No. 1 overall, here came the second such athlete, a No. 1 pick who was expected to strap a desperate franchise on his back and carry it back to prominence. Hollywood would have requested that Perreault come out of retirement for one night, returning to the Aud and performing an Olympic-style passing of the torch to Turgeon. Of course that was the perception the Sabres—and Turgeon—wanted to debunk. They knew the comparisons would be relentless.

"I knew he was very good in Buffalo," Turgeon said early in his rookie season of Perreault. "I just want to play my game. Some people make comparisons, but I don't. I like [Wayne] Gretzky and [Mike] Bossy and [Mario] Lemieux, but when you play, you don't think, 'I'll play like this guy or that guy.' I play like Pierre."

But Turgeon being Turgeon simply wasn't good enough for the hockey fans of Buffalo, who'd grown accustomed to the brilliance of Perreault and the way he played. Turgeon was a different player, and while he enjoyed a few decent years, he wound up being traded to the New York Islanders as part of the deal that brought Pat LaFontaine to Buffalo. Turgeon has largely been forgotten in western New York since.

"There were very high expectations on Pierre because he was going to be the guy who was going to come in and be the next Gilbert Perreault," said Craig Ramsay. "It was too bad. Pierre was a very good player, but he wasn't a Gilbert Perreault. He didn't have the skating ability to do that, but he had great passing skills and he needed good people to play with. But in Buffalo, everybody had that feeling that, 'Here we go again, we're going to have another Gilbert,' and imagine coming into a situation like that. That's unreasonable for anybody. He went on to do some great things in the NHL."

All-Time First-Round Picks

Year	Player		Year	Player
2012	Mikhail Grigorenko (center)		1990	Brad May (left wing)
	Zemgus Girgensons (center)		1989	Kevin Haller (defense)
2011	Joel Armia (right wing)		1988	Joel Savage (right wing)
2010	Mark Pysyk (defense)		1987	Pierre Turgeon (center)
2009	Zach Kassian (right wing)		1986	Shawn Anderson (defense)
2008	Tyler Myers (defense)		1985	Calle Johansson (defense)
	Tyler Ennis (center)		1984	Mikael Andersson (left wing)
2006	Dennis Persson (defense)		1983	Tom Barrasso (goaltender)
2005	Marek Zagrapan (center)			Normand Lacombe (r. wing)
2004	Drew Stafford (right wing)			Adam Creighton (center)
2003	Thomas Vanek (left wing)		1982	Phil Housley (defense)
2002	Keith Ballard (defense)			Paul Cyr (left wing)
	Dan Paille (left wing)			Dave Andreychuk (left wing)
2001	Jiri Novotny (center)		1981	Jiri Dudacek (right wing)
2000	Artem Kryukov (center)		1980	Steve Patrick (right wing)
1999	Barrett Heisten (left wing)		1979	Mike Ramsey (defense)
1998	Dimitri Kalinin (defense)		1978	Larry Playfair (defense)
1997	Mika Noronen (goaltender)		1977	Ric Seiling (right wing)
1996	Erik Rasmussen (center)		1975	Bob Sauve (goaltender)
1995	Jay McKee (defense)		1974	Lee Fogolin (defense)
	Martin Biron (goaltender)		1973	Morris Titanic (left wing)
1994	Wayne Primeau (center)		1972	Jim Schoenfeld (defense)
1992	David Cooper (defense)		1971	Richard Martin (left wing)
1991	Philippe Boucher (defense)		1970	Gilbert Perreault (center)

In his four full seasons with Buffalo, Turgeon scored 14, 34, 40, and 32 goals; had 42, 88, 106, and 79 points; and missed only six regular season games. And the Sabres—who had failed to reach the playoffs during the two years before he arrived—made it to the postseason in all four of his seasons with the team, though they never advanced past the first round.

By the time he retired as a member of the Colorado Avalanche (his sixth NHL team) in 2007, Turgeon's final tally was 515 goals (three more than Perreault), 812 assists (two fewer than Perreault), and 1,327 points (one more than Perreault). He also won the Lady

Byng Memorial Trophy for sportsmanship in 1992–1993, which Perreault had also won in 1972–1973.

So was Turgeon the next Perreault? No. Was he a terrific player for two decades with a résumé that should land him a spot alongside Perreault in the Hall of Fame? Absolutely.

"Had he had [Rick] Martin, [Rene] Robert, [Danny] Gare, maybe that would have helped," said Ramsay. "He had [Alexander] Mogilny for a while, but the team wasn't the same kind of team. Pierre was a highly skilled player, but he needed other people around him to take advantage of those skills."

47 Thomas Vanek

The Sabres didn't have to go very far to scout the player they ultimately picked in the first round of the 2003 NHL Draft. In fact, he came to them.

Thomas Vanek was a freshman at the University of Minnesota, a perennial NCAA Division I college hockey powerhouse, when the Gophers advanced to the Frozen Four in 2003 (fortuitously hosted by Buffalo at HSBC Arena).

Vanek put on quite a show that weekend, scoring the game-winning goal in overtime of Minnesota's 3–2 semifinal victory over Michigan. He also scored what proved to be the winner in the Gophers' 5–1 rout of New Hampshire in the national championship game.

Vanek, who led Minnesota in scoring that season with 31 goals and 62 points (most points by a Gophers freshman since Aaron Broten's 72 in 1979–1980), was named the tournament's most outstanding player. That sent Sabres general manager Darcy Regier scurrying to find out more about the Austrian-born winger.

Regier learned that Vanek had left his homeland as a 14-year-old to seek a career in the NHL. His journey began in tiny Lacombe, Alberta, a town located roughly halfway between Calgary and Edmonton, where he played midget AA while trying to learn English.

"I'll always remember getting off that plane in Canada and asking myself that question: 'What am I doing here?'" Vanek told the *Buffalo News*.

His next stop was Rochester, New York, where, ironically enough, Buffalo's farm team in the American Hockey League, the Rochester Americans, was located. He was hoping to play for the fledgling Rochester Junior Americans, who were in their first season of existence in the North American Hockey League. "They were a new franchise and I thought I had a pretty good shot of playing there even though I was so young," Vanek said.

A student visa problem prevented him from enrolling in school, so after just 14 games he moved on to Sioux Falls, South Dakota, to play in the United States Hockey League. For the next two-and-half years he was a star for the Stampede with 46 goals and 91 points in 53 games during his last season. That led him to being recruited to Minnesota, where his game continued to soar. The Sabres didn't need much convincing when their turn to pick at No. 5 came up.

"We saw a lot of his games," coach Lindy Ruff said. "We saw him score highlight-reel goals, big goals in a lot of different games. He's just a pure goal scorer from the tops of the circles down. Some of his goals on the rush were goals not many players can score. He's just got that knack around the net."

Vanek was thrilled that Buffalo selected him, saying, "I love the rink; I've won a championship there already, and hopefully there's more to come. I'm real happy I'm in Buffalo. Hopefully I can get to Buffalo soon and win some games and get Buffalo back on top."

Vanek opted to play one more year at Minnesota, then turned pro. He returned to Rochester to play for the Americans, scoring 42

Buffalo's Thomas Vanek scores the decisive shootout goal on Boston Bruins goalie Manny Fernandez in a 3–2 Sabres victory on October 21, 2008. Vanek was the first Austrian to play in the NHL All-Star Game.

goals and 68 points in his only minor league season and earning a promotion to Buffalo for the 2005–2006 season.

Vanek was a 43-goal-scorer by his second season. When Edmonton tried to pry him away from Buffalo with an eight-year, $50 million offer sheet, the Sabres exercised their option to retain him despite that hefty price tag. Clearly he turned out to be a bargain; today he is Buffalo's most dynamic scorer.

In 2009, when he became the first Austrian to play in the NHL All-Star Game, Vanek reflected on his magnificent journey. "The All-Star Game was so special to me as a kid that it was something I never dreamt," Vanek said. "The dream was always playing in the NHL—one game. When I watched the All-Star Game, I guess you can dream big. That was a little too big, especially for an Austrian who never made it before."

Razor

On the evening of March 11, 2003, all the sports highlight shows were airing a clip of the newest Ottawa Senator doing what he had been doing his entire career—taking a penalty.

For Rob Ray, those two minutes he was assessed for interference gave him 3,191 career penalty minutes, fifth most in NHL history. Incredibly, his first 3,189 penalty minutes were earned during his career with the Sabres—the most in history by one player on one team.

It was a strange sight that night watching Ray battle the Boston Bruins in the uniform of the despised Senators—about as weird as seeing former Buffalo Bills great Thurman Thomas wearing the uniform of the despised Miami Dolphins during the 2000 NFL season. For Sabres fans, seeing Ray in Ottawa skating on the same line with archenemy Chris Neil was also a stark reminder of the Sabres' financial plight at the time.

General manager Darcy Regier was looking to trim payroll from a team that barely *had* a payroll thanks to the Rigas family scandal that ultimately plunged the franchise into bankruptcy. But he also wanted to give Ray—who was likely to retire at season's end—one last shot to win a Stanley Cup.

"When they asked me if I wanted to go to another team if something came up," Ray recalled, "I said, 'Yeah,' because I didn't think there was a shot in hell of me going anywhere. Darcy said, 'If you want to go, we'll make the arrangements. If you don't want to go, we'd love to keep you.' He gave me the opportunity to say 'yes' or 'no.' So I thought about it and talked to a lot of people in a short period of time and decided to go."

However, as he said at the time, "This is home. I'm not leaving home. I'm just going away to work for a little bit. This is where my life is. My wife is from here, and this is where we make our home. We'll be here forever."

And sure enough, Ray retired after Ottawa was knocked out of the playoffs. The Sabres honored him the following October with an appreciation night, an honor that only the great Gilbert Perreault has been given in team history.

Ray played 889 games with Buffalo to rank fourth on the team's all-time list, and very few of them were easy. He scored only 40 goals and 50 assists for 90 points, but his job was never about scoring. From the time he came up to the Sabres during the 1989–1990 season, Ray was Buffalo's hammer, its enforcer. Whenever the team needed dirty work done, Ray was sent over the boards to do it, and he did it proudly, effectively, and sometimes bloodily.

"It's a thankless job night after night," said former Sabres captain Stu Barnes, who was traded the same day as Ray to the Dallas Stars. "He doesn't get to play a lot of minutes or score goals, but he has a very difficult job to do and he does it night after night. He's a character in the [locker] room, he's a great leader, and he cares very much not only about how the team is doing and the franchise, but he cares about things in the community."

Ray knew his role and reveled in it. His teammates appreciated it, and the fans adored him for it. True to his word, he has never left Buffalo, and through his charity work, his endorsements, and his presence on the Sabres' telecasts, he is one of the most popular ex-athletes in the city's history.

"For the people, I think it was the style you played on the ice that leaves a big impression," Ray said. "When you talk to people, they're not talking about goals you scored or your playmaking or anything like that. It was how they were entertained by the way you played. I played longer than I ever, ever dreamed of. I dreamt of playing, but I never ever thought it would be a reality.

Getting the chance to play one game was more than I ever thought I'd get."

49 First-Round Flopping

On the eve of Buffalo's 1992 first-round playoff series against Boston, Dave Andreychuk was one of only two players on the Sabres roster who were with the team the last time they won a playoff series (Mike Ramsey was the other).

"If you just take a look around the room, there's not too many guys that were here for that," said Andreychuk of the Sabres' 1983 three-game sweep of Montreal.

Lucky them.

The Sabres had become well-known for their first-round failures, and they would do it again in this series, losing in seven games to the Bruins. That made seven consecutive playoff exits in the first round.

The misery began in 1984, when the Sabres, with 103 points to finish second in the Adams Division, lost three games to none by a cumulative score of 13–5 to a Quebec team that had finished nine points behind them. "We didn't do very much, but we didn't do very well against them in the season either, so it wasn't as if it was a surprise," said coach Scotty Bowman. "We've got young guys and when you get young guys, you've got to build up their confidence."

The following year, the Nordiques were the better team in the standings by a point, giving them home-ice advantage. After winning the first two in Le Colisee, they lost twice at the Aud as Buffalo scored 13 goals. The Sabres then took a 5–3 lead early in the third period of the deciding fifth game, only to give up three goals in a row, the last by Brent Ashton with 1:09 left, to end their season.

Buffalo missed the playoffs the next two years, then returned in 1987–1988, only to get bounced out by Boston in six games despite seven goals by John Tucker, six of them coming in Games 3 and 4 when the Sabres rallied to tie the series after dropping the first two in Boston.

The Sabres were bursting with confidence the following year; they truly felt they were better than Boston after going undefeated against the hated Bruins (5–0–3) during the regular season. "The playoffs are completely different," said Bruins coach Terry O'Reilly, and he was right. Buffalo won the opener 6–0, and then Boston won the next four to close it out. "We had 36 weeks of good hockey and one week of bad hockey," said Sabres coach Ted Sator. "Your fortunes are determined in the playoffs, and that pains me deeply."

In 1989–1990 the Sabres rolled through the regular season, finishing with the third-most points in the league (98) under new coach Rick Dudley. This meant they would have home-ice advantage against Montreal. Again, there was confidence bursting from the Buffalo locker room prior to the series. "This is not the team that lost out in the first round," said Mike Foligno. "This is a new Buffalo Sabres team. We've got to go into this with a new frame of mind and a positive feeling." But it was not to be: Montreal won it in six games.

By now Sabres fans were furious and naturally expected the worst when it came to the postseason, especially when the 1990–1991 team won only 31 games (14 fewer than the previous season). Montreal was the opponent again in the opening round, and as Rick Vaive said, "We want to win it bad, but we don't look back and say, 'We owe these guys one.' We haven't won in the first round since 1983. That's enough pressure." And the pressure got to them: the sixth straight first-round flop was complete in six games.

John Muckler took over for Dudley early in the 1991–1992 season. This Sabres team became the only one in franchise history to earn a playoff berth with a losing record (31–37–12), benefitting from the horrible seasons of division rivals Hartford and Quebec. With no expectations, the Sabres gave it a great effort, extending Boston to seven games before losing the deciding game at Boston Garden 3–2.

The futility finally ended in 1992–1993, when the Sabres eliminated the Bruins in four straight games, closing it out with Brad May's dramatic overtime goal at the Aud—the famous "May Day, May Day" goal.

50. The Muckler-Nolan Feud

For their laudable work on the ice, the 1996–1997 Sabres became known as "the hardest working team in hockey"—a moniker that fit them perfectly. To win the Northeast Division with a roster comprised of an all-world goaltender and a bunch of muckers and grinders, none of whom scored more than 53 points, the Sabres had to work hard to win games. And that's exactly what they did, 40 times.

But in the months that followed their thrilling first-round playoff victory over Ottawa and their predictable loss to a much more talented Philadelphia club, the Sabres earned a new and far less flattering calling card: "Team Turmoil."

"I watch *Days of Our Lives,* and this is another soap opera for my list," said center Derek Plante.

This should have been a team riding a wave of pride over accomplishing so much during a year when most observers thought they wouldn't even contend for a playoff berth, let alone win a division crown. Instead, the franchise was only a few threads away from being completely torn asunder thanks to a series of incidents that transpired during a summer of chaos.

The foundation of the trouble was rooted in the discontent between general manager John Muckler and coach Ted Nolan.

Muckler had been asked by management to slice the payroll, and as the coach, Nolan obviously had big problems with some of the personnel decisions Muckler made. They were at each other's throats, dating back even before the start of the season. Team president Larry Quinn brought an end to the sniping by firing Muckler in mid-May, a day before Muckler was named NHL executive of the year by *Sporting News.*

"We felt we had to improve the communication within our organization," Quinn said in announcing the dismissal of Muckler, who had given Nolan his first break in coaching when he hired him out of obscurity in 1995.

Of course that was just the beginning of the upheaval. A month later, after Darcy Regier was hired to replace Muckler and Nolan was named the NHL's coach of the year, Nolan's future in Buffalo was thrust into doubt. His contract was set to expire, and with Muckler out of the way, bringing back the reigning coach of the year should have been a pretty easy negotiation. It wasn't.

Like any new GM, Regier certainly wanted to bring in his own coach, but he realized Nolan had some leverage. Nolan was also a popular figure in town, considering he'd just guided a team low on talent to the second round of the playoffs. Regier decided to offer Nolan a one-year contract worth a reported $500,000, saying he and Nolan needed "time to build a relationship." Nolan was furious that he wasn't given more job security, and he promptly rejected the offer.

Here's where it really got crazy. While all this was going on, the Sabres were in the midst of a messy ownership transfer. John Rigas was attempting to buy the team from the Knox family, which was now represented by Northrup Knox after the death of his brother, Seymour, a year earlier. Quinn and Northrup were in favor of Regier's one-year contract offer to Nolan, while Rigas was a staunch Nolan backer. So, too, was Jean Knox, the wife of the late Seymour.

After the contract offer and Nolan's refusal to accept it became public during a clumsily handled press conference, a rally was organized a few days later in front of Marine Midland Arena. Among the more than 200 people on hand to lend support to Nolan was Mrs. Knox.

"If Seymour was alive, he absolutely would have signed Ted by now," she said while wearing an eagle feather that Nolan, a Native American, had given to her at Seymour's funeral.

Yes, it was absolutely bizarre, and there never was a resolution. There were no further offers to Nolan. Regier moved on, hiring Lindy Ruff, one of the most popular former Sabres players, to be the team's new coach. Ruff had been working as an assistant coach in Florida.

The Hasek-Nolan Feud

Ted Nolan was certainly one of the most polarizing figures in Sabres history. There were some who loved him and others who hated him. Dominik Hasek was in the latter category, and that became perfectly clear during the summer of 1997.

During the 1997 playoffs, Hasek suffered what to this day remains a mysterious knee injury in Game 3 against Ottawa. He never played again in the postseason, and there were some in the organization who felt that he quit on the team because he did not like Nolan.

Hasek was angered when general manager John Muckler was fired, and shortly after Darcy Regier was hired to replace Muckler, Hasek went on the record regarding his opinion of Nolan. "I cannot respect him," Hasek said. "That's my problem. I don't want to play for someone I don't respect."

Hasek had just become the first goalie in 35 years to win the NHL's MVP award—and now he was saying he didn't want to play for Nolan. That statement surely carried some weight when Regier decided to offer Nolan a paltry one-year contract, and in the end, Hasek was pleased when Nolan opted not to return.

Of course most of the players loved Nolan, and they were not happy with Hasek's stance. Matthew Barnaby was the most outspoken; he promised to "run" Hasek when training camp commenced.

But Barnaby never made good on that promise, and in the end, new coach Lindy Ruff managed to get everyone on the same page, making the next two years among the best in Sabres history.

"The thing was, we accomplished something last year," said the team's most tenured player, Rob Ray. "We should have been building on that. But everything that's gone on away from the ice has taken away from that. It was unfortunate, but everyone realizes it's a business."

51 The End of the Spectrum Jinx

On the evening of November 10, 1977, general manager Punch Imlach was sitting up in the press box at The Spectrum while his team skated onto the ice surface to begin warming up for its game against the big, bad Philadelphia Flyers.

Imlach was looking at the Sabres 1977–1978 schedule and noticed that after this game, the club wouldn't be back in the City of Brotherly Love until March 18, 1978. The then 59-year-old, who had undergone major heart surgery six years earlier and whose health was sometimes questionable, looked at a couple of the Sabres beat writers and jokingly said, "I may not live long enough to see this thing end."

"This thing" was the Sabres' jinx in Philadelphia, a laughable winless streak that extended back to the birth of the franchise in 1970. In their previous 20 games in The Spectrum, the Sabres' record was 0–18–2, including three losses in the 1975 Stanley Cup Finals.

"It was a jinx," said Rene Robert. "There were games where we deserved to win. The first two games of the Finals, we deserved to win both of those games. There's always teams that for some reason give you a harder time than somebody else. We used to beat the Canadiens when no one else could, but we couldn't beat the Flyers. How do you beat the Canadiens and not beat the Flyers? It was all psychological for us."

But everyone knew something was up on this night, when the little-used Terry Martin, who hadn't played in six games because of a back injury, assisted on a second-period goal by another fourth-line player, Fred Stanfield, then scored the go-ahead goal himself early in the third as the Sabres broke through for a 3–2 victory.

Just like that, "this thing" came to an end—seven years of frustration and a 15-game losing streak in the Spectrum finally over. Before that evening, Buffalo hadn't earned a point on Broad Street since pulling out a tie on March 16, 1972.

"This is a tremendous win for the team as far as attitude goes," said Gilbert Perreault, who, along with his French Connection linemates Rick Martin and Rene Robert, was held scoreless. "Before, everybody was saying we couldn't beat the Flyers in Philadelphia. But now that we have beaten them, it makes us think we can beat them again."

Terry Martin had been up in the press box at Madison Square Garden the previous night watching Buffalo's 8–4 loss to the Rangers. Sitting nearby were a couple of Flyers scouts who were no doubt snickering about Buffalo's performance and figuring the Flyers would have little difficulty with the Sabres—especially in the house that had long haunted Buffalo.

"They were pretty cocky," Martin said of the scouts. They were pretty humbled 24 hours later.

During their 20-game unbeaten streak, the Flyers had outscored the Sabres 85–33, 11–3 in the two teams' three Stanley Cup games. After this one-night reprieve, the Spectrum continued to be a cursed place for Buffalo until the Flyers finally moved into their new building across the street in 1996. Through the end of the 1970s, this remained Buffalo's only victory against the Flyers, with their record against that team going to 1–24–5. Ultimately, the Sabres finished with an all-time record of 12–40–8 and were outscored 225–152 at The Spectrum. No team in the NHL was happier to see that place blown up.

Road Warriors

During the month of January 1984, the Sabres never lost a game, compiling a 13-game unbeaten streak that ranks as the second-longest in team history. Included in that streak were six straight victories on the road. Coupled with four straight victories away from the Aud in December, the Sabres set a team record that season with 10 consecutive road victories.

Rookie goalie Tom Barrasso, who grew up in Boston, lost his first start as a professional at Boston Garden with the Sabres back in October 1983. On the night at Boston Garden when the 10-game road streak began, Barrasso did not play. But the 18-year-old earned his first victory in his hometown by making 27 saves in the record-setting 10th-straight road win on January 23, 1984. The Sabres broke a 3–3 third-period tie with goals by Dave Andreychuk and Paul Cyr 10 seconds apart with about two minutes remaining.

Buffalo played its next three games at home and had two ties and a 7–3 victory over Pittsburgh, but the 13-game unbeaten streak and 10-game road streak ended on February 2 in Boston when the Bruins pulled out a 5–3 victory.

On the flip side of all that success on the road was the misery of 2011–2012, when the Sabres lost a team-record 12 consecutive road games—every one of them in regulation play—before finally ending it with a 2–1 shootout victory in New Jersey on January 24, 2012.

"Whenever I walked through that big, black door leading into the visiting locker room at the Spectrum, I thought I was walking through the gates of Hell," former Sabres defenseman Mike Robitaille said.

52 Mike Ramsey

These days, there are all kinds of statistics that track the play of defensemen in the NHL. Fans can go online, pick any game, call up the stat sheet, and see how much ice time a defenseman has logged, as well as how many hits, blocked shots, or takeaways he has earned.

According to his old teammate John Tucker, had Mike Ramsey played in this era, he would have been a stat-sheet marvel.

"Rammer was an unsung hero kind of guy," said Tucker, who played with Ramsey for eight of Ramsey's 14 seasons in Buffalo. "We didn't have the stats that they have today, but if they would have kept all that stuff, Rammer would have been ranked up there pretty high."

Ramsey was the quintessential defenseman's defenseman, a 6', 200-pound rock who stood sentry at the Buffalo blue line and made even the greatest players of his era—men like Wayne Gretzky, Jari Kurri, Mario Lemieux, Mike Bossy, and Steve Yzerman—work for their goals and points. He'd pound opponents into the end boards, level them in open ice, or lay down in front of the most wicked of shots if it meant preventing a goal.

"Mike was a warrior," said former Montreal Canadien Mario Tremblay, who later coached with Ramsey under Jacques Lemaire for the Minnesota Wild. "If you had your head down, you were going to get hit. That's why I always gave him a few shots when I could."

But Ramsey was often overlooked because he played at the same time as Edmonton's Paul Coffey, Boston's Ray Bourque, Chicago's Doug Wilson, and his own teammate, Phil Housley. It became chic during the 1980s for defensemen to lug the puck out of their own zone—ala Bobby Orr—and kick-start the offense. None were better at this than Hall of Famers Coffey and Bourque, and few were worse than Ramsey.

Even though Ramsey could skate and handle the puck, he usually preferred not to because he wanted to concentrate on his play in his own end. Rather than pinch in at the line, he'd peel back to make sure the opposition didn't get odd-man rushes. He was the ultimate stay-at-home defenseman.

Sabres defenseman Mike Ramsey, shown here in action against the Hartford Whalers in 1991, was a member of the 1980 Miracle on Ice U.S. Olympic Hockey Team and a Sabre for 14 years.
Photo courtesy of Getty Images

This style, of course, didn't do much for Ramsey's Q-rating, a point that was hammered home by a humorous incident that took place after the 1985 All-Star Game in Calgary. Lemieux scored the game-winning goal for the Wales Conference team and was named game MVP, while Bourque played a sublime game with four assists. Afterward, a TV reporter and his cameraman stopped Ramsey and asked for an interview.

"We must have been talking for three minutes before the guy says, 'Tell me about your assists,'" Ramsey remembered. "So I said, 'I didn't get any assists.'" Startled, the reporter said, "You mean you're not Ray Bourque?" Ramsey's reply was no, and at that point the camera clicked off and the two men walked away, not the least bit interested in Ramsey's contribution to the victory.

Ramsey was born in Minneapolis and became a Minnesota legend during both his stellar high school career and the one season he played at the University of Minnesota, where he helped lead the

Gophers to the NCAA championship before earning a spot on the 1980 Miracle on Ice Olympic team.

Scotty Bowman took over the Sabres operation in the summer of 1979 and Ramsey became Bowman's first draft choice, No. 11 overall, making him the second U.S.-born player to be selected in the first round.

Ramsey, who will always be remembered for the role he played in helping the U.S. win the gold medal, finished his career with 79 goals, 266 assists, and 345 points in 1,070 games. We can only guess how many shots he blocked, how many checks he delivered, and how many goals and scoring chances he prevented. If those numbers were available, perhaps he'd get some well-deserved consideration for the Hockey Hall of Fame.

Sauve's Double Shutout

Before the start of the Sabres' best-of-five opening-round playoff series in 1983 against Montreal, goaltender Bob Sauve warned anyone who would listen that a team like the Canadiens, with nine 20-goal scorers on its roster, "only needs one goal to get going."

But by the time the Canadiens scored that one goal, the series was already just about over. Sauve pitched back-to-back shutouts at the fabled Montreal Forum to give the Sabres a commanding two-game lead. And even though Sauve finally relented 7:25 into the second period of Game 3 when Mats Naslund beat him, it wasn't enough. The Sabres went on to a 4–2 series-clinching victory, the highlight of Sauve's eight-year career as a Sabre.

"You have to understand, if you grow up in the Montreal region, you either dream of playing for the Canadiens or of playing for someone else and facing the Canadiens in the playoffs," said Sauve, who hailed from Quebec. "But I'm not crazy enough to say I thought I could blank them even one game, let alone two, especially at the Forum. I think about it now and it was just amazing."

The Canadiens had never been shut out in back-to-back games at the Forum, and had only been shut out once in back-to-back playoff games (in 1961 when Chicago blanked them once at the Forum and then again at Chicago Stadium in the NHL semifinals).

In the first game, Montreal goalie Rick Wamsley was almost Sauve's equal. But Wamsley allowed one goal, by Brent Peterson with 17:30 left in the third period, and that was all the Sabres needed. Sauve turned aside all 24 Montreal shots. The key to the game, and perhaps the entire series, was the first 20 minutes of play. As expected, Montreal came out buzzing, played most of the period in the Buffalo end, and outshot the Sabres 10–2. Sauve made a number of big saves to keep the game scoreless, and he rode that early momentum for the rest of the week.

"Bob Sauve was great," said Sabres coach Scotty Bowman. "When we got out of the first period of the first game in Montreal with a shutout, it set the tenor of the play for us."

In Game 2 the Sabres jumped on Montreal right away. Dale McCourt scored 1:47 after the puck was dropped. When Gilles Hamel and Mal Davis scored 36 seconds apart in the second period, the game was out of reach. Sauve was completely in the zone, turning aside all 22 Canadiens shots.

The Sabres came back home to an electrified Aud two nights later; as Tony McKegney said, "Some of the veterans were saying they hadn't heard so much noise since 1975 [the year of Buffalo's first trip to the Stanley Cup Finals]." When Montreal finally scored its first goal, it wasn't even clean: Naslund fired a shot from the left faceoff circle that deflected off Buffalo defenseman Bill Hajt's stick and snuck past Sauve. "I put my stick out and it hit my stick and went through Bobby's legs," said Hajt. "That was the only way they could score on Bobby."

Buffalo surged into the lead when John Van Boxmeer and Lindy Ruff scored 1:05 apart near the end of the period. The Canadiens tied it on a legitimate goal by Steve Shutt midway through the third, but the Sabres responded when McKegney scored the winner off a rebound.

"It's pretty tough to win a series, or any game for that matter, with just two goals," Montreal coach Bob Berry said. "Sauve made the big saves. That was a tremendous record to have in the playoffs. He played super."

54 "Wowie"

Scotty Bowman created quite a stir during the 1982 NHL Draft when, after picking 18-year-old defenseman Phil Housley right out of a Minnesota high school with the sixth overall pick, he said, "He is the nearest thing to Bobby Orr I've seen."

And as if that wasn't enough to ruffle the feathers of many Canadians, who were proud that their countrymen held the vast majority of the spots on NHL rosters at the time, Housley had the audacity to add, "I think I can fill Orr's shoes some day."

More than three decades after limping through his final NHL season on his badly damaged knees, Orr is still considered one of the greatest players in history. Some would argue that when he was healthy during the late 1960s and early 1970s, no one—not Wayne Gretzky, not Gordie Howe—was as talented as Orr.

Housley never truly filled Orr's shoes, but what he did do during a remarkable 21-year NHL career was play in 1,495 games and score 338 goals and 894 assists for 1,238 points—figures that dwarfed the injury-plagued Orr's totals in every category.

During the first three years of Bowman's stewardship in Buffalo, the one missing piece to the jigsaw puzzle he was assembling was a puck-carrying, playmaking defenseman—and Housley was certainly that. Bowman didn't mind that Housley was often a liability on defense; he had terrific stay-at-home defenders in Mike Ramsey, Bill Hajt, and Jim Schoenfeld, who covered wonderfully for Housley. Bowman wanted Housley to jump-start Buffalo's offense from the back end, not only as a playmaker but as a goal scorer, and for eight years in Buffalo and 13 seasons elsewhere, that's exactly what he did. Housley was just a baby-faced kid when he first showed up, but he was so dynamic that Sabres broadcaster Rick Jeanneret used to call him "Wowie" when he scored.

"I saw one game and that was enough for me to make sure we got him," Bowman said of scouting Housley. "We knew what we needed, and obviously that was it. He was a talent, especially on the power play. He was a quarterback, the way he brought the puck up the ice, the moves he made in the neutral zone. He had super skills. He could really accelerate. He was one of the better skaters I've ever seen."

Sabres coach Lindy Ruff, who was Housley's teammate for six years during the 1980s, shared with writer Randy Schultz what he thought when he first saw the kid at training camp in 1982:

> I remember hearing that Scotty had drafted this 18-year-old kid out of high school. I wasn't sure what Scotty was thinking. I didn't know that much about high school players at the time, other than the fact that I didn't think they could make the jump directly into the NHL. And when I saw Phil at training camp, I wasn't sure that he would even survive the physical play of the NHL. But once he hit the ice, that was a different story. He could fly. He managed to avoid the big hits. And Phil was a marked player. He could handle the puck very well. It wasn't long into his first season in the NHL that he earned the respect of his teammates.

Housley scored 19 goals and 66 points as a rookie, then scored a career-high 31 goals in 1983–1984. As Bowman said, "As a 19-year-old, even with Bobby Orr you didn't see that."

Housley ended up playing for eight NHL organizations during his career. When he retired in 2004, he was the leading American-born scorer in NHL history. He never won a Stanley Cup, but he did win an Olympic silver medal playing for the United States in 2002 at Salt Lake City.

The seven-time All-Star has earned induction into the Sabres Hall of Fame and the United States Hockey Hall of Fame, and it seems only a matter of time before he receives the ultimate honor with a place in the Hockey Hall of Fame.

As Housley told Schultz:

> I knew that being a U.S. kid fresh out of high school, I would be a marked individual. But I think once teams saw me play, I was accepted a little more. I knew going in that because of my size [5'10" and 170 pounds], opponents would try to take the body a lot more than usual. But I remember having three teammates on the Sabres at the time who protected me. If anybody tried running me, they would have to answer to Mike Foligno, Lindy Ruff, or Larry Playfair. And that seemed to work.

55 Hometown Heroes

When the NHL played its annual All-Star Game in Buffalo for the first (and still only) time in 1978, the Sabres were represented by two-thirds of their famed French Connection line: Gilbert Perreault and Rick Martin. But Sabres general manager Punch Imlach wasn't so sure his two star scorers deserved to be playing in the NHL's showcase game.

To that point in the 1977–1978 season, the French Connection had not played particularly well, and Imlach wasn't the only one who'd taken notice of the recent slippage.

Allen Stanley, a trusted Imlach confidant who had played for Punch during the 1960s when the Maple Leafs won four Stanley Cups, had been hired to assist head coach Floyd Smith in 1976–1977. At the end of that season, when Imlach fired Smith after the Sabres were swept out of the playoffs in the second round by the Islanders, he asked Stanley to give him his honest appraisal of the team. Stanley was brutally honest: with the exceptions of Craig Ramsay, Don Luce, and Danny Gare, most of the players were given poor reports. He felt that Perreault, Martin, and Rene Robert were spiraling downward and not trying as hard as they could.

When the 1977–1978 season began with Marcel Pronovost installed as the new coach, Imlach still felt that the French Connection was playing lethargically. In his book, *Heaven and Hell in the NHL*, Imlach revealed that he wrote a note to himself right around the time of the All-Star Game that read: "French Connection—you're playing lousy, no drive, no fight, and the fans see it and I see it."

Well, what the fans saw at the sold-out Aud on the night of January 24, 1978, was Martin scoring the tying goal for the Wales Conference with 1:39 left to play and Perreault then netting the winning shot 3:55 into overtime to produce a thrilling 3–2 victory over the Campbell Conference.

"A fitting end," Martin said of the dramatic finish that had the building rocking with glee. "The game won't be back in Buffalo for 18 years, if ever, and when it comes back, I won't be playing. I'll never score another goal here in an All-Star Game, so I really enjoyed that one. Nice for the fans and for me and Gil."

It seemed the Wales had no luck that night. Islanders goalie Billy Smith, a Sabres tormentor who was booed throughout the evening—especially when it was announced that he had been chosen as the game's MVP—was tending net. He played the first 30 minutes and stopped all 16 shots he faced. Philadelphia's Wayne Stephenson played even better as the Wales began to dominate a game in which they ended with a whopping 40–12 advantage in shots.

Bill Barber of the Flyers scored 1:25 into the game against Montreal goalie Ken Dryden to give the Campbells a 1–0 lead, and Denis Potvin of the Islanders scored later in the period on a slap shot from just inside the blue line. Toronto's Darryl Sittler scored on a power play late in the second, but Stephenson's play was outstanding for most of the third. It appeared that the Campbells were going to escape with victory in a game in which they had been thoroughly outplayed.

That is until Martin, who had won the MVP award in the 1977 All-Star Game in Vancouver, scored on a backhander off his own rebound to send the game into overtime for the first time since overtime had been instituted five years earlier. That set the stage for Perreault's winner, though it certainly wasn't the kind of goal Perreault usually scored. His centering pass from the right boards was accidentally deflected into the net by opponent Phil Esposito.

"We got lucky," said Perreault. "I was just trying to pass out to the middle, but Espo was cutting in the middle and it went off his stick. It was good for me, and Buffalo, too. You don't see something like that too often, two guys from the home team scoring the tying and winning goals in overtime in an All-Star Game."

56 Schony

If Jim Schoenfeld's playing career in Buffalo was all you had to go by, you'd consider him one of the best—not to mention most interesting—men to ever don the blue-and-gold uniform. Mix in his bizarre dealings with Scotty Bowman, and Schoenfeld instantly becomes one of the most compelling figures in Sabres history.

"We were like oil and water," Schoenfeld once said of his relationship with the man who is considered the greatest coach in hockey history.

Schoenfeld had already forged a notable career with Buffalo when Bowman arrived on the scene as the team's new coach and general manager in 1979. Schoenfeld had been a first-round draft pick in 1972, and his physical style and much-needed toughness helped take the Sabres to the playoffs during his first season.

Throughout the 1970s, Schoenfeld was a leader on the ice and off, serving as captain of the club for three seasons. But when Bowman left Montreal to take over the Sabres, he had a vision to remake the team with youth, and Schoenfeld was not a part of that plan.

Bowman had already jettisoned such popular players as Rene Robert, Rick Martin, Jerry Korab, and Don Luce (eventual Sabres Hall of Famers all) when he stunned Sabres fans by dealing two more future franchise Hall of Famers, Schoenfeld and Danny Gare, to Detroit in a blockbuster trade. A devastated Schoenfeld, moved to tears, said the best part of leaving was that he wouldn't have to put up with Bowman anymore.

Eyebrows were raised across the region a few years later when Bowman turned to Schoenfeld to see if he'd be interested in coaching

Buffalo's American Hockey League team in Rochester. By then he had moved on from Detroit to Boston, and had just announced his retirement in the spring of 1984.

Schoenfeld was wary of Bowman, but he also decided it was an opportunity he couldn't pass up. "I was offered the job in Rochester, but I didn't think I would be interested," recalled Schoenfeld, who really hadn't considered a career in coaching. "I had a friend who said, 'Why don't you try it and if you hate it, at least you'll know that's what you don't want to do and you can move on to something else.' So I said, 'What the hell, I might as well try it.' I had no other plans."

Schoenfeld's Amerks got off to a scintillating 17–6–2 start, but when the Sabres started poorly, Bowman asked Schoenfeld to ditch the suit and tie for a blue-and-gold sweater because the Sabres needed help on defense. Schoenfeld finished out the season as a player. After the Sabres were bounced from the playoffs by Quebec, he retired again, and this time Bowman asked him to stay in Buffalo and coach the Sabres—even though he'd only coached 25 games at the AHL level. "I didn't expect that at all," said Schoenfeld.

Of course he didn't expect what happened three months later, either. With the team idling at 19–19–5, Bowman fired Schoenfeld and took back the coaching reins for the rest of the season—the first in 12 years in which Buffalo did not qualify for the playoffs. That was it for Schoenfeld in Buffalo. "All my ties are severed right now," he said. "There's nothing I would consider doing with the organization." And he never has, though he did accept the honor of being inducted into the Sabres Hall of Fame in 1995.

Schoenfeld played 584 games as a Sabre, accumulated 228 points and 1,025 penalty minutes, and earned the respect of every teammate he played with.

"He was a genuine heavyweight, a tough guy, and very visible on the ice with his red hair, no helmet, and his opinions," said Craig Ramsay. "Then he became one of the best shot blockers in the business; he'd dive in front of anything, anytime, and then he turned himself, by hard work, into a really versatile defenseman. His career shows you don't have to be the most talented guy on the block, you just have to want it bad enough."

Schoenfeld has been in and out of hockey in the quarter century since Bowman dismissed him, serving as head coach in New Jersey, Washington, and Phoenix. He made big news one year during the playoffs when an angry dispute with referee Don Koharski resulted in Schoenfeld calling the official "a fat pig" and telling him to "have another doughnut."

Nothing Schoenfeld ever said about Bowman made national news, but one can only imagine the kinds of things he must have said about Bowman in private to friends and family.

"I was extremely proud to be a Buffalo Sabre," he said. "The one regret, and it will always be with me, is that we didn't give the Buffalo fans a championship season. It's something that the Buffalo fans deserve. They gave us such great support, and have continued to give the team great support, so you'd like to see that rewarded."

57 Gerry Meehan

If Punch Imlach hadn't plucked Gerry Meehan off the Philadelphia Flyers' unprotected player list in the 1970 expansion draft, the 23-year-old was ready and willing to join the working force in the "real" world.

"I wasn't going to bang around the minors anymore," Meehan recalled. "I was going to stay at home in Streetsville [Ontario]. I had been offered a position with a local drug company as a management trainee, and I would go to school in the evenings."

Meehan held firm on going to school in the evenings, eventually receiving his undergraduate degree from Canisius College and a law degree from the University at Buffalo. But his schooling became secondary—not to a pursuit of pharmaceutical management, but to a pursuit of pucks—when Imlach rescued Meehan's flagging hockey career on that June afternoon in 1970 as part of building the Buffalo franchise.

"I believed it was my last chance to play in the NHL," Meehan said of the expansion draft. "If I wasn't picked up by another team, I was not going to go to training camp [with the Flyers]. I had decided that summer that if I didn't play in the NHL that year, I wasn't going to continue playing. And then I got drafted, and being drafted by the Sabres and playing here basically gave me my career."

Meehan wound up playing in Buffalo for four years, and spent another five split between Vancouver, Atlanta, and Washington. By the time he retired in 1979, his résumé included 670 NHL games and 180 goals. Not bad for a guy who had nearly given up the game a decade previously.

Meehan scored 24 goals that inaugural 1970–1971 season in Buffalo to rank third on the team, but his contributions went well beyond goals and assists. Imlach saw Meehan as a heady player and a natural leader; when Floyd Smith retired early in 1971–1972, Imlach passed the captaincy of the team on to Meehan, who wore the "C" until his trade to Vancouver early in 1974–1975.

He chipped in a career-best 31 goals in 1972–1973 as he and linemates Jim Lorentz and Hugh Harris provided a strong complement to the French Connection. "That was a year when I was able to capitalize playing basically in a second-line position behind Perreault," Meehan said. "We didn't get as much quality ice time as Gilbert's line, and deservedly so—they were the Connection—but we were able to chip in some pretty decent numbers as a second unit."

Meehan's production dipped the following year, and when Imlach went searching for what he felt the Sabres really needed—a hard-shooting defenseman—Meehan was part of the bait. He and Mike Robitaille were shipped to Vancouver in exchange for Jocelyn Guevremont and Bryan McSheffrey.

Meehan's days in Buffalo were far from over, however. After retiring just before Christmas 1978, Meehan returned to Buffalo, finished law school, and accepted a position in the Buffalo law firm headed by Sabres board member Robert Swados. By 1984 he was dabbling in the Sabres' legal affairs.

"When I originally got to Buffalo, I spent a couple years enjoying the life of being in the NHL and not having to worry about where the money was coming from, so I played golf in the summers and worked at a few hockey schools," Meehan said. "But after I got traded from Buffalo, I realized this was going to be it, I wasn't going to be able to waste my summers anymore."

Meehan was hired by the team to be general manager Scotty Bowman's assistant in 1984, and when Bowman was fired in 1986, it was Meehan who moved into the big office, where he remained for six-and-a-half years. During his tenure he brought players such as Dominik Hasek, Alexander Mogilny, Rick Vaive, Dale Hawerchuk, Pat LaFontaine, Grant Fuhr, Pierre Turgeon, Rob Ray, Derek Plante, Donald Audette, Brad May, and Brian Holzinger to Buffalo via trades and the draft.

He turned over the GM role to John Muckler when he was promoted to executive vice president of sports operations in 1993, but his ultimate goal of becoming team president was shattered when the Knox brothers hired Doug Moss for that position in 1994. Meehan left the Sabres in the summer of 1995.

"I became aware, as a result of Doug Moss' hiring, that there had been a ceiling placed on my career aspirations," Meehan said.

58 Captain Clutch

The Sabres have won 31 sudden-death overtime games in the Stanley Cup playoffs through the 2011–2012 season, and four of those game-winning goals carried even more drama, as they wrapped up a series triumph.

The goal Chris Drury scored on May 4, 2007, did not win Game 5 of Buffalo's Eastern Conference semifinal series against the New York Rangers, nor did it send the Sabres on to the next round, but it was without question the biggest goal of that series.

The high-scoring Sabres, whose 308 goals during the regular season were their most since 1992–1993, had suddenly gone into an offensive coma against Rangers goalie Henrik Lundqvist. After winning the first two games at HSBC Arena, Buffalo lost the next two at Madison Square Garden, scoring just once in each game as Lundqvist performed a dead-on impersonation of a brick wall.

Back in Buffalo for the pivotal fifth game, Lundqvist was once again unbeatable. When Martin Straka scored against Ryan Miller with just 3:19 left to play, it looked as if the Sabres—the President's Cup–winning Sabres, who'd compiled a franchise record–tying 113 points during the regular season—were on their way to a crushing and potentially season-killing 1–0 defeat.

Cue Captain Clutch: Drury, one of the best big-game players to have ever played in Buffalo. With 17 seconds remaining and Miller pulled for an extra attacker, Drury lost a faceoff in the Rangers zone. Winger Dainius Zubrus managed to corral the loose puck along the boards. Zubrus shoveled it to Drury, who was below the goal line, and Drury found Tim Connolly at the top of the left circle.

Tim Connolly jumps on Sabres teammate Chris Drury's back after Drury's game-tying goal against the New York Rangers in the third period of their playoff game on May 4, 2007, in Buffalo. The Sabres ended up winning 2–1 in overtime.

Connolly unleashed a slapshot that Lundqvist stopped, but the rebound jumped out to Drury, who had circled out front, and he whipped it into the net with 7.7 seconds left as the Arena exploded in celebration.

"With three minutes left, we could have just said, 'Aw, the heck with it. We had a good effort. We had almost 40 shots. Let's just pack it in,'" Drury said. "But we stayed with it. Lindy [Ruff] called a timeout, and we regrouped. I think it was pretty gutsy to come back and win in OT."

Drury got the game to overtime tied at 1–1. Maxim Afinogenov, whom Ruff had benched for Game 4 because of lack of production, ended up scoring the winner 4:39 into the extra period when he ripped a slap shot that deflected off New York's Jed Ortmeyer and past Lundqvist.

"It goes along with the season," Ruff said. "We've had a lot of victories where it kind of looks like you're down and out and all of a sudden you come back and you tie it and then minutes later you win the game. I think it's appropriate. I don't like it. I was a little bit uptight on the bench, but you've got that belief it can be done."

Yes, it can be done, especially since Ruff had Drury—a player who thrived in the biggest games and on the biggest stages—in his lineup.

59 The Bowman Showcase

The western New York region can never be compared with Canadian provinces such as Ontario and Quebec when it comes to producing NHL-level hockey talent. But a growing number of kids coming out of the Buffalo and Rochester areas are now making their mark in the NHL.

One need only look at two of the most storied franchises in the league, the Montreal Canadiens and the New York Rangers, for proof of this. In 2011–2012 both teams were captained by Rochester born-and-bred players, Brian Gionta in Montreal and Ryan Callahan in New York. And in Chicago you can find one of the NHL's rising stars, the player who scored the Stanley Cup–winning goal for the Blackhawks in 2010: Buffalo's own Patrick Kane.

In 2005, when NHL players were locked out in a contract dispute with the owners and there was no professional hockey being played in Buffalo, the Sabres organization thought it was as good a time as any to try to put a spotlight on the area's burgeoning youth talent. This was the motivation behind the creation of the Scotty Bowman Showcase.

The idea was to pit two high school all-star teams from Buffalo and Rochester (one team comprised of juniors, the other of seniors) against one another in a doubleheader at HSBC Arena with the intention of giving them exposure to potential college recruiters and Junior A and B coaches from America and Canada.

"We are always surprised at the number of kids who play hockey in Buffalo and yet [at the same time] the real lack proportionately of Division I scholarships and NHL players," said Sabres managing partner Larry Quinn. "What we've been consciously trying to do here with the Sabres is develop a program from the grass roots, which [youth hockey manager] Pat Fisher has been running for some years now, to start to correct some of that. This is one step."

That first year, Sabres general manager Darcy Regier and ex-Sabre Rob Ray coached the Rochester senior team against a Buffalo squad led by Sabres coach Lindy Ruff and ex-Sabre Larry Playfair. Buffalo won the first game easily, 9–1, in front of about 2,000 fans at the arena. The Buffalo juniors, coached by ex-Sabres Grant Ledyard and Darryl Shannon, were also victorious, 2–0, over a Rochester team led by Danny Gare and Ric Seiling.

"It was a wonderful evening," said Bowman, who has long maintained a home in the Buffalo suburb of East Amherst and is easily able to attend Sabres events. "We all miss hockey, and this was a good replacement."

Harry Neale, a *Hockey Night in Canada* employee at the time who now works on Sabres broadcasts, served as the master of ceremonies, while Buffalo's legendary broadcaster Rick Jeanneret and his partner, Jim Lorentz, did play-by-play.

The Showcase has grown in stature since its creation. Today it also incorporates music in the form of a student Battle of the Bands that takes place during game intermissions. The best student band in the area is chosen by a panel of music industry professionals from a group of six finalists from over 150 western New York schools.

The event is no longer free, but for a modest $5 admission, fans get to see the best high school players in the region playing in two games with great music in between. Actually, it's quite a bargain.

The Underappreciated Hall of Famer

Only one player in Sabres history has scored more points for the team than Dave Andreychuk, and his name was Gilbert Perreault—the greatest player in the history of the franchise. And only two players have scored more goals for Buffalo than Andreychuk: Perreault and Rick Martin. Perreault and Martin, two-thirds of the famous French Connection line, are considered icons in Buffalo, and their numbers are retired and hanging from the rafters at First Niagara Center. But Andreychuk? Well, let's just say his name rarely comes up in the same breath as those two legends, which makes the big winger the most underappreciated player to ever wear the Sabres uniform.

But after many years of serving as the face of the often-underachieving Sabres teams he played on during the 1980s and early 1990s, when he was an inexplicable favorite of the boo birds, Andreychuk finally got his just due from Sabres fans. In October 2008, when he was inducted into the team's Hall of Fame, the fans gave him a heartfelt standing ovation, celebrating a career that, by the time it was finished, included 23 NHL seasons, 640 goals (14th-most in NHL history), 1,338 points (tied for 28th with Denis Savard), and a Stanley Cup championship (with Tampa Bay in 2004).

"That was somewhat unexpected, to be honest with you," Andreychuk said of the welcome he received. "I went on to bigger and better things from here and I always felt I cheated the fans for some reason. After winning [the Cup], you realize what it does for the community. It's just too bad, really, I couldn't be a part of it here."

Andreychuk was part of Scotty Bowman's draft bonanza in 1982, the 16th overall pick in the first round of the same draft in which Bowman also chose Phil Housley sixth and Paul Cyr ninth. Big things were expected from the big guy (who stood 6'4" and weighed 225 pounds), and for the most part he delivered. During his 12 years in Buffalo, he had seven 30-goal seasons, twice surpassing 40, and he led the team in goals four times. "I look back and the numbers are pretty good here," said Andreychuk, who still holds the

One for the Thumb

The Sabres have been in existence for more than four decades and have played more than 3,600 regular season and postseason games through the end of the 2011–2012 season. But only once has a Sabre ever scored five goals in one evening. That was Dave Andreychuk on February 6, 1986, in a wild 8–6 victory over the Bruins at Boston Garden.

"My concern near the end of the game was that I might get five goals and the team would not win," Andreychuk said, recalling the Bruins' rally in the third period when they pulled to 7–6. "That would have spoiled the whole night."

Andreychuk scored twice in the first period and three times in the second, but was foiled in his attempt to tie the modern NHL record of six goals, which is shared by six players (the most recent being Darryl Sittler of the Maple Leafs in 1976). The all-time record of seven goals was set by Joe Malone for the Quebec Bulldogs in a 10–6 triumph over the Toronto St. Pats in 1920 at Quebec City.

"I dreamed about it," he said that night. "Everybody dreams about it. It was just one of those nights when I happened to be there at the right time. I was just wondering when it was going to end. I started getting nervous."

Coach Scotty Bowman made this prediction that night: "I think he's capable of eventually scoring 50 goals. Dave's going to be a great goal-scorer." Andreychuk did score 50 goals in a season, but he did it only once, with the Toronto Maple Leafs in 1993–1994. And, yes, he became one of the game's all-time great goal scorers, ending his 23-year career with 640.

Sabres single-game record of five goals, and remains No. 1 all-time in power-play goals with 161.

But he scored a somewhat disappointing 12 goals in 41 play-off games during his primary time in Buffalo (he also played the 2000–2001 season with the Sabres and had one goal in 13 playoff games that year). And the Sabres won only one playoff series during his time there, a best-of-three series in his rookie year (1982–1983) in which he barely saw any ice time.

Rick Dudley, who coached the Sabres for a little less than three seasons between 1989–1990 and 1991–1992, was one of Andrey-chuk's biggest fans—not only in Buffalo, but also during his time as general manager in Tampa Bay, where he acquired Andreychuk to help lead a young Lightning team in 2001–2002. Andreychuk finished his career there, and captained the 2004 championship team.

"Dave was wonderful," Dudley recalled. "I ran a tough training camp and he kind of led the charge. He bought into it, worked his ass off, and from that point on I realized there are guys that can lead, and this is one of them. I thought he was the most influential player on our team then, and he was the reason the Tampa Bay Lightning won the Stanley Cup, because of his leadership."

When asked why he thought Andreychuk got such a raw deal in Buffalo, Dudley said, "People change, people mature, people grow into something. I heard all the things about Dave Andreychuk and the Buffalo Sabres and how they were a lazy team and there was a country club atmosphere, but I got none of that."

61 Steady Bill

If Phil Housley was the prototypical "offensive defenseman," then Bill Hajt—the man they called Steady Bill—was certainly the preeminent stay-at-home defenseman for the Sabres. Hajt was perhaps one of the most overlooked players in team history, a man fans never seemed to notice on the ice. Of course, in retrospect, that's exactly what a defenseman hopes for—to escape notice—since the mistakes of the guys in the back end can be so glaring.

"I wasn't a star player," Hajt said the night he was inducted into the Greater Buffalo Sports Hall of Fame. "People didn't come to the hockey game to watch me. I just gave whatever I had. I gave the best I could every day. Maybe it wasn't enough some days, and on my best days it wasn't All-Star caliber, but I gave what I had. Not everybody is great, some people are better than other people at certain things. Whatever you're doing, you just do the best you can."

Well, the ever-modest Hajt was far better than he ever gave himself credit for.

"People talk about me being lucky with my drafts—first picks like Perreault, Martin, and Schoenfeld—but they never mention Hajt," Sabres general manager Punch Imlach once said. "That was really fortunate. Everybody knew those others were good. But apparently not everybody realized Hajt was good. I think he's going to be an All-Star."

Interestingly, Imlach let his chief scout, John Andersen, talk him out of picking Hajt in the second round of the 1971 draft because Andersen really liked winger Craig Ramsay. Overcoming his legendary stubbornness, Imlach took Andersen's advice and chose Ramsay—which turned out to be a pretty good decision. However, when it came time for the third round, Hajt—much to the surprise of Imlach—was still there, so he got the man *he* wanted, too.

It took a little time, however, for Hajt to finally join the fold. Imlach and Hajt could not agree on a contract; without any remaining junior eligibility, Hajt sat out the entire 1971–1972 season. He finally decided to take what Imlach was offering the next year, and after spending two seasons honing his game at AHL Cincinnati, he earned a permanent spot in Buffalo in time for the memorable 1974–1975 season.

With the French Connection at its peak, the Sabres were the second-highest scoring team in the NHL that year. But what gets lost in all that goal-scoring wizardry is that the defense was sixth-best in the league even though the goaltending wasn't what anyone would consider elite.

Hajt was one of the main reasons for the defensive success of that team, as he and Jim Schoenfeld, Jerry Korab, Lee Fogolin, Larry Carriere, and Jocelyn Guevremont joined forces to lock down the opposition. His plus-47 rating was the best among that group, and third-best on the team.

Over the next 13 years, Hajt was Mr. Reliable. Only once in his career did he finish a season with a negative plus/minus rating, that being a minus-4 in 1978–1979. He was plus-30 or better seven times, and he finished his career with a plus-321. With 854 NHL games on his résumé, every one of which he played for Buffalo, Hajt ranks fifth on the team's all-time list behind only Gilbert Perreault, Craig Ramsay, Mike Ramsey, and Rob Ray.

"I was very fortunate," Hajt said. "I played in an era when the Sabres had a lot of great players, a lot of great characters, a lot of class individuals. I was much more comfortable just staying in the background trying to help the team win games."

And he did so very well.

62 The Bottle Cap Bisons

Ruby Pastor was clearly a man ahead of his time. When the owner of the Pepsi-Cola Bottling Company of Buffalo purchased Buffalo's minor league hockey team in 1956, one of the first things he did was change the team's logo, emblazoning "Buffalo" across a red and blue bottle cap where the words "Pepsi-Cola" would normally appear.

That logo—the bottle cap logo as it came to be known—was one of the most distinctive in hockey, if not all sports. It proved to be an effective marketing strategy for Ruby and his brothers and business partners, Al and Sam. Not only did their bottling plant business do well, but the Bisons wore that logo proudly until the team was folded to make room for the Sabres' entrance into the NHL.

Professional hockey had been played in Buffalo as far back as the late 1800s, and the city fielded two minor league pro teams known as the Fort Erie Bisons and the Buffalo Majors before Louis M. Jacobs, owner of Jacob's Concessions, acquired the Syracuse American Hockey League franchise and moved it to Buffalo in time for the 1940–1941 season.

Playing in the recently built Memorial Auditorium, Buffalo was an early powerhouse in the AHL, winning the Calder Cup championship in 1943, 1944, and 1946 and losing in the Finals in 1948, 1951, and 1955. The Bisons were owned by their parent team in the NHL, the Chicago Blackhawks, at that time, but the Pastor brothers bought the team for a reported price of $125,000.

They slapped that logo on the sweaters and guided the Bisons through a successful stretch that produced four more appearances in the Calder Cup Finals, including championships in 1963 and 1970 with Fred Hunt managing the club, and future NHL coaching greats Bill Reay (1963) and Fred Shero (1970) calling the shots behind the bench.

During their time in the AHL, the Bisons were affiliated with the Blackhawks, the Montreal Canadiens, and the New York Rangers. A number of future distinguished NHL players wore their famous jersey, including Jacques Plante, Brad Park, Toe Blake, Doug Harvey, Pierre Pilote, Harry Lumley, Denis DeJordy, Barclay Plager, John McKenzie, Camille Henry, Gilles Villemure, and Terry Crisp.

Some of the old Bisons even returned to Buffalo to play for the Sabres in the early days of the franchise, including Mike Robitaille, Roger Crozier, Larry Hillman, Dave Dryden, and Larry Mickey.

63 Luuuuuuuce

Glenn "Chico" Resch, a former goaltender who spent 14 years stopping pucks in the NHL (primarily for the New York Islanders and the New Jersey Devils), obviously has an appreciation for guys who pay attention to defense.

As he watched the Devils on a nightly basis as the team's television color analyst, there was no one he respected more than New Jersey's former tandem of defensive forward stalwarts, Jay Pandolfo and John Madden. So when Resch used to say "Jay Pandolfo is the Donnie Luce of today's hockey, and John Madden is the Craig Ramsay," it was high praise indeed.

Luce and Ramsay. Ramsay and Luce. "You would have thought their last name was Ramsayluce," Resch said with a smile, recalling the dynamic defensive duo that dominated shifts for a full decade in Buffalo. "Everybody talks about Perreault-Martin, Bossy-Trottier, Gretzky-Kurri, but it's the same thing with those defensive players. They come in pairs, and those two guys were as good as there's ever been."

Luce began his career in the New York Rangers system, but in November 1970 he was dealt to Detroit, and then in May 1971 he and defenseman Mike Robitaille came to Buffalo for goalie Joe Daley. It was a perfect scenario for Luce: on the established teams he had previously played for, there were veterans in place filling the role he was born to play, the role that ultimately defined his 10-year tenure in Buffalo.

"I was happy to get to a team that I felt I would get a chance to play for and that I could play in the league," Luce said.

Luce instantly endeared himself to Punch Imlach and Joe Crozier with his stickier-than-syrup defensive style and magnificent penalty-killing skills. The fact that he could put the puck in the net—he topped 20 goals in six straight years from 1974 to 1979—was a nice bonus.

"At any important time in a game when I needed to win a draw in my own end or I needed someone checked, Luce would be on the ice, that's all there was to it," said Crozier, who might as well have been speaking for every coach Luce ever played for. "His skating wasn't as good as some of the other guys, but he had good hands, he could score goals, and he could check anybody."

How good were Luce and his partner in crime, Ramsay? Damn good, said Rick Martin, who had to face them on a daily basis as part of Crozier's prolific scrimmages.

"Those guys didn't get half the credit they deserved," Martin said. "We always got a lot of attention as the French Connection. When we'd go on the road, it was always, 'The French Connection is coming to town.' But those guys were great checkers, and guess what, we had to play against them in practice every day. They wanted to stop us in practice; they didn't want us to score. We were playing against some of the best checkers in the game, and it made us better, as I'm sure we made them better."

What separated Luce from the other great checkers of his day—or any other day—was his ability to transition from defense to offense.

"I looked at it a little differently than just being a checker," said Luce. "Coming from junior when I was a scorer, I looked at it as a way to take advantage of a situation offensively. You're playing against the other team's top scorers, and usually the top scorers don't worry about defense. Therefore they're a little lax in their own end and some of them aren't very good defensively."

In 1974–1975, with Ramsay and Danny Gare on the so-called checking line, that trio combined for 90 goals. Luce set two Sabres records that still stand when he netted eight shorthanded goals and finished with a plus/minus rating of plus-61, a mark that may never fall. He also won the NHL's Bill Masterton Trophy, presented to the player who best exemplifies the qualities of perseverance, sportsmanship, and dedication to hockey.

Luce scored 216 goals and 527 points in Buffalo before being traded along with Martin to the Los Angeles Kings in March 1981. He played briefly in Los Angeles and Toronto, retired, and after spending a few years out of the game, returned to the Sabres as a scout in 1984. He spent some time behind the bench as an assistant coach for Jim Schoenfeld and Scotty Bowman, then went back upstairs and served as director of player personnel until 2006.

The Saga of Perreault's Retirement

For all the grace that Gilbert Perreault displayed on the ice at Memorial Auditorium during his 16½ years with the Sabres, there was no grace in his departure from the organization.

At the end of the 1985–1986 season, Perreault looked around the Sabres locker room and realized that his brilliant career had come full circle. He just wasn't ready to start all over with a team that wasn't going to contend for a playoff berth, let alone a Stanley Cup.

So at the age of 35, two months after missing out on the playoffs for just the fourth time since he came to Buffalo as its inaugural player in 1970, Perreault announced his retirement in the middle of June 1986. He opened his press conference at the Aud by saying,

"It was a tough decision to make, but there's a time for everything, and today's the day."

Reporters had barely turned off their tape recorders and put away their notebooks when the man who had lived and breathed hockey for the better part of three decades—half that time in Buffalo as the face of the Sabres—began waffling about his decision. "Right now, I don't feel like playing hockey too much, but once September comes, you never know," he said. "Sometimes with the right offer and everything, you might change your mind."

And that's what happened. Coach/general manager Scotty Bowman coaxed him into playing for one more year with a one-year contract. But everything Perreault had thought at the end of 1985–1986 regarding the quality of the team slapped him in the face in the first month and a half of 1986–1987, and when the Sabres stumbled out of the gate a league-worst 4–13–3, Perreault knew it was time to call it quits for good.

"If the team had been going good, maybe things would have been different," said Perreault at his second and final retirement announcement. "But after the start we had, I decided I had enough and it was time to make a change. You need a certain feeling, a special eagerness to want to practice and want to play the game. I had lost that. I just couldn't find it this season."

Perreault really didn't have a game plan for his immediate future, but the way he tells the story, he was led to believe that he'd be offered a position in the hockey department whenever he did retire. When he was instead asked to serve as a public relations ambassador for the club, Perreault angrily refused. So began a painful estrangement from the team.

He stayed away from Buffalo for nearly three years, but when he was inducted into the Hockey Hall of Fame in the fall of 1990, the Sabres initiated a full-court press to make amends to their greatest player, and it succeeded. "We had some good meetings and we patched everything up," Perreault said.

With the relationship mended, a ceremony to retire his No. 11 jersey was immediately organized. On October 17, 1990, Perreault returned to the Aud to a sellout crowd that gave him a three-minute standing ovation. During the 42-minute celebration of Perreault's career, team owner Seymour H. Knox III presented Perreault with a silver hockey stick and declared, "There is no player who has meant more to his team than the man we honor tonight."

65 Mike Foligno

When General Manager John Muckler used the Senators' first-round pick in the 2006 Entry Draft on Sudbury Wolves left winger Nick Foligno, he admitted the kid's surname had "something to do with it."

Nick, of course, is the oldest son of one of the most beloved players in Buffalo sports history, a man who spent 10 of his 15 years in the NHL with the Sabres. Mike Foligno used to have the fans at Memorial Auditorium jumping out of their seats the same way he jumped out of his skates after every one of the 247 goals he scored for the blue and gold.

"Good bloodlines," Muckler said of young Nick, who moved on to the Columbus Blue Jackets in summer 2012 as a free agent after five years with the Senators. "His dad played in the NHL for many years and had a great career. Nick plays somewhat similar to his father, with a lot of heart. That's something that we were looking for."

When Scotty Bowman pulled the trigger on the infamous 1981 trade with Detroit, he was scolded for trading away the team's heart and soul, Jim Schoenfeld and Danny Gare. As it turned out, however, Bowman had found a new heart and soul in Foligno. Few players have worn the Sabres crest more proudly, and even fewer performed with more distinction than the man with the bulbous helmet, the discombobulated nose, and the unique goal-scoring celebration.

His goal total ranks sixth in team history, his 264 assists are 10th, his 511 points are eighth, and just as important to Sabres fans, his 1,450 penalty minutes, which defined his rugged style of play, rank second only to Rob Ray.

Detroit picked Foligno No. 3 overall in the 1979 draft. He never played in the minors, moving right into the Red Wings lineup and scoring a team-high and rookie-record 36 goals during his first season and finishing second in the NHL's rookie of the year voting to Boston's Ray Bourque.

He slipped to 28 goals in 1980–1981 and had 13 goals in 26 games in 1981–1982, when he was sent to Buffalo. Bowman paired Foligno with Gilbert Perreault almost immediately, and they were linemates on and off until Perreault called it quits in 1986. "I had a really good time with Mike," said Perreault. "He put a lot of life in the dressing room and on the ice."

Foligno scored at least 20 goals in his first eight seasons with Buffalo, and for much of that time he served as the team captain. He was the epitome of hard work—because nothing came easily for him. When he scored a goal, you knew he worked for it. And when he got into a scrap, he got his money's worth every time.

On the night that Perreault scored his historic 500th career goal, Perreault felt like he'd gotten into a fight with Foligno. It was Foligno who drew the primary assist on the play, and when Perreault deposited the puck in the net, Foligno's excitement more than made up for Perreault's typically laconic reaction. "I can still feel the slap he gave me," Perreault said with a laugh. "It was a thrill to play with him."

Foligno, who was inducted into the Greater Buffalo Sports Hall of Fame in 2005, was traded to Toronto just before Christmas 1990. He played there for three years and finished his career with one season for the Florida Panthers before retiring in 1994.

Sabres right winger Mike Foligno skates to the puck during a game versus the Detroit Red Wings at the Auditorium in Buffalo during the 1990–1991 season.
Photo courtesy of Getty Images

Watching Nick Foligno play today, it's easy to see that the apple didn't fall far from the tree. The Sabres hope another Foligno, Mike's younger son, Marcus, who had 13 points after being called up from the minors in 2011–2012, can carry on the family name in Buffalo.

"I picked up my dad's love and respect for the game," Nick said. "They kept him in the NHL so long because he loved the game, and I try to take that with me every time I step on the ice. I learned a lot of great things from my dad, but that's what influenced me the most."

Foligno Family Reunion

While Mike Foligno wasn't thrilled that he'd been fired from his position as assistant coach of the Anaheim Ducks two weeks earlier, the timing of that disappointment allowed him to be present on the night his two sons, Nick and Marcus, played against each other in the NHL for the first time.

On December 20, 2011, the Sabres called up 20-year-old Marcus—a fourth-round draft pick who was one of their top young prospects playing at AHL Rochester—to fill in during an injury crisis. Marcus' first NHL game was against the Ottawa Senators, a contest in which his 24-year-old brother Nick, a former first-round pick, would be playing in his 303rd game. About 30 family members and friends were present at ScotiaBank Place that night, including Mike, the former captain of the Sabres.

"Nick was pretty pumped," said Marcus. "Nick's excited. I think he's a little more excited than I am. It's awesome. It's kind of unreal how it works out to be like this. My first NHL game and it's against my brother."

Neither of the Folignos, both of whom were born in Buffalo while their dad was starring for the Sabres, scored a point in the game, but it's still a memory that they will cherish for a lifetime.

66 Sabres University

For nearly 30 years, the Sabres had a wonderfully convenient American Hockey League affiliation with the Rochester Amerks, a team that was located just 70 miles east on the New York State Thruway.

It was a picture-perfect arrangement for the Sabres, in that they could easily monitor the progress of their players—in person if they chose. And if they needed to bring someone up on an emergency recall because of an injury, the player could be in Buffalo in a flash. Sabres fans who were interested in seeing how Buffalo's top prospects were doing could jump in their cars and head to the War Memorial Auditorium in downtown Rochester, where dozens of players who later became mainstays in Buffalo cut their professional teeth.

From 1979, when the Sabres bought the Amerks, until 2005, which included the first 10 years the Amerks were owned by Steve Donner and his limited partners, the Sabres stocked the Rochester team with its players. For three years after that, the Sabres shared Rochester with the Florida Panthers—an ill-advised concept from the start, as the two teams' coaching philosophies, player usage, and development styles often clashed.

When financial difficulties struck Donner, creating situations in which the Amerks couldn't pay their creditors—including the Sabres—Buffalo had the perfect out. They bailed on Rochester and the cumbersome dual affiliation, opting instead to work out a new deal with the Portland (Maine) Pirates.

It was a dark day for the Amerks, to be sure, as their fan base really didn't have much of an interest in the Panthers' prospects. Rochester is in Sabres territory, where thousands of fans spend their winter evenings watching the Sabres on TV. Further, Florida's players weren't as good as Buffalo's, and the Amerks sank in the AHL standings, as did their attendance. For a 20-year period starting in 1984, the Amerks averaged about 6,000 fans per night; but by the last season with Florida, attendance had dipped to 3,872 per game.

The Amerks franchise, which was purchased by millionaire businessman Curt Styres in 2008, was bleeding money. That's when new Sabres owner Terry Pegula—who purchased the team in the spring of 2011—met with Styres.

Pegula realized that having Rochester as the Sabres farm team made enormous sense for the player development and convenience reasons, but also from a marketing standpoint. When Pegula made an offer of approximately $5 million, Styres gladly agreed, thus reuniting Buffalo and Rochester.

"This is not an affiliation, this is a unification," Sabres president Ted Black said when the deal was announced at a news conference in Rochester. "We're one market, we are one team, and we have one vision. It's no secret we very much want to win a Stanley Cup for the Sabres Nation, and we consider Rochester to be a suburb of the Sabres Nation."

Pegula, whose wife Kim was raised in Rochester and was an Amerks fan, has taken to calling the Amerks the Sabres University. Rochester is just fine with that—the city and the Amerks are thrilled to be back.

"It was an attitude that was everywhere," said Ron Rolston, who was hired by Pegula as the Amerks coach in 2011. "Every stop we had, the first thing you heard was how happy people were to be back in Buffalo, especially with Terry Pegula's ownership. They're excited about the resources and what they're going to put in the program here. There's a good buzz."

67 The Owners

When Terry Pegula was officially announced as the new owner of the Sabres in the spring of 2011, he looked out at a large gathering of reporters, employees, and fans in the lobby of First Niagara Center and uttered the comment that will be attached to him for as long as he's the boss.

"Starting today," Pegula said, "the Buffalo Sabres' reason for existence will be to win a Stanley Cup." It was music to the ears of Sabres fans, who have been frustrated for 40 years by the franchise's inability to achieve that lofty goal.

Pegula's pronouncement had hearts fluttering throughout western New York, and there were other reasons to rejoice, as well. The team was no longer financially constrained, meaning there would be no excuses for not winning. With a net worth of more than $3 billion, coupled with his passion for the game of hockey and his will to win a championship, Pegula made it perfectly clear that he wasn't in the hockey business to make money.

"If I want to make money, I'll go drill a gas well," said the founder of Pennsylvania-based East Resources, a natural gas drilling company that he eventually sold for $4.7 billion. "We'll put the pedal to the metal as capably as we can. I don't know if it's wise to spend to the cap every year. But we're not in this to save money, that's for sure."

To which NHL commissioner Gary Bettman replied, "This is a dream come true for him, but it's also a dream come true for the league because we know this franchise is in great hands."

That has actually been the case throughout most of the Sabres' four-plus decades in the league. Solid and stable ownership—with the exception of the dark period in the early 2000s—has been a hallmark of the club since its birth in 1970.

After a rejected attempt by the Knox family to bring a team to Buffalo during the NHL's six-team expansion in 1967, the brothers Seymour and Northrup Knox refused to let their dream die. They convinced the NHL that Buffalo was worthy when the addition of two teams was targeted for 1970—and this time the league agreed.

For the next 28 years, the Sabres were a well-oiled machine at the top of their game. The Knoxes ran the team with absolute class. While it was true that they could not compete financially with some of the bigger-market teams, their club rarely suffered in the standings; the Sabres made the playoffs 22 times, with three of the misses coming within four years of their birth.

But as the cost of doing business in the NHL rose, the Knoxes struggled to make ends meet; it was reported that the team lost $32 million in their final three years of ownership. Seymour passed away in May 1996, and Northrup died in 1998, though the machinations behind the transfer of ownership to John Rigas, the founder of Adelphia Communications, were already in motion.

Rigas and his sons, Timothy and Michael, were basically in charge of the team starting in 1997–1998, and during those first few years, it appeared to be as seamless a transition as the Sabres could have dreamed for. The team advanced to the Eastern Conference Finals in 1998, then to the Stanley Cup Finals in 1999, and was less than two minutes away from making it back to the Eastern Finals in 2001 before a stunning turn of events in their series loss to Pittsburgh.

And then it happened: a scandal so catastrophic that the Sabres were thrust into bankruptcy and, at one point in 2002, even seemed in danger of leaving town. Rigas and his sons were arrested in July 2002 on charges that they had embezzled more than $2 billion from Adelphia, and the ripple effect of this corporate corruption nearly buried the Sabres under a tidal wave of adversity.

While the Rigases concentrated on their legal defense (which ultimately went for naught, as John and Timothy were sent to federal prison), the NHL stripped the family of its ownership rights, took over stewardship of the beleaguered franchise, and tried to find a new owner. It was an arduous process, but that man—a "white knight on a white horse," according to Bettman—wound up being Tom Golisano, a billionaire from just down the Thruway in Rochester who ponied up $92 million.

Golisano is recognized as the savior of the Sabres, and rightly so. Without him, the team might have relocated. During his eight-year tenure the Sabres enjoyed two of their most exciting seasons, 2005–2006 and 2006–2007, when they advanced to the Eastern Conference Finals. There were some outstanding players who suited up in the familiar blue-and-gold uniforms that Golisano eventually reinstated (the team had changed colors and logo when it moved into its new arena in 1996 and changed back in 2007), and there were certainly some thrilling moments.

Passing of the Patriarch

On the night the Sabres turned out the lights at the Aud one last time, Seymour Knox closed his remarks by looking around the building and saying, "Farewell, old friend." Barely a month later, the Sabres, their fans, and all of western New York were saying the same thing to Knox when he passed away at the age of 70 on May 22, 1996, after a long battle with cancer.

Play-by-play announcer Rick Jeanneret served as the emcee for the closing ceremony at the Aud, and knowing Knox's health was declining, he admitted, "I almost had the feeling that night that Seymour was saying good-bye to everyone, not just the building. It was a very emotional night."

Five months later, Jeanneret had a microphone in his hand again, only this time he was standing on the ice at Marine Midland Arena. While the night was meant to celebrate the future of the Sabres organization and the opening of their new 18,000-seat playpen, Jeanneret felt it was only appropriate to also pay homage to the past—and the man who provided Sabres' fans with that past.

"I remember saying on that night that all of this—meaning the new arena—came about because of one man and one man only," Jeanneret said. "I never mentioned Seymour's name, I just said, 'one man,' and the whole crowd stood up and gave him a standing ovation. They knew. That was pretty neat."

Simply put, Knox was one of the most influential and important citizens to ever call Buffalo home, and his contributions to life in western New York extended far beyond the Sabres. But while he was known for his philanthropy, his business success, and the art gallery that carries his family name, bringing the Sabres and the NHL to Buffalo is what he will be most remembered for.

"Although he did not live to see the opening of the new Marine Midland Arena, its presence will be a lasting, and fitting, legacy to the man who was such an integral part of bringing and keeping NHL hockey in Buffalo," said Dennis Gorski, the Erie county executive at the time.

But at his core, Golisano was a businessman, and he ran the team like a company. He and his partners, Larry Quinn and Dan DiPofi, were always conscious of the payroll, which tied the hands of general manager Darcy Regier in his pursuit of free agents with which to upgrade the roster.

When Golisano quietly began looking for an exit, in stepped Pegula. This Pennsylvania native, who had once been a Sabres season-ticket holder, made an offer of $189 million. Golisano took it, netting himself a tidy profit, indeed.

With Pegula in charge, there are no worries about the team leaving town, or that it won't spend money to improve the product. In his first full year, 2011–2012, Pegula got right to work, giving free-agent defenseman Christian Ehrhoff a 10-year contract worth $40 million, then shelling out another $27 million over six years to forward Ville Leino.

Clearly a new era had begun, and if Pegula is a man of his word, he's not going to stop spending until the Stanley Cup resides in Buffalo. And even then, one visit from Lord Stanley's chalice won't be enough.

68 Roger the Dodger

The punch line would have been: "If you watched the Buffalo Sabres play on a regular basis during their first two years in the NHL, you'd have had an upset stomach, too."

But Roger Crozier's upset stomach was no joke. The little goaltender from Bracebridge, Ontario, who helped give the Sabres credibility at their birth and a chance to win every night he was able to play during those early years, suffered from stomach ailments throughout his 14-year career.

His frequent bouts with pancreatitis forced him to miss large portions of almost every season he played in the NHL, and was just the precursor to the ultimate battle he eventually lost with prostate cancer, which took his life at the age of 53 in 1996.

But when Crozier did play, he was often spectacular. His Buffalo teammates knew that without him in the franchise's first two seasons, the already woebegone Sabres might have set unbreakable NHL futility standards.

"Roger really made the difference for the Sabres that first year," recalled Floyd Smith in a story written by Randy Schultz for NHL. com. "It was Roger who kept us in many games that first season. There were nights when he faced as many as 50 to 60 shots, and he stopped many of them. He kept us respectable."

Don Luce, who joined the Sabres in their second year in a trade from Detroit, agreed. "Roger was unbelievable in goal," Luce told Schultz. "He was so quick and so fast. He was almost impossible to beat when he was on top of his game. Roger's ability to stop the puck helped the Sabres team grow in those early days."

Crozier played a handful of games in three different seasons for the old Buffalo Bisons during the early 1960s before he made his dazzling NHL debut in 1964–1965 with the Detroit Red Wings. That year he won 40 games with a 2.42 goals-against average to earn the league's rookie of the year award. Then in 1965–1966 he backstopped the Red Wings to the Stanley Cup Finals, winning the Conn Smythe Trophy as playoff MVP even though the Wings lost to the Montreal Canadiens in six games.

Hockey legend Gordie Howe remembered one particular save Crozier made in a playoff game against Chicago that he said typi-fied Crozier's style. "Bobby Hull fired a drive that hit him on the shoulder and Roger almost did a cartwheel, but he got in front of it," Howe said. "That's the way he played. He was the only reason we got to the Finals in 1966."

Because of his health issues, Crozier never played more than 38 games during his last three years in Detroit, and the Red Wings were willing to trade him to the expansion Sabres in 1970. Punch Imlach knew Crozier would not be an iron man, but he also knew without an established NHL goalie there was a chance the Sabres would get blown out every night.

Sabres goalie Roger Crozier wipes his face during Game 6 of the Stanley Cup Finals against the Philadelphia Flyers on May 27, 1975. Though the Sabres fell to the Flyers in the series 4–2, Crozier was a big part of Buffalo's early success.

"Roger was the foundation of the Buffalo Sabres franchise," Smith said. "The minute Punch got Roger from the Red Wings, it gave the Sabres instant credibility. And Punch knew that the strength of the Sabres would be built from the goal out. Roger provided that foundation in goal to work from."

Crozier went 9–20–7 during his first year in Buffalo, and 13–34–14 in 1971–1972, the only one of the six years he spent in Buffalo during which he was relatively healthy. His goals-against averages during those seasons were 3.68 and 3.51—numbers that would buy him a ticket to the minor leagues these days, but were downright heroic playing behind Buffalo's horrendous defense.

"Roger was certainly a major contributor to the early success of the franchise," said former Sabres co-owner Seymour Knox III upon hearing the news of Crozier's passing (only four months prior to his own). "He was the one who made us competitors in the games we played in our early years. He was a great athlete, very acrobatic, and known for his many saves he had to make practically every game he played in."

69 Wounded Knee

Dominik Hasek was undeniably a great goaltender, a Hall of Famer who began to forge his legacy during his years in Buffalo and later cemented it with a Stanley Cup in Detroit.

But for all his brilliance in the goal crease, Hasek was a complex man, and there were several incidents that occurred while he was a member of the Sabres that left his teammates shaking their heads in wonderment.

One that stands out like a red flare on a dark highway occurred during the first-round playoff series against Ottawa in 1997. Hasek and coach Ted Nolan were barely on speaking terms during that season. But the bickering with Nolan seemed to have no effect on Hasek's performance, as he was the primary reason why a fairly ordinary team won the Northeast Division. But things came to a head during this tumultuous playoff series.

After the teams split a pair of 3–1 victories in Buffalo, they traveled up to Ottawa for the first home playoff game in the history of the five-year-old Senators franchise. The day of the game, Hasek was unusually on edge. He had skipped the optional morning skate, the team meeting, and team breakfast, something he rarely did. In the pregame warm-up he lost his temper, slamming his stick against the goal post, when he failed to stop a shot, and twice during the shoot-around he skated out of the crease in frustration and had to be cajoled by teammates.

When the game started, Buffalo grabbed a 1–0 lead, but in the second period, Ottawa's Sergei Zholtok took a shot that deflected off a Sabre defender and sailed past Hasek to tie the score. Hasek immediately grabbed his knee, then skated directly to the locker room before the trainers could even get onto the ice. Backup Steve Shields had to go in cold. In one of the great clutch performances in Sabres history, Shields allowed only one goal—that just 2:08 after he had entered—and Buffalo rallied to win when Dixon Ward broke a 2–2 tie with 19 seconds remaining in the third period.

As thrilling as the victory was, the postgame talk all centered on Hasek's condition; privately, some players questioned whether he was even really hurt. As respected columnist Jim Kelley wrote in the *Buffalo News,* "There may well be other forces at work here, but what we've seen so far is scary enough. I don't for a moment believe that Dominik Hasek intentionally bailed out on his coach and his teammates Monday night, but I do believe the pressure of having to be unbeatable may well be more than even he can bear. If that's the case, there may be more than a slightly sprained knee to worry about."

Shields started Game 4, battling Ottawa's Ron Tugnutt to a scoreless 60-minute draw only to lose in overtime on a goal by Daniel Alfredsson. Ottawa then went back to Buffalo and rolled to a 4–1 victory to grab a three-games-to-two lead. Meanwhile, the Hasek situation had exploded out of control.

Hasek had announced before Game 4 that he probably wouldn't be able to play until the next series (if Buffalo made it that far). Yet the team doctors indicated that Hasek's status would be judged on a day-to-day basis. The day after Game 4, Hasek read a prepared statement trying to clarify his position, but it only clouded the situation more. After that, his teammates—led by Rob Ray—read a prepared statement of their own in support of Hasek, though no one knew about it until it was actually being read, a clear indication of the unrest in the locker room.

On the morning of Game 5, Hasek held another press conference, saying that if team management had not backed him, he would have left the organization. He remained upset with Nolan, however, because the coach did not publicly support Hasek against charges that he wasn't really as injured as he was letting on.

It was a mess. After the game, emotions were raw and Hasek's boiled over. When he spotted Kelley outside the Buffalo locker room, he attacked him, grabbing and ripping his shirt and spewing

The Scoreboard, Not the Walls, Came Tumbling Down

Boston Bruins fan William Beeke, then a 34-year-old from Westfield, Massachusetts, drove 375 miles from his home to downtown Buffalo to watch his beloved Boston Bruins take on the Sabres on November 16, 1996, in Buffalo's brand-new home, Marine Midland Arena.

That was a long way to go to *not* see a game. A few hours before the scheduled opening faceoff, workers were lowering the JumboTron scoreboard for routine maintenance when a cable snapped and the $4.5-million, 40,000-pound unit crashed to the ice.

"It was incredible," said one arena worker who witnessed the incident. "It was like a loud groan, and then another groan, and another, and then it dropped."

The damage to the ice was irreparable, so the game had to be postponed. It was later played on March 17, 1997, and the Sabres won 5–1. For the rest of that season the Sabres played at the Arena without a JumboTron, and the gaping void above center ice was certainly an odd sight to see.

One of the JumboTron screens that never hit the ice and was therefore undamaged was erected on top of the lower bowl at one end of the rink, allowing most of the crowd to watch instant replays. About four rows of seats had to be removed to make room for the screen.

"Everyone told me not to come up, that there would be 30 inches of snow," Beeke told the *Buffalo News*. "There's not snow. But there's no game."

profanities before being pulled off by a reporter, a security guard, and teammate Jason Dawe.

Incredibly, the Sabres regrouped and won Game 6 in Ottawa as Shields pitched a shutout, and then Buffalo pulled off a 3–2 overtime victory to win the series in what remains the only Game 7 victory in franchise history.

Hasek did not play again that year. The Sabres were blown out in the second round in five games by Philadelphia. Nolan lost a power struggle with general manager John Muckler during the off-season, quitting when he wasn't offered a multiyear contract extension— which surely pleased Hasek.

70 Larry Playfair

After losing to the Broad Street Bullies in the 1975 Stanley Cup Finals, it was pretty obvious to Rick Martin that the one ingredient the Sabres lacked was toughness.

"We needed a cement head," Martin said. "Not that we didn't have any tough guys, but all our tough guys were good players. [Jim] Schoenfeld and [Jerry] Korab were more valuable on the ice than they were in the penalty box. If someone had gotten ahold of us after we lost to the Flyers and maybe just done a little tweaking… You didn't have very many soft games, and we needed that one hammer."

What the Sabres needed was Larry Playfair, but they didn't get him until the 1978–1979 season, which was a little too late for that dynamic mid-'70s Sabres team that never reached the pinnacle.

Playfair played his junior hockey for the Portland Winter Hawks; during his last year in the Western Canadian Junior Hockey League, he piled up 402 penalty minutes in 71 games.

"It was a role that I found I needed to play back to when I was 15," said Playfair, who stood 6'4" and weighed a rugged 215 pounds. "We had a bunch of young kids playing against some older guys, they were smacking us around a little bit, and it just became obvious to me that it was a need."

Sabres general manager Punch Imlach took notice of that, and he used the 13th overall pick in the first round of the 1978 NHL Draft to make sure those fists would be flying in Buffalo.

"As descriptive as anyone has ever been with me, that was Punch," said Playfair. "The day they drafted me, I was at a friend's place working on my car, and the phone rang in the office. I went in to answer it, and it was Punch, and he said, 'Congratulations, we drafted you in the first round. We understand you're a big kid and you play aggressive, and that's why we drafted you.' And then the

The Campbell Check

Brian Campbell was one of the last guys the Sabres ever depended on to provide an intimidating physical presence during his eight years with the organization.

But on April 22, 2006, in the Sabres first postseason game since 2001, it was Campbell, the smooth-skating, offensive-minded defenseman, who unloaded a thunderous mid-ice check on Philadelphia rookie center R.J. Umberger that set a tone for Buffalo's first-round series against the historically nasty Flyers.

"It wasn't quite like scoring a goal, but I couldn't believe how much it was going around," said Campbell of the buzz that he generated with that hit, which knocked Umberger out of the game. "I couldn't go anywhere in Buffalo without people saying, 'Nice hit.'"

Campbell crunched Umberger in the first overtime period, and Daniel Briere—who left Buffalo a few years later to sign a rich free-agent contract with Philadelphia—scored the winning goal in the second overtime for the Sabres. Buffalo went on to win the series in six games, and ultimately advanced all the way to the Eastern Conference Finals before losing in seven games to eventual Stanley Cup champion Carolina.

To this day, when the Sabres put together pregame video montages before their home playoff games, the Campbell check is still shown, and it draws loud roars every time. It very well may be the most famous check in team history, albeit from one of the most unlikely of sources.

phone went dead. So he called back and said, 'Listen, I hope that was just an accident, because if that's not how you play, then we just made a mistake with our draft pick.'"

But Imlach had not made a mistake, a fact he confirmed at training camp when Playfair proved his mettle in an exhibition game in Kitchener, Ontario, against Toronto.

"Dave Hutchison ran Ric Seiling, and I was on the ice, so I went over, and we got into a bit of a scrap," Playfair recalled. "After the game, Punch came over and shook all of our hands, and he stopped at me and said, 'Okay, that was good, that's what I like, but the guys I want you to take care of are those three,' and he pointed to the French Connection. But I never felt I had to be told that, anyway."

Playfair started his first season with Hershey in the American Hockey League, then was called up to Buffalo at midseason and never played another minor league game. He was Buffalo's enforcer for the next seven and a half years before Scotty Bowman traded him to the Los Angeles Kings. After three and a half years in Hollywood, he returned to Buffalo and closed out his career in 1989–1990.

Playfair later worked on Sabres broadcasts with Rick Jeanneret, was inducted into the team's Hall of Fame in 1998, and has been the longtime president of the Sabres Alumni Association.

"If you ask any of the guys I played with, I probably made it a little more comfortable for them to play," he said.

And he's right.

71 Attend a Party in the Plaza

One of the most enduring images of the Sabres' run to back-to-back appearances in the Eastern Conference Finals in 2006 and 2007 were the thousands of loyal fans who didn't have tickets to get into HSBC Arena, but went downtown to stand outside and watch the playoff games on a 9' × 12' video screen.

During every game, live shots of the crowd going crazy outside when the Sabres scored a goal were shown on the JumboTron inside the arena, adding an increased level of excitement that was undeniable in the already pulsating environment.

These outdoor gatherings became known as the Party in the Plaza, and with the addition of beer tents, concessions, and live music, what had begun with fans just coming to watch the game with other Sabres fans morphed into a full entertainment experience.

The genesis of this activity is rooted in Buffalo's appearance in the 1999 Stanley Cup Finals, when folks who could not get tickets to the games were invited to sit in the city's baseball stadium, where the Triple A Buffalo Bisons played—then called Dunn Tire Park—to watch the games on the big video board for a modest $2 admission fee, money that was split between Sabres and Bisons charities.

The Party in the Plaza was rejuvenated in 2006, when the Sabres made the playoffs for the first time since 2001. The organization invited fans to come down to watch Game 3 of the team's second-round series against Ottawa. The atmosphere was electric because Buffalo had won the first two games in Ottawa over the heavily favored Senators.

Team owner Tom Golisano made an appearance at the party, telling the crowd, "I wish we had an arena that could seat 40,000 people so we could get you all in here."

The following year the parties returned, but there was some controversy. After some alcohol-related incidents during the first-round series against the New York Islanders, the Sabres attempted to do away with beer sales at the event during the second-round series against the New York Rangers, hoping for a more family-friendly atmosphere.

Naturally, the fans in attendance were irate, so the Sabres relented for the next party and the taps were turned back on with a three-beer limit—a "hat trick maximum," if you will. As one happy partygoer remarked, "Nobody wants to stand for three hours watching a hockey game and not be able to drink."

The Party in the Plaza concept was expanded in intervening years to include Opening Night for each season, and then in 2011–2012—the first full season under the ownership of Terry Pegula—a 3,200-square-foot party tent was constructed for the entire season, and the Tailgate Tent Party became the place to be for fans who had tickets to the games.

A $10 admission (which includes one drink) provides attendees with the chance to drink, eat, and listen to live music, as well as the opportunity to meet special guests—often Sabres players who are injured or not playing in that night's game.

This idea was hatched when Pegula and his wife, Kim, saw the excitement that was generated at the outdoor Party in the Plaza during the playoffs in the spring of 2011. "Terry, Kim, and I continue to be blown away by the extraordinary support of the Sabres Nation," Sabres president Ted Black said in announcing the Tailgate Tent Party experience.

Hockey, beer, food, music, camaraderie: what's not to love?

72 A Hero's Welcome

The 1980 United States Olympic hockey team has been immortalized in every possible way, and for good reason. That group of college students delivered a story so compelling and improbable on its way to capturing the gold medal in Lake Placid that, even more than 30 years later, their Miracle on Ice is still considered the greatest sports team achievement in history.

With three of those Olympians belonging to the Sabres, imagine the excitement in Buffalo when the Games were over and those players were free to move on with the rest of their hockey careers.

Punch Imlach, who built the Sabres in the early years with top-notch draft picks, made his final draft in 1978 a memorable one by choosing Larry Playfair and Tony McKegney in the first two rounds, then Olympians Rob McClanahan (third round) and Eric Strobel (eighth). And then in 1979, when Scotty Bowman was in charge of the draft, the first selection he made as the Sabres general manager was Mike Ramsey, another Olympian, with the 11th overall choice.

Ramsey, McClanahan, and Strobel all played their college hockey at powerhouse Minnesota under Herb Brooks, who was also the Olympic coach. They made the U.S. team and played vital roles in the Americans' run through the tournament, so everyone in Buffalo knew who they were and couldn't wait to get a glimpse of them.

The city got its chance to take a look at Ramsey and McClanahan on March 9, 1980, in a game against the St. Louis Blues at Memorial Auditorium, and what a night that was for the usual 16,433 paying customers. Old pros Rick Martin and Gilbert Perreault did their best to upstage the arrival of the newbies as Martin scored four goals and Perreault tied his own team record with five assists in Buffalo's 9–4 romp. Yet despite Martin and Perreault's greatness, this night was all about the Olympians, who received a thunderous standing ovation before the game when they were presented with a commemorative gift by team owner and President Seymour Knox III.

The Olympians gave the Sabres a shot of adrenaline throughout the game. "Ramsey and McClanahan gave us a little something extra," associate coach Roger Neilson said.

Neilson played McClanahan on the fourth line with Bob Mongrain and then a rotating member, usually Danny Gare, while

Ramsey logged much more ice time as part of the three-pair defensive rotation. "It wasn't that I was trying to give them confidence. I just thought they could do the job," said Bowman, who coached behind the bench for the first time in nearly two months in this game while Neilson sat in the press box communicating with his walkie-talkie.

Ramsey was just happy to get his NHL debut out of the way. Of the fame he and his Olympic teammates had garnered, he remarked, "I'll be glad to be done with all the hoopla and just play hockey again." McClanahan nodded in agreement.

Ramsey went on to become one of the greatest Sabres, playing 14 of his 18 NHL seasons with the team. His 911 games are the most ever for a Buffalo defenseman. He also played in four NHL All-Star Games, was a member of two U.S. Canada Cup teams, and was inducted into the United States Hockey Hall of Fame in 2001. He also served as an assistant coach with the Sabres for a few years during the late 1990s.

McClanahan's star, on the other hand, fell quickly. He played 13 games with the Sabres upon joining the team in 1980, scoring two goals, and in 53 games with the club the following year he scored only three goals. At the end of that season he was left unprotected and was selected by Hartford in the waiver draft. After brief stints with the Whalers and the New York Rangers, he retired in 1984 having scored only 38 NHL goals.

That was 38 more than Strobel, however, whose professional career never got off the ground. He played a half season for the Rochester Americans after the Olympics, then promptly retired from hockey, figuring he wasn't going to get a shot with the Sabres, and returned to the University of Minnesota to earn his degree.

73 King Kong Korab

When you scan down the roster of any NHL team in this day and age of the super-sized athlete, you don't even blink when you see someone who stands 6'3" and weighs 220 pounds. "Today you go to any game and you can pick a dozen guys who are bigger, so it's commonplace now," former Sabres defenseman turned broadcast analyst Mike Robitaille said.

But back in the 1970s, a player that big was considered a veritable monster. Such was Jerry Korab, a man who earned the nickname "King Kong" because that's about how big he looked to the opposition.

"There were very few players that were his size, and it was freakish to see anyone that big," said Robitaille, a rugged 190 pounds when he played but no match for Kong. "I played against him in junior hockey, and you can imagine how big he looked in junior hockey. He kept you honest, and every now and then his eyes would spin out of his head and he could lay the wood on you, and you wouldn't forget it for a while."

Korab spent parts of nine seasons rattling the glass at Memorial Auditorium with his booming body checks on pitied enemy skaters. And even in an age when NHL players are bigger and physically stronger than ever before, Kong would still have made some of today's so-called power forwards melt into the ice.

"He was a big guy and he gave us a little toughness and size that we needed," Rick Martin said of Korab, who came to the Sabres in 1973–1974 from Vancouver, was traded to Los Angeles by Scotty Bowman in 1980, and then came back to Buffalo to wrap up his career for two years during the mid-1980s. "Jerry could be pretty mean, and the other teams didn't want to rile him up, they'd prefer to just let him sleep. But when he got fired up, he was tough and he didn't mind dropping 'em."

And when Korab wasn't busy implanting opponents' profiles into the boards, he was scaring the hell out of goalies. "Jerry Korab had a shot that would hurt you," said former Islanders goalie Chico Resch. "You hear about guys who have a heavy shot. His was a heavy shot."

Korab began his NHL career in Chicago in 1970 and was part of teams that lost to Montreal in the 1971 and 1973 Stanley Cup Finals. He was dealt to Vancouver before the 1973–1974 season, and less than halfway through the year he was on the move again, this time to Buffalo in exchange for Tracy Pratt and John Gould,

Sabres defenseman Jerry "King Kong" Korab slashes at the Rangers' Rick Middleton as he goes for the puck during a game on January 28, 1976, at New York's Madison Square Garden. Photo courtesy of Getty Images

a deal that created a stir in Buffalo. Pratt had been a popular player, and the fans were irate at general manager Punch Imlach for trading him away. But in time, this proved to be one of the best trades in team history, as Korab became one of the Sabres' top blueliners.

Korab set team scoring records for a defenseman his first full year with the club in 1974–1975, when he scored 12 goals and 56 points. He followed that with 13 goals in 1975–1976 and 14 in 1976–1977, and his 67 career goals are third-most in team history for defensemen behind only Phil Housley (178) and Mike Ramsey (73).

When Scotty Bowman came to Buffalo in 1979, Korab had an inkling that he wouldn't be around much longer, mainly because he lacked the mobility Bowman demanded from his defense. Sure enough, in March 1980, just days after Ramsey joined the Sabres following the 1980 Olympics, Korab was dealt to Los Angeles for the Kings' first-round draft pick in 1982 (which wound up being No. 6 overall, and enabled Bowman to select Housley).

74 Impact Trades

The undeniable No. 1 trade in franchise history was the December 2, 1981, deal that sent Jim Schoenfeld, Danny Gare, and Derek Smith to Detroit in exchange for Mike Foligno, Dale McCourt, and Brent Peterson. But of course there have been many other trades that have had a major impact on the Sabres.

On January 14, 1972, Jim Lorentz was acquired from the Rangers in exchange for a 1972 second-round draft choice that became Larry Sacharuk. Punch Imlach made this deal from his hospital bed while recovering from a heart attack, and it was one of his best. Lorentz won a Stanley Cup in Boston in 1970 as a fourth-liner, but he was never a regular until arriving in Buffalo, where he scored at least 20 goals in four seasons. After retiring, Lorentz went on to work on Sabres' broadcasts as an analyst for 30 years.

On March 4, 1972, Eddie Shack was sent to Pittsburgh for Rene Robert, a slam dunk if ever there was one. Shack's career was just about finished, while Robert became the third and final member of the famed French Connection.

On November 12, 1988, Tom Barrasso, the former No. 1 draft pick, was sent to Pittsburgh along with Buffalo's third-round draft slot in 1990 in exchange for Doug Bodger and Darrin Shannon. Barrasso enjoyed a few very good years in Buffalo, but he played on some poor teams at the end of his stint and struggled. He went on to win two Stanley Cups with Pittsburgh, while Bodger and Shannon were solid Sabres for several years.

On March 7, 1989, former captain Lindy Ruff was traded to the Rangers for a fifth-round pick in 1990 that became Richard Smehlik. Ruff was the heart and soul of the Sabres, but general manager Gerry Meehan, knowing Ruff and coach Ted Sator did not get along, decided to make the deal. "[Sator's] perception of me as a hockey player is different from my opinion," Ruff said. "Maybe he wanted more finesse players. I've got a burning desire to just prove to myself and whoever was doubting my ability that I can still play the game."

On June 16, 1990, Phil Housley, Scott Arniel, Jeff Parker, and a 1991 first-round draft choice that became Keith Tkachuk were sent to Winnipeg for Dale Hawerchuk and a 1990 first-round pick that Buffalo used to select Brad May. Hawerchuk was a superstar in Winnipeg and built most of his future Hall of Fame legacy there, but he also scored 110 goals and 275 assists in four and a half seasons with the Sabres.

On October 25, 1991, Pierre Turgeon, Uwe Krupp, Dave McLlwain, and Benoit Hogue were dealt to the Islanders for Pat LaFontaine, Randy Wood, and Randy Hiller. This trade comes the closest to the Gare/Schoenfeld deal in magnitude. Turgeon was the No. 1 overall pick in the 1987 draft, but never really lived up to that billing in Buffalo. LaFontaine was a four-time All-Star who was holding out, looking for a trade. "I only can think of two players you can name right off the bat; you think of Lemieux, you think of Gretzky. After that, he's got to be considered with anybody else," coach Rick Dudley said of LaFontaine. "That's a pretty high-quality player. That's a dominant player." LaFontaine's time in Buffalo was marred by injury, but he had a big enough impact to have his No. 16 jersey retired.

On August 7, 1992, Dominik Hasek was acquired from Chicago for Stephane Beauregard. It seemed like a nothing swap of goaltenders at the time, and it wound up being that for the Blackhawks. For the Sabres, it became the greatest steal in team history. Hasek began to build his Hall of Fame resume in Buffalo, becoming the greatest goalie the Sabres have ever seen.

On July 8, 1995, Alexander Mogilny and a fifth-round pick were traded to Vancouver for Michael Peca, Mike Wilson, and a 1995 first-round choice that became Jay McKee. Mogilny was beginning to fade, while Peca became a captain and the guts of Buffalo's late 1990s playoff teams, including the Stanley Cup runner-up in 1999. McKee also had a solid career in Buffalo.

On March 11, 2003, Daniel Briere came to Buffalo from Phoenix in exchange for Chris Gratton. Gratton had been acquired a few years earlier and never really panned out. Briere was a middling player in Phoenix, but he became a star in Buffalo, leading the Sabres to back-to-back conference finals appearances before bolting for Philadelphia in free agency.

75 The Hardest-Working Spectacle in Hockey

Rob Ray would prefer to remember the electricity that flowed through Marine Midland Arena the night the Sabres made their return to the postseason and the building hosted its first Stanley Cup playoff game, an exciting 3–1 victory over Ottawa.

He would prefer to remember the way the Sabres rallied from a three-games-to-two deficit in that first-round series against the upstart Senators by winning Game 6 in Ottawa, and then recording the first and still only Game 7 victory in franchise history on Derek Plante's unforgettable overtime goal.

He would rather talk about the bonds forged by player-friendly coach Ted Nolan's second and last Sabres team during a shocking season when Buffalo overachieved to such a degree that it won a division title, earned the second seed in the Eastern Conference bracket, and was deservedly branded "the hardest-working team in hockey."

Instead, what Ray remembers most was the chaos that engulfed the organization all year.

"There were so many things going on behind the scenes that people to this day don't even know about," said Ray. "It was quite a year."

If nothing else, the 1996–1997 Sabres were a sportswriters' dream. If it was story lines you were looking for, the Sabres never stopped providing them that season. You could make a case that the combination of tumult off the ice and excitement on it made this the most memorable year in the team's history.

It started in early October, when the Sabres moved into Marine Midland Arena. On the night they won their first game in the building, superstar Pat LaFontaine suffered a concussion that effectively ended his career with the team—he appeared in only seven more games that season and was traded to the New York Rangers before the following season.

In November the JumboTron scoreboard crashed to the ice during a routine maintenance check, and the wreckage at center ice seemed like a fitting microcosm for what was happening to the organization. Amidst the difficult transfer of ownership from the Knox family to the Rigas family, there was unprecedented (at least to that point) front-office turmoil, including the dismissal of Doug Moss as team president, with Larry Quinn sliding into that position, and the constant bickering between general manager John Muckler and the man he had handpicked as the team's coach, Ted Nolan.

Through it all, a Sabres team that had missed the playoffs the year before for the first time since 1987, a team that wasn't even supposed to be a playoff contender, somehow overcame the adversity they faced to win the Northeast Division title, then fended off more trouble in the series against Ottawa when Dominik Hasek's mysterious knee injury in Game 3 sidelined him for the rest of the playoffs.

The Sabres went 40–30–12, and those 92 points—eight more than runner-up Pittsburgh—were rather amazing when you consider the leading scorer on the team was Derek Plante, who had a mere 53 points.

"We were a pretty tight group of guys," said Ray. "The style of game we played kind of brought everybody together. We made it difficult for teams to play against us and we got a little momentum and once we gained a little confidence, for a young group of guys who don't know any better, it's amazing what you can do when you have that confidence. There were times where we thought we could beat anybody and we were going into the games thinking that way."

Alas, their average talent was unmasked in the second round by Philadelphia as the Flyers ended Buffalo's crazy season in five games.

The New Home of the Sabres

The Sabres certainly didn't catch a break from the NHL schedule-maker in 1996–1997 when they were told to christen brand-new Marine Midland Arena with a game against the Detroit Red Wings.

The Wings had produced a league-record 62-win regular season the previous year, but all that hard work went for naught when they were upset in the Western Conference Finals by archrival Colorado. Needless to say, the Wings felt like they had some unfinished business to tend to, and they showed no mercy on Buffalo's big night on October 12, 1996.

They toyed with the overmatched Sabres for 60 minutes, spoiling the opening of the new arena in front of what was the largest hockey crowd in Buffalo history at that time (18,595). "It was ugly. There is no excuse for it," said Buffalo coach Ted Nolan, who could not believe his team had been that badly outclassed.

Things would improve that year. The Sabres earned a playoff berth, then won a first-round series with the Arena's first great moment, Derek Plante's Game 7 overtime winning goal against Ottawa.

76 The Sabres Store and the Buffalo Sports Hall of Fame

Two of the most popular attractions at First Niagara Center—besides the actual ice surface where the games are played—are certainly the Sabres official team store and the Greater Buffalo Sports Hall of Fame display area located in the main lobby in front of the store.

The team store offers the largest selection of Sabres merchandise anywhere, including jerseys with the names of players past and present sewn in, T-shirts, hats, sweatshirts, and jackets in all sizes.

The store also carries hockey equipment and collectibles, including items such as bobble-heads, coffee mugs, jewelry, posters, pennants, team media guides, yearbooks, and books that have been written about the team, including the 40th anniversary book that was published in 2010.

The store is open weekdays from 10:00 AM to 5:00 PM, and whenever there is a Sabres game or a Buffalo Bandits indoor lacrosse game, the doors remain open throughout the evening. Whenever the building is open, fans are also welcome to visit the Hall of Fame in the west end of the lobby. Though it's a rather small display, it's a place where Buffalo sports fans can spend hours looking at the collected memorabilia.

There had been talk of creating a Sports Hall of Fame in Buffalo for many years, but nothing ever came of it until a Buffalo business-man named John Kapelewski got things moving in the fall of 1990. Kapelewski had previously helped to create the Syracuse Sports Hall of Fame. Upon moving to Buffalo and learning that Buffalo did not have a Hall of Fame, Kapelewski began recruiting members of the community who shared his interest in history.

Incorporated as a nonprofit organization, the Greater Buffalo Sports Hall of Fame group began meeting regularly in 1991, and that's when plans were formulated for an inaugural induction din-ner that was ultimately held in 1991. The event was emceed by longtime television sports anchor Van Miller, then the legendary voice of the Buffalo Bills.

The first class of 11 inductees in 1992 included the original Sabre, all-time leading scorer and Hockey Hall of Famer Gilbert Perreault; Buffalo Bills superstar and Pro Football Hall of Famer O.J. Simpson; St. Bonaventure basketball great and pro basketball Hall of Famer Bob Lanier; and two Buffalo native Baseball Hall of Famers, longtime New York Yankees manager Joe McCarthy and pitcher Warren Spahn, the all-time winningest left-hander.

Through 2012, more than 250 men and women—all of whom live, or have lived and worked or played in western New York—have been inducted, and the dinner has become one of the premier events on Buffalo's sporting calendar.

Part of the proceeds from the 2011 dinner and ceremony, which was held in the main ballroom of the downtown Hyatt Regency hotel, were donated to local athletic groups through the Hall's Amateur Sports Development Fund (donees included Annunciation School, the Cazenovia Park Hockey Association, the Depew Lacrosse Club, Niagara Frontier Volleyball, the Northwest Buffalo Community Center, the South Buffalo Baseball Association, and the Town of Aurora Parks and Recreation). Through the years, the Hall of Fame has donated more than $80,000 to such organizations.

77 The One That Got Away

Throughout the timeline of a sports franchise's existence, there are certain major events that can change a team's fortunes. These include the drafting of a future superstar, a change in coaching or management that turns a team from a loser into a winner, or a triumph in a playoff series that sets a team off on a dynastic run.

And yes, there are some events that fall on the negative side of the ledger, such as the drafting of a future bust, a change in coaching or management that turns a team from a winner into a loser, or a galling defeat in a playoff series that sends a team spiraling into an abyss.

For the Sabres, one of those positive events was beating Ottawa in Game 7 of the first round of the 1997 playoffs—without the great Dominik Hasek. That victory kicked off a run that saw the team reach the Eastern Conference Finals in 1998 and then the Stanley Cup Finals in 1999. And conversely, their gut-wrenching Eastern Conference semifinal series loss to the Pittsburgh Penguins in 2001 launched a domino effect that ended Hasek's career in Buffalo and began the darkest period in team history, one that included

Masters of Heartbreak

The Sabres have definitely endured some tough times in the NHL playoffs, not the least of which are two losses in the Stanley Cup Finals, one to Philadelphia in 1975 and the other to Dallas in 1999.

They also had a stretch in the mid-1980s and early 1990s during which they qualified for the playoffs seven times and were bounced out in the first round on each occasion.

However, perhaps the most gut-wrenching aspect of Buffalo's playoff history has been its horrific record in Game 7s. The franchise has played seven of them and has won only one.

In 1983 Boston's Brad Park ripped a slapshot from the point past Bob Sauve 1:52 into overtime at Boston Garden after the Sabres had blown a 2–0 second-period lead in the second-round series.

Down 3–1 in the first-round series against the Bruins in 1992, the Sabres battled back with 2–0 and 9–3 victories. But they went back to Boston Garden and dropped a 3–2 decision as Dave Reid scored the game-winning goal on Tom Draper.

After the Sabres won the epic four-overtime sixth game in 1994, they went back to New Jersey, where Dominik Hasek stopped 44 of the 46 shots he faced. The problem was, Martin Brodeur allowed only one goal. The Sabres lost 2–1 and were out in the first round again.

It was 1997 when the Sabres took the only Game 7 they have ever won. Derek Plante blew a slapshot through Ron Tugnutt in overtime at the new Marine Midland Arena to oust Ottawa in the first round.

In 2001 pesky defenseman Darius Kasparaitis scored a soft goal in overtime on a long wrist shot that somehow got past Hasek at the Arena to give Pittsburgh a 3–2 victory.

The Sabres enjoyed a magical season in 2006, the first year after the NHL lockout, reaching the Eastern Conference Finals. But injuries ravaged their defensive corps, and they blew a third-period lead in Carolina and lost 4–2.

In a hard-fought series that Buffalo led 3–2, the Sabres wasted a chance to wrap it up on home ice in their 2011 Game 6, losing in overtime, and then the Flyers rolled to a 5–2 victory in the deciding game as Ryan Miller was pulled for the first time in 47 career playoff appearances.

a bankruptcy, an owner sentenced to prison, and a four-season absence from the playoffs.

The 2000–2001 team earned 98 points during the regular season, then bounced Philadelphia in a stirring six-game first-round playoff series capped off by an 8–0 clinching victory. Buffalo lost the first two games against a talented Pittsburgh team led by "Super Mario" Lemieux, then rallied to win the next three. The team was clinging to a 2–1 lead late in Game 6 when disaster struck. Thanks to a lucky bounce, Lemieux was in the right place at the right time to bang in a loose puck from just outside Hasek's crease with 78 seconds left in regulation to tie the score. Martin Straka staved off elimination for the Penguins by scoring in overtime to force a seventh game back in Buffalo.

In the deciding game, the Sabres took a pair of one-goal leads only to see Pittsburgh answer each time, then watched in shock and disbelief as one of the NHL's all-time pests, defenseman Darius Kasparaitis, beat their all-world goaltender with a seemingly harmless wrist shot from the high slot to bring a sudden and bitter end to Buffalo's season.

If you were to take a vote, as galling as the Kasparaitis goal was, it was the Lemieux goal that left the Sabres feeling sick.

"I'll definitely be remembering that one not for just this summer but a long time," defenseman Rhett Warrener said. "We dug ourselves a hole to start [the series] with, and that was tough enough. We climbed out of it and we were playing very well. We had things under control. It was that one minute, 18 [second] goal that haunts us. They got a bounce, a break."

Captain Stu Barnes agreed, saying, "We feel shorted, there's no question. To start the series down 2–0 and to battle back to the position we were in in the last game with 78 seconds left to go, they tie the game on a lucky bounce. But that's hockey. To finish like we did is disappointing."

When the game ended, the media expected to do what it always did—wait for Hasek to work out his frustrations on the stationary bike. Instead, he was the first player dressed and hustling out the door when he stopped briefly to share his thoughts. When asked if that might have been his last game as a Sabre, he replied, "It's very possible. I mean, right now I'm still thinking about the game. Give me two, three weeks and I'll make the decision."

Soon enough, the decision was made: Hasek was gone. Sadly, after winning six Vezina Trophies (for best goaltender) and two Hart Trophies (for league MVP), the last on-ice memories Sabres fans had of the greatest goaltender in franchise history were the Lemieux goal and the Kasparaitis goal, one as depressing as the other.

The Joker Is Wild

The Sabres have been chasing the elusive Stanley Cup for more than four decades, but the one thing they have never lost during this often-frustrating pursuit is their sense of humor—as evidenced by a series of wonderfully creative practical jokes they have perpetrated through the years.

The most famous occurred during the 1974 NHL Entry Draft, when the team's light-hearted public relations director, Paul Wieland, talked general manager Punch Imlach into "picking" a Japanese player who did not exist: the immortal Taro Tsujimoto.

At that time, each team had to call Commissioner Clarence Campbell and inform him of their selection, and then Campbell would announce the pick. As the story goes, the draft was dragging on as it always did, and Imlach was growing impatient with the process. Director of scouting John Andersen proposed picking a player who wasn't eligible for the draft as a way to irritate the NHL, but then Wieland took it a step further, suggesting that they select a player who didn't even exist. Imlach agreed to go along with the joke, figuring that a 10th-round choice stood almost no chance of making it in the organization anyway.

The men chose Taro as the first name for their fictional player because it was a popular Japanese name. Tsujimoto was the name of a Buffalo-area Asian market. As for Taro's team, they came up with the Tokyo Katanas when they were told *katana* was a loose translation for sabre in Japanese.

Interestingly, co-owners Seymour and Northrup Knox were not informed of the gag, and Wieland played it right to the end. Tjusimoto's name was listed with the other draft picks and was included on the training camp roster. He had a stall set up at the practice rink in St. Catharines, Ontario, and equipment manager Rip Simonick even issued him a full set of equipment.

The final chapter came at the team hotel in St. Catharines when Wieland and coach Floyd Smith, who had been let in on the gag, spied a Japanese man entering the restaurant where Seymour was dining. Wieland and Smith asked the front desk to page Taro Tjusimoto, and when Seymour heard the page and saw the man, he was about to approach him when Wieland and Smith intervened with big smiles on their faces. Knox took it good naturedly—no one was fired.

Running a close second to the Taro incident was one of Wieland's April Fools jokes. He issued a press release informing the league that the team was replacing the ice at the Aud with a revolutionary plastic surface called Sliderex.

Wieland wrote that the Prime Minister of Canada had invented Sliderex, and the lone drawback was that a lit cigarette could burn a hole in it. Wieland did include in the release that it needed to be held until April 1, but at least one media outlet didn't pick up on that hint and went with the story on its 11:00 newscast.

Another classic came in 1976 when the *USS Little Rock* was decommissioned. The Sabres announced that they were purchasing the vessel and were going to use it as their team yacht. CBS spoke with Imlach about the deal, who said the paperwork wasn't final and the Sabres were still considering other ships.

79 Takin' It to the Streets

If you were a hockey-loving kid who grew up in the Buffalo area during the 1970s, there are two wintertime memories you will surely never forget: snow banks piled up on either side of the street you lived on, and those mounds of snow framing the street hockey game you and your friends were playing.

Back then, as hockey was growing in popularity in the western New York region—in large part due to the excitement the Sabres were creating in the community with their rapid ascent in the NHL standings—there were still very few actual ice rinks.

While youth hockey wasn't nearly as popular as it is today, the alternative for kids of all ages (mostly boys but also some girls) was to take to the streets to play the game. Every Christmas, the most popular kid on the block was the one who received one of those red plastic nets for which you fit the posts and crossbar together and then string the net around it.

Invariably that net would tear within about three days, so then you started using hockey tape or string to patch up the holes. But it didn't matter—that was better than using two pails or boots or whatever else you could find in the garage to serve as a goal.

The condition of the street (or the church or school parking lot) dictated which equipment you used. If there was a coating of hard-packed snow and/or ice, you could use an orange plastic puck, or a black rubber puck, because they would slide along the surface pretty well, and you'd use your wooden stick with the blade wrapped in tape.

But if you were down to the asphalt or tar, you went with the orange hockey ball or tennis ball and your older stick that had the wooden shaft but the attachable plastic blade—because the ground would tear the wooden blades to shreds after about a week's time.

On the weekdays, the games started as soon as you got home from school, and if the street lights in your neighborhood were really bright, you could even play after dinner. Imagine that: a world without all those electronic gadgets in which kids were dying to get out of the house to play.

For more than a decade, the Sabres have been re-creating these thrills of street hockey—albeit a version played on the streets around First Niagara Center in the middle of the summer in which T-shirts and shorts replace gloves, hats, and parkas.

In August 2012 the 11th-annual Buffalo Sabres Street Hockey-Fest was held. More than 200 teams made up of kids ranging in age from five to 17 years old participated in the event, with more than 3,000 spectators taking in the action over a two-day weekend. There were only 32 teams on the docket for the inaugural tournament in 2001; the tournament has grown remarkably since its inception and is likely to continue to do so in the years to come.

Each team consists of up to five players. For the $125 entry fee, at least three games are guaranteed and each player gets a hat and a T-shirt, while division winners receive trophies. Just contact the Sabres community relations office to sign yourself and your teammates up.

80 The Ripper

The guy who should really be writing this book is Rip Simonick. After all, he's the only member of the Sabres organization who has been there since day one.

Simonick got his first taste of life around a professional hockey team as a teenager, serving as a stick boy for the Buffalo Bisons in the American Hockey League starting in 1964.

Simonick was in college by the time the Sabres were granted an NHL franchise that would begin play in 1970. But he knew hockey was in his blood, and he wanted to be a part of the Sabres operation any way he could.

So he went down to the Aud one day and asked for a job, and general manager/coach Punch Imlach hired him. Simonick served as an assistant to trainer Frank Christie and was also the team's gofer boy. One of his primary duties in those early years was to fetch coffee at a shop on Main Street—because there was no coffeemaker anywhere in the Aud. For that and other mundane tasks, his starting salary was $100 a week. But to be honest, he didn't even care about the money.

"I was just happy to be working in the NHL and meeting the players who were in the NHL when I was 12 and 13 years old," he said. "Jean Beliveau and Henri Richard were playing for the Canadiens. Stan Mikita with the Blackhawks. They were superstars. That was my payment, not the cash. It was meeting guys I idolized my whole life."

Simonick worked his way up and ultimately became the equipment manager, a position he still holds more than 40 years later, making him the longest-tenured manager in the NHL.

"It's really a dedication to the organization and the sport," said Lindy Ruff—who had been in his own position for 15 years, the longest-tenured coach in the NHL, through the 2011–2012 season. "A lot of times, it's a thankless dedication. His devotion to the team is behind no one. Ripper is on everybody's side, is everybody's backer. He just goes about his business of helping, and that goes for whether you're No. 1 or No. 20."

Ruff began his NHL playing career with the Sabres in 1979, and he told the *Buffalo News* that he still remembers meeting Simonick at the training camp rink in St. Catharines, Ontario, during his rookie year. "Rip was somebody you could talk to as a young player when you were intimidated by the players around you," recalled Ruff. "He was really probably the first guy who made me feel comfortable. It was almost as if you walked in and had a father figure. You had someone who would take care of you, help you out, and tell you a couple stories."

And, oh, the stories he could tell. Simonick has witnessed more than 3,600 Sabres games, flown by his estimation more than two

Frank Christie

For the first 16 years of their existence, the Sabres were bandaged and mended by head trainer Frank Christie, one of the first men Punch Imlach hired when the franchise was born in 1970. But in the 25 years before that, Christie was doing the same thing for the old Buffalo Bisons, earning a reputation as one of the best in the business.

"He has always been an asset to the sport, and his popularity with the players is well known," Imlach said when he announced that Christie would be the Sabres trainer. "It would almost be unthinkable for a club representing Buffalo to take the ice without Frank Christie in attendance."

When Christie was posthumously inducted into the Greater Buffalo Sports Hall of Fame in 2005, former Sabres great Rick Martin accepted the honor on behalf of Christie and his family.

"He was a father to me," said Martin of Christie, who passed away at the age of 63 in 1986 after a battle with cancer. "Anybody that played for Frank could approach him and Frank would help him. You could go anywhere with Frank and people would recognize Frank. Frank might have been small in size, but he was big in heart."

Christie, a New York City native, began his career in hockey in the 1930s as a stick boy for the New York Americans of the NHL. After serving in World War II, Christie came to Buffalo when the Bisons offered him a position as trainer—and he never left.

Christie, who was instrumental in getting the word out to potential Buffalo-area investors that an NHL expansion club could be had, once said his role in the locker room went beyond taking care of the players' physical ailments. "It's a hard life, and a lot of these kids are scared," Christie once remarked. "They've got to have someone they can talk to." That guy was very often Christie.

million miles with the team, and has gathered enough tales to keep the folks at Wikipedia busy for quite a long time.

Fans remember the great Gilbert Perreault for the way he flew up and down the ice, but do they know he drank five cups of coffee and smoked a pack of cigarettes before every game? "It was literally a pack," Rip said. "People don't believe me when I tell them these guys had their own ashtrays on the road with their numbers on them. Gilbert, Jerry Korab, Rene [Robert], Rico [Rick Martin], all of them. Now they have six beers [for the entire team] after a game. Back then, it was more like six cases."

Simonick has seen just about every practical joke imaginable. He saw rookie Danny Gare being hauled away in handcuffs, after which the team went to the police station to inform him that it was all a hoax. He also witnessed Jim Schoenfeld hazing rookies by waiting until they were dressed, then summoning them back near the shower room, where he'd douse them with a bucket of water. Simonick remembers Ruff being tipped off to that prank and putting on Schoenfeld's clothes before walking back. "Schony bombarded his own suit," Rip roared.

Beyond the fun, there has been the joy of victory, the agony of defeat, and everything else in between for Simonick. Now all he lacks is the one thing every other member of the Sabres organization lacks: a championship for his hometown to call its own.

81 The First Game

What a weekend it was for the bars, restaurants, and hotels of the Steel City—and the proprietors had Buffalo sports fans to thank for their spike in business during that special weekend of October 10–11, 1970.

It just so happened that the very first Sabres game was scheduled for a Saturday night at the Pittsburgh Civic Center against the Penguins, and that the Buffalo Bills were going to be in town on the very next day to play the Pittsburgh Steelers at Three Rivers Stadium.

Excited to be a part of this unique experience, thousands of Buffalonians made the three-hour trek to Pittsburgh to see the birth of the Sabres and to watch the Bills play their fourth game in the newly merged National Football League.

Sadly, it wasn't such a great day for the Bills, who lost to the Steelers 23–10. That game snapped a 16-game Pittsburgh losing streak that dated back to early 1969. Rookie quarterback Terry Bradshaw earned his first career NFL victory despite completing only three of 12 passes for 24 yards and being benched for half the game.

But there was plenty to celebrate the night before, as the Sabres pulled out a 2–1 victory when Gilbert Perreault scored the game-winning goal with 8:24 left to play in his first NHL game, delighting the more than 1,500 newly minted Sabres fans who helped Pittsburgh achieve a record hockey crowd of 11,189.

"I told them they would need more than a 100 percent effort, they needed to put out 120 percent, and they did," said coach Punch Imlach. "Some of the rookies made errors, but [Roger] Crozier was always there to pull them out of trouble. What can I say, the boys said it out there on the ice for me."

Said Crozier: "Punch didn't say anything special to us before the game, just how to play this team. But the guys really wanted to win this one."

The first goal in team history was scored by defenseman Jim Watson when he whistled a 50-foot slap shot past Pittsburgh goalie Les Binkley at 5:01 of the second period. A little more than a minute later, Wally Boyer tallied the first goal against the Sabres, beating Crozier with a backhander.

That left it to the 19-year-old Perreault to do what he was brought to Buffalo to do: score. Gerry Meehan missed the net with a high shot, the puck caromed back in front, and Perreault was there to swat it in. And boy did those Buffalo fans make their presence known.

"I remember we played a pretty good game," Meehan said. "I just remember the momentous feeling of being part of a new franchise. It was quite a thrilling experience."

No one was more responsible for the victory than Crozier. As Imlach had said when he acquired Crozier from the Detroit Red Wings: "I want a major league goaltender, a guy with major league credentials who has proved he can do the job up here, and Crozier is the man. For us to win, we must get superior goaltending."

On this night—and on many nights during that inaugural season—that's exactly what Crozier gave the Sabres.

Of course stealing a game from Pittsburgh, a franchise in just its fourth year, was one thing. Doing it against the powerhouses of the league…well, let's just say Meehan was glad that first game was against the Penguins.

"We had played Pittsburgh a few times in the preseason, so we went into that game with sort of an expectation that we could do pretty well," said Meehan. "It wasn't as scary as it might have been had we played the Rangers or the Canadiens."

82 Tom Barrasso

Tom Barrasso grew up dreaming of one thing: winning the Stanley Cup. So when he completed his fabulous high school career in suburban Boston and was asked to try out for the United States'

Olympic team that would be going to Sarajevo in 1984 to defend the gold medal won by the 1980 Miracle on Ice team, he did so with mixed emotions.

Barrasso had a college scholarship to Providence locked up, and he was a cinch to follow in fellow Boston native Jim Craig's footsteps as the goalie of the U.S. team. But college and Olympic hockey had never been his priority. So when Buffalo used the fifth overall pick in the 1983 draft to select Barrasso—the highest choice ever used on a goalie—the wheels started spinning in the teenager's head.

"I came to realize I didn't fit the Olympic mold," he said. "For me, the NHL was my primary goal." After leaving Olympic training camp in late August to attend his sister's wedding, Barrasso decided he wasn't going back. Instead, he came to an agreement with Buffalo and was at Sabres' training camp a few weeks later to begin his NHL career at the ripe old age of 18.

Sadly, Barrasso's career began amidst a barrage of bad press, but he didn't let it get to him. "It really didn't bother me what they wrote," Barrasso said of the negative articles and the hate mail he received from people who felt he had betrayed his country by not playing for the Olympic team. "That's their opinion, they're entitled to that. But for me, I can't say that the Olympic players are any more American than I am. They're playing for the Olympic team because that's what they chose to do. And I'm playing pro hockey because that's what I chose. And isn't that what living in the United States is all about: the right to choose?"

Barrasso was a tremendously talented player, and Scotty Bowman—who had drafted him for the Sabres—fully believed he would be the goalie who would lead the Sabres to the Stanley Cup.

"Tommy came in and he had an air of cockiness about him, and people always faulted him for that, but I always thought that's what made him so good," said Ric Seiling. "His cockiness made him challenge guys, and he was so cocky, so competitive even in practice, he hurt our team's scoring. Guys would lose confidence because they weren't scoring on him in practice because they never had a goaltender try that hard in practice. Every shot was like the Stanley Cup to him."

Barrasso's career started brilliantly: he won the NHL's rookie of the year award, as well as the Vezina Trophy as the league's top goalie in 1983–1984, and then combined with Bob Sauve to help the Sabres lead the league in fewest goals allowed in 1984–1985. But the Sabres were bounced out of the playoffs in the first round by Quebec in both seasons, and when Barrasso gave up three goals in the final nine minutes of the deciding game against the Nordiques in 1985, his efforts were largely forgotten.

After that, the team around Barrasso began to struggle and he couldn't overcome it. In 1985–1986 his goals-against average was almost a goal higher than it had been the year before. It was marginally worse in 1986–1987, when the Sabres finished dead last in the league and gave up a franchise-worst 308 goals. The Sabres missed the postseason during both of those years.

Following a decent 1987–1988, in which Barrasso had a 25–18–8 record and a 3.31 GAA, the Sabres returned to the playoffs. But Barrasso didn't play well, and Boston eliminated the Sabres in six games. Finally, after a slow start in 1988–1989, general manager Gerry Meehan dealt Barrasso to Pittsburgh in a trade that brought back defensemen Doug Bodger and Darin Shannon.

Barrasso went on to play for 12 years in Pittsburgh. And while it didn't happen in Buffalo, Bowman was proved correct when Barrasso won Stanley Cups with the Penguins in 1991 and 1992.

"Tommy was a wonderful kid, but he was very cocky," said Larry Playfair. "With goaltenders you expect some of that, but when they traded Tommy, I thought it was the right move for our team to get him out of here. He had a bit of an arrogant attitude. He had a demeanor that wasn't one that a lot of the vets appreciated."

83 The Other Guy

It wasn't Ric Seiling's fault that Sabres general manager Punch Imlach came to the conclusion that Buffalo had more than enough goal scorers and really didn't have a need for a right winger named Mike Bossy prior to the 1977 NHL Entry Draft—even though the kid from Quebec had scored 309 goals in four junior seasons.

But for much of his underappreciated nine-year career in Buffalo, Seiling bore the brunt of the fans' displeasure over Imlach's decision to use the 14th pick of the first round on him when it became clear that Bossy—who was chosen with the very next pick by the New York Islanders—was going to become one of the greatest goal-scorers in NHL history and a shoo-in for the Hall of Fame.

"We could have had him when our first pick came up," Imlach once explained. "We thought about it hard. But the main point with us was that we weren't all that hungry for scoring and that Ric Seiling, whom we took instead, fitted better what we needed. The last bloody thing we needed was another guy who could score goals."

The Sabres were one of the highest-scoring teams in the league at that time, led by wondrous offensive players such as the members of the French Connection—Gilbert Perreault, Rick Martin, and Rene Robert—as well as Danny Gare, Andre Savard, Don Luce, Craig Ramsay, and Jim Lorentz. But they weren't very good at preventing goals, and outside of solid two-way forwards such as Ramsay, Luce, and Lorentz, they were a bit lackadaisical when it came to back-checking.

"What we needed was to make the team more defensive-minded," Imlach went on. "That's why I chose Ric Sciling over Bossy. Seiling had checking ability and a willingness to mix it up."

Seiling was no slouch in the offensive end, either, as he'd scored 118 goals in junior, including 50 with the St. Catharines Fincups in 1976–1977, the year he was selected by Imlach. And as natural a goal scorer as he was, Bossy was considered a soft player; Imlach didn't think he would be able to play that way in the rugged NHL and still score all those goals. Seiling, meanwhile, would score goals and provide some much-needed grit.

Well, Punch got it wrong with Bossy. By the time their careers were finished, Seiling had 179 goals and Bossy had 573, not to mention four Stanley Cups.

What was really strange about the treatment Seiling received in Buffalo is that 12 other teams passed on Bossy, including the New York Rangers and the Toronto Maple Leafs, twice each. Of course down in Manhattan, Rangers fans could have cared less about Seiling; they were too busy spending years lamenting the decision of the Broadway blue shirts—who hadn't won a Cup since 1940—to select Lucien DeBlois (eighth overall) and Ron Duguay (13th) instead of Bossy.

"I'm considered one of the biggest busts because they could have had Mike Bossy," said Seiling. "But let me ask you this: who was he going to play with here? You weren't breaking up the French Connection, you weren't breaking up Luce/Ramsay/Gare, so where was he going to play? Punch knew why they had been losing games, and he knew I could play both ends of the rink. I was a 50-goal scorer in junior, and we won the Canadian championship, so I had proven I could win. That's why he drafted me."

84 Michael Peca's Holdout

In March 2002, when Michael Peca played his first game at Buffalo's HSBC Arena since his trade from the Sabres to the New York Islanders the previous summer, he knew what to expect: booing. Lots of booing. And that's what he got.

"I'd been hoping that people would reflect on the things I did for this organization and this community rather than how they viewed a contract negotiation," Peca said. "But that's the way it goes."

Peca was jeered roundly every time he touched the puck that night; the only cheer he drew was when he lost an edge and tumbled clumsily to the ice. Oh well, so much for that "C" he wore on his Sabres sweater, and for the Selke Trophy he won in 1997 for being the NHL's best defensive forward, and for the leadership he provided during Buffalo's run to the Stanley Cup Finals in 1999.

Peca's Buffalo career was a short one: five years on the ice and one in limbo during which he and team management couldn't come to a contract agreement, prompting him to sit out the entire 2000–2001 season. During those five years he established a true connection with Buffalo fans, who appreciated his blue-collar work ethic. But it all went out the window during his bitter contract squabble, during which he asked for what many fans thought was too much money and then refused to back down when the Sabres wouldn't meet his demands.

Peca had made it clear during the 1999–2000 season that he was looking for a big pay raise; when the year ended, he and his agent, Don Meehan, asked for $4 million per season. The Sabres countered with $2.5 million and refused to budge, a stance that angered a faction of fans who didn't understand why they were low-balling the team captain. Peca came down to $3.5 million, but general manager Darcy Regier stayed firm, leaving Peca to sit idle all year.

As the 2001 NHL Draft approached, Regier realized Peca wasn't going to play for the Sabres anymore, so he worked feverishly to make a trade. He found a willing partner in the New York Islanders, who exchanged Tim Connolly and Taylor Pyatt for Peca.

"I can't have any bad feelings toward the fans because they're part of the reason I enjoyed playing there so much," said Peca on the day of the trade. "I think all in all it's a shame that it went this far. I think this is a deal that could've been accomplished a long time ago, but for whatever reason it didn't. I'm just happy now that I can move on, and my family can look forward to moving on, as well."

During his time in Buffalo, Peca played 363 games and had 96 goals and 121 assists for 217 points. He became a fan favorite because he was an undersized player who played with grit and edge. Still, once you change teams, you're just another guy to dislike, and Peca found that out every time he played in Buffalo after his departure.

85 Gretzky's Big Night

On the night that her eldest son, Wayne, stood on the brink of National Hockey League history, Phyllis Gretzky was in Quebec, watching her youngest son, Brent, competing in a pee wee hockey tournament.

Wayne and his Edmonton Oilers were playing in Buffalo, barely a two-hour drive from the Gretzky home in Brantford, Ontario, and Wayne was one goal away from breaking Phil Esposito's record for goals in a season—one of the NHL's most sacred accomplishments.

But what's a mother to do when two of her boys are playing games on the same night? Well, Phyllis surmised that she couldn't let 10-year-old Brent down, so Wayne's father, Walter, made the trip to Buffalo on February 24, 1982, while Phyllis trekked north to Quebec to watch Brent.

Phyllis looked on with glee as Brent helped his team to a victory. But she missed seeing Wayne score the record-breaking goal with 6:36 left to play, then tack on two more exclamation point goals to put away a 6–3 Edmonton victory over the Sabres that, despite the final score, stands as one of the most exciting nights the Aud ever hosted.

"Nobody could believe it, but that's the way it was in my family," Wayne recalled. "One of our parents tried to be at every game. My mom always tells people, 'Wayne isn't the only hockey player in this family.'"

Maybe not, but he sure was the best; in fact, some would argue that he was the best hockey player in *anyone's* family, ever.

When asked to rate Gretzky on a scale of one to 10, Bobby Orr (who is also on the list when it comes to discussing the greatest player of all, along with Gordie Howe and Mario Lemieux), replied, "He's about a 60."

During the 1981–1982 season, Gretzky put on an unprecedented scoring display, scoring 92 goals and assisting on 120 others for a total of 212 points in 80 games, all single-season NHL records at the time (he later broke his own assists and points marks). As Oilers assistant coach Billy Harris said: "That's like hitting 80 home runs in one season or rushing for 3,000 yards in one year."

On the momentous night Edmonton arrived in Buffalo, the Sabres decided to honor their captain and greatest player, center Gilbert Perreault, who had become Buffalo's all-time leading goal scorer a week earlier. There was already an overload of electricity coursing through the creaky walls of the arena in anticipation of Gretzky possibly breaking Esposito's record. The added emotion of the tribute to Perreault had the sellout crowd—which included Esposito, as well as movie stars Burt Reynolds and Goldie Hawn, who were in Buffalo shooting scenes for the film *Best Friends*—whipped into a frothing frenzy.

Perreault, usually an emotionless player, was duly stoked for this showdown, and he put on a show by scoring three goals, the last coming early in the third period and tying the game at 3–3. Meanwhile, Sabres goalie Don Edwards was having a great night, making a few stupefying saves on Gretzky. It was starting to look like Esposito would be following Gretzky on to Edmonton's next stop in order to be present for the eclipse.

"I had no goals but two assists and I kept looking up at Esposito," Gretzky recalled. "I could see the look on his face: 'C'mon, Wayne, I didn't pack enough clothes for this trip.' But it wasn't my fault, it was Don Edwards' fault. He started pretending he was Grant Fuhr or Ken Dryden."

And then it happened: Sabres winger Steve Patrick gloved a pass and fumbled the puck as he tried to drop it to the ice. Gretzky swooped in, took it away from him, and skated in on Edwards. With Buffalo's Richie Dunn hooking him from behind, Gretzky managed to get a low shot away and the puck skipped past Edwards' right pad and into the far side of the net.

"I didn't want him to score when I was on the ice," Patrick said. "It's history now, but I felt bad when it happened. I don't know how he got it. I didn't know if the ref was going to blow the whistle or what, I was just holding it there [against his stomach]. When I dropped it, he just sort of batted it out of the air. I didn't even see where he came from."

Gretzky wasn't through. After the Sabres put heavy pressure on the Oilers trying to get the equalizer, Gretzky put it away with another goal, then capped the night with 17 seconds remaining to match Perreault's hat trick, giving him a goal on each of his last three shifts.

86 The Voices of the Sabres

From high above the ice at First Niagara Center, Rick Jeanneret bellows into his microphone night after night, describing Sabres action like no one else ever has or ever will, just as he has done for 40 years as the team's play-by-play announcer.

Jeanneret's perch is named the Ted Darling Memorial Press Box. There's a certain apropos symmetry to that, as Darling was the other half of what has to be one of the greatest one-two combinations in broadcasting history.

When the Sabres came into existence in 1970, Darling was given the job of broadcasting the games on the Sabres radio network, WGR. He had been working in radio for years in Canada, and had most recently been the intermission host for *Hockey Night in Canada*, but play-by-play was his true passion. He put together an audition tape of a fake Sabres game against the Montreal Canadiens to give to Punch Imlach, and Imlach hired him on the spot.

Darling worked the Sabres broadcasts, first on radio and then later on television, until he was forced to retire during the 1991–1992 season because he was suffering from an illness called Pick's Disease, a degenerative condition similar to Alzheimer's. A member of the Sabres Hall of Fame who was also enshrined in the Hockey Hall of Fame in 1994 as the recipient of the Foster Hewitt Memorial Award, Darling died in 1996 at the age of 61, just a few months after the Sabres moved into what is now called the First Niagara Center. The organization promptly named their new press box after him.

"He was so visible, both on the air and in the community, that next to Gil Perreault, he was arguably the most recognizable figure representing Buffalo Sabres hockey," Paul Wieland, the team's former director of communications, told the *Buffalo News* in 1994. "He was a hard worker, had great pipes, and had a wonderful sense of humor."

Jeanneret is also blessed with great pipes, albeit of a different sort from Darling's. While Darling had an elegant, toned-down cadence while calling a game, Jeanneret has a booming voice and an exciting and energetic style that has made him a legend in hockey broadcasting. His good friends call him Rodney because he bears a resemblance to the late comedian Rodney Dangerfield. But while Dangerfield's shtick was that he never got any respect, Jeanneret has plenty of that as the longest-tenured broadcaster in the NHL.

A Toronto neighbor of Jeanneret's worked at a radio station, and that's what first piqued his interest in the profession. He went to the MidWestern Broadcasting School in Chicago for a 13-week course, then came home and landed work at several radio stations, eventually becoming a disc jockey in Niagara Falls, Ontario, in 1963.

When the play-by-play announcer for the junior hockey team in Niagara Falls was felled by illness, Jeanneret filled in, and away he went. He joined the Sabres organization in 1971 for their second season, sharing broadcasting duties with Darling. For radio-only games the two worked together, while televised games had Darling doing the telecasts and Jeanneret on the radio.

Darling certainly had his share of great calls in his day, but Jeanneret's are the ones that no one will ever forget. His "May Day, May Day" call after Brad May's series-winning goal against Boston in 1993 has become a Sabres anthem, and his "LaLaLaLaLaLaLa-Fontaine" whenever Pat LaFontaine scored could almost qualify for release as a single on iTunes.

To the newest generation of fans, Jeanneret is the voice of the Sabres. But the man himself disagrees, saying, "I think that title should always belong to Ted. In my mind, he always will be the voice of the Sabres. He was taken away from us far too soon as far as I'm concerned, and he deserved that adulation. I'm perfectly comfortable with being called the Sabres announcer. I'm good with that."

Jeanneret paid homage to Darling on the night in 2011 when he joined his dear late friend in the Sabres Hall of Fame, closing his remarks by telling the fans, "No. 1, this is the only job I've ever wanted, and No. 2, this is the only place I ever wanted to be. From my lips to your ears, thanks for listening."

87 Shackie

His Sabres career consisted of 106 games, and he never played a full season in Buffalo, joining the club a third of the way through the inaugural 1970–1971 season and leaving it three-fourths of the way through 1971–1972.

While his number will never be retired and he will never be enshrined in the Sabres Hall of Fame, Eddie Shack proved to be one of the most important players to ever wear the Sabres crest—and it had nothing to do with goals, assists, and penalty minutes.

"Shackie gave the team color," Punch Imlach wrote in his book *Heaven and Hell in the NHL.* "He put the show on the road and the people in the seats. That first year, Roger Crozier, Gilbert Perreault, Reggie Fleming, and Eddie Shack made our team exciting."

Shack, who left school after the third grade and never learned to read or write, was 15 years old and working in both a coal mine and a meat market as a butcher when he tried out for the Guelph Biltmores of the Ontario Hockey Association. He made the team, and for the next 25 years—17 of which he spent in the NHL—he made his living in ice arenas as a pretty decent player and a brilliant showman.

They called him Eddie the Entertainer—not because of the 1,047 games and 239 goals he scored in the NHL for the Rangers, the Maple Leafs, the Bruins, the Kings, the Sabres, and the Penguins, or the four Cups he helped Imlach and the Leafs win—but because of the way he entertained the crowds. "Shackie can play all three forward positions, but his problem is he tries to do it all at the same time," Imlach said.

"He reveled in doing things that were different, and he found ways to get attention," said Mike Robitaille, who played against Shack, as well as with him briefly when their paths crossed in Buffalo. "He was always the loudest guy in the locker room, and he was always relaxed. I'd be all tied up as tight as could be, and he'd be laughing and having a great time, and I was wishing I could be like that."

Shack once said, "I only played half the season and entertained the other half." But when he wasn't being a comedian, he could actually play. He enjoyed five 20-goal seasons, including 25 goals in only 56 games during his first year with Buffalo.

"If he was dead serious and they gave him the ice time and he didn't want to clown around so much and put a show on, he was an automatic 20-goal scorer," said Robitaille. "He was big and he could be intimidating and he took on a lot of comers because everybody wanted a piece of him. But he stood the test of time."

While languishing on the bench and contributing nothing on the ice, Shack would stand up and start waving his arms to get the crowd into the game—and they always responded. He'd hear chants in Maple Leaf Gardens of "We Want Shack." The fans roared with delight when he did his little pirouette celebration after a goal or performed his mad dashes onto the ice if he was named one of the game's three stars.

One time in the Aud, Minnesota goalie Gump Worsley was injured and needed a stretcher to take him off the ice. As the medics rolled it out, Shack lightened the mood in the place by hopping on and pretending to row a canoe.

Shack came to Buffalo in November 1970 along with another old Imlach crony from Toronto, Dick Duff. They were playing for Los Angeles at the time, and Punch obtained them from the Kings in exchange for Mike McMahon.

The story goes that Shack and Duff were at the airport bar in Los Angeles because their flight had been cancelled, which gave them time to debate the pros and cons of joining the expansion Sabres. Shack finally stood up and said, "Well, Duffy, will we go and pull that asshole Imlach out of another hole?"

Shack, though unwittingly, played an even bigger role in the building of the team in March 1972, as it was Shack whom Imlach traded to Pittsburgh for Rene Robert.

It was not a popular move at first, as the fans hated to see Eddie the Entertainer leave. But the story had a happy ending: this guy Robert, who no one had ever heard of, who had scored only seven NHL goals to date, became the final third of the famed French Connection line, joining Perreault and Rick Martin.

88 Les Nordiques

The Sabres have never really maintained a consistent rivalry with any one team. At various points it was the Bruins who were their chief antagonists, and the Flyers have certainly played that role (especially since it was Philadelphia that defeated Buffalo in 1975 in their first trip to the Stanley Cup Finals). Toronto has long been a rival based primarily on geography, and of course Ottawa was the most hated team for a few years.

One team that sometimes gets left out of the discussion—mainly because it no longer exists—is the Quebec Nordiques. But long-time fans probably haven't forgotten the frustration coach Michel

Bergeron and his trio of Stastny brothers created for Buffalo during the mid-1980s.

In 1983–1984 and 1984–1985 the Sabres and the Nordiques were co-inhabitants of the old Adams Division, and there was no team Sabres fans hated more after Quebec eliminated Buffalo during the first round of the playoffs in both of those seasons.

"I don't think you appreciate it as much until you're done playing and you look back on it, but you wish we could have done a bit better," said John Tucker. "But at the time they were such quick series, best-of-five, and we always seemed to go up against a team that had our number—Quebec those first couple years, then Boston."

In 1983–1984 Buffalo piled up 103 points—fourth-most in the league but only second-best in the Adams, as Boston won the division with 104 points. Still, Quebec placed third, nine points behind Buffalo, so the Sabres had home-ice advantage for the first-round series. But the Nordiques had dominated the regular season against the Sabres, going 6–1–1 and outscoring Buffalo 35–18. In the first-round series, they swept Buffalo out in three straight by scores of 3–2, 6–2, and 4–1.

"We didn't do very much, but we didn't do very well against them in the season either, so it wasn't as if it was a surprise," said coach Scotty Bowman. "We've got young guys, and when you get young guys, you've got to build up their confidence."

That following year, Buffalo managed to go 3–4–1 against Quebec, but on the final night of the season, with a first-round rematch already set, the Sabres had a chance to earn home-ice advantage. They trailed the Nordiques by a point, but lost 5–4 at the Aud to Montreal, which gave Quebec the privilege of hosting the first two games.

Predictably, that did not go well. The Nordiques won the first two at Le Colisée and came to Buffalo looking to wrap up another three-game sweep. The Sabres finally showed some life, erupting for a combined 13 goals to win both games in Buffalo. Back in

Quebec for the deciding game, they opened a 5–3 lead 1:27 into the third period on a goal by Phil Housley. But just when it seemed as if the Sabres were going to rid themselves of the curse of Quebec, the Nordiques scored three times in the final nine minutes, the last coming off the stick of Brent Ashton with just 69 seconds remaining, sending the Sabres to a crushing defeat in what proved to be their last playoff game until 1988.

Tucker chalked it up to Quebec having more savvy veterans.

"They had some older guys and we had a lot of young guys," said Tucker. "They had the Stastnys, [Michel] Goulet, and we had [Dave] Andreychuk, myself, [Mike] Foligno, Lindy [Ruff], Housley—all young guys. The experience factor was a big difference in those series."

89 Support the Sabres Foundation

The Buffalo Sabres Foundation is the primary arm of the Sabres' charitable work. Since it was reinvigorated in 2004, when the team was owned by Tom Golisano, more than $250,000 has been raised for the foundation's beneficiaries through a variety of activities.

The foundation has focused its philanthropy in three main areas: youth hockey, children's health and wellness initiatives (specifically those that serve the underprivileged and handicapped), and nonprofit organizations that provide vital services to those in need in the western New York community.

The foundation donated $100,000 to Buffalo's Women's and Children's Hospital in 2005. In 2006 a $30,000 grant was awarded to Hasek's Heroes and a $15,000 grant went to Skating Athletes Bold at Heart. Other grant recipients have included Kelly for Kids,

Sisters of Mercy Hospital, the Kaleida Health Foundation, the Make a Wish Foundation, the Amherst Community Foundation, Tender Wishes, Big Brothers/Big Sisters of Niagara, the Buffalo Zoo, the Hunters Hope Foundation, Ronald McDonald House, the Buffalo Public School Foundation, the Teammates for Kids Foundation, the Lawrence D. Jacobs Foundation, and The United Way.

Sabres fans have a chance to participate in a number of events throughout the year that fund the foundation's gifts.

The Corporate Hockey Challenge is an annual 16-team, three-on-three tournament held at First Niagara Center. Men and women representing area businesses get some help for their teams from Sabres alumni. The list of those who have played runs the gamut from Hall of Famer Gilbert Perreault to pugilist Andrew Peters. Every team member and a guest are invited to a Sabres game prior to the Challenge, and a live "Alumni Draft" is conducted to match up teams with former Sabres. The tournament features a full day of play followed by a happy hour and dinner in the evening.

The Aces and Blades Gala is a popular casino gaming night held in the Harbor Club at the arena. Sabres past and present serve as dealers and hosts for games such as poker, blackjack, and roulette. They also put together gift baskets that are bid on during a Chinese auction, and sports memorabilia is also auctioned off.

The Sabres Golf Tournament, held at the prestigious Park Country Club in the Buffalo suburb of Williamsville, gives fans an opportunity to play 18 holes with players and alumni. Numerous sponsorship opportunities are available, and the day includes lunch, dinner, and a post-round open bar. Similar to the golf tournament is the Bowl-a-Rama, which pairs fans with alumni for an evening of bowling, auctions, prizes, live entertainment, and food and beverages, including an open bar.

Those who wish to inquire about any of the foundation's events can call the Sabres or visit sabres.com for more information.

90 Scoring Frenzy

The box score looked like something straight out of the National Lacrosse League: 14 goals in one game, nine in one period. But Buffalo's professional indoor lacrosse team, the Bandits, wasn't born until 1992, a full 11 years after this game was played.

"It seemed like the puck went in every time we got into their zone," said Buffalo right wing Danny Gare, who had two goals and an assist during the Sabres' head-shaking 14–4 cremation of the Toronto Maple Leafs on March 19, 1981.

The Sabres tied their own team mark for goals in a game that night at the Aud—a record set in 1975 against Washington—and established an NHL record for most goals in a period, a mark that remains unbroken more than 30 years later. The 12 combined goals in that period by the Sabres and Leafs, and the 23 individual points Buffalo players totaled in the period, also remain tied for the most in NHL history.

Hard to believe? You betcha, especially when you look at the NHL today, in which goaltenders have become so proficient and coaches have devised devious defensive schemes like the neutral zone trap to limit scoring chances.

But the NHL was playing a different game back in 1981, and the Sabres were one of the league's most prolific offensive machines. That season they scored 327 goals, fourth-most in team history, but only the seventh-best total in the NHL that year behind the Islanders, St. Louis, Los Angeles, Montreal, Calgary, and Edmonton.

Such was life back in the days when an offensive player could actually skate, stickhandle, and shoot without one defender clutching at his body, another grabbing his stick, and still another standing in front of the net waiting to block shots while wearing space-age protective gear.

Incredibly, this game began in a mundane fashion as Buffalo's John Van Boxmeer scored the lone goal and the teams combined for only 14 shots in the opening period. But when the second period began, it seemed as if it would never end for the Leafs. Gilbert Perreault started the fireworks by neatly stealing the puck from Wilf Paiement, zipping past Borje Salming, and deking goalie Bunny Larocque to the ice before beating him with a backhander. Then the goals started flowing like Niagara Falls. Four minutes later Derek Smith scored off a nice feed from the corner by Tony McKegney, and over the next three minutes Ric Seiling and Perreault made it 5–0, those three goals coming on successive shots. Toronto answered with two scores on goalie Don Edwards within 31 seconds. After Craig Ramsay scored at 13:24, Leaf captain Darryl Sittler answered with his second of the game 42 seconds later to make it 6–3 Buffalo. Toronto was still fighting, but when Andre Savard banged one past Larocque off a feed from McKegney at 15:50, the Leafs folded like laundry. Before the period ended, Perreault completed his hat trick and Gare and Savard scored to make it 10–3, Savard's goal enabling Buffalo to break the single-period mark of eight shared by five other teams.

"I really thought Bunny played well that night, considering the score," said Edwards. "He didn't have any help that night. The Leafs defensive system seemed to collapse in front of him. He faced a lot of shots both on and off the net, plus he stopped four or five breakaways."

Larocque was playing just his fourth game for Toronto after having come over in a trade from Montreal, and this was his first loss. He stayed on the bench when the third period began, and with backup goalie Jiri Crba in net, the Sabres did not back off. They fired 22 shots at Crba, with Smith, Gare, Gilles Hamel, and Savard [completing his hat trick and a career-best six-point performance] all scoring.

"It was a great, beautiful night," said Savard.

Thirteen Sabres registered points in the game. In the Buffalo locker room, resident goon Larry Playfair—who pulled off the rarity of having more points in a game (three) than he did penalty minutes (two)—deadpanned, "I don't think they particularly liked it."

91 The First One Against the Great One

Daren Puppa couldn't have scripted a more daunting challenge for his NHL debut with the Sabres. He also couldn't have scripted a more remarkable result.

Called up from the minor league Rochester Americans to fill in for injured backup Jacques Cloutier, Puppa took to the ice for the first time at Northlands Coliseum in Edmonton on November 1, 1985. Yes, Edmonton—home of Wayne Gretzky, Mark Messier, Jari Kurri, Paul Coffey, and the rest of the two-time defending Stanley Cup champion Oilers.

Seven months earlier Puppa had been backstopping Rensselaer Polytechnic Institute to the NCAA Division I national championship with 21 saves in a 2–1 victory over Providence at Detroit's Joe Louis Arena. Now here he was being tapped by Sabres coach Jim Schoenfeld to start against the dynastic Oilers because starter Tom Barrasso was due for a rest. It seemed like a recipe for disaster, but instead Puppa stopped 37 shots to post a stunning 2–0 shutout victory, Edmonton's first shutout loss since February 1984 and its first at home since March 1981.

"This is extra special," Puppa said that night to reporters as his teammates chanted his name in the locker room. "I knew three days ago I was going to play the Oilers. I knew I couldn't be in awe of them or I'd be in trouble. I just wanted to go out and play my best."

Lindy Ruff scored the game's first goal after only 61 seconds of play. The Oilers spent the rest of the evening trying to get the equalizer, but never did. Finally, Gilles Hamel relieved some of the pressure for Puppa when he scored in the final minute.

Edmonton managed only 18 shots in the first two periods and really didn't test Puppa too often outside of one breakaway by Gretzky. But that changed in the final 20 minutes, when the Oilers began buzzing on offense like only they could. They peppered Puppa with 19 shots, and the 20-year-old stopped Gretzky twice more on breakaways.

"There's not really anything you do differently against a guy you've never faced before," explained Coffey, "except you worry a bit. You know that he's either going to be red hot or he's going to be terrible. There's never any in-between with guys making their first start."

Obviously, Puppa was the former on that unforgettable night.

Floyd Smith

Floyd Smith knew that his days as an NHL player were just about over, but he had no idea that they were going to end with the suddenness that they did.

On the morning of January 7, 1972, Smith came to the Aud fully expecting to practice with the rest of his teammates, just as he had for the first season and a half that he was with the expansion Buffalo team.

Among his NHL stops throughout the 1960s was a brief stint with Toronto while Punch Imlach was the Leafs' coach, and Imlach signed the wily veteran to serve as the captain of the inaugural Sabres team in 1970. Smith and Imlach shared a similar philosophy about the game, and Punch trusted him so thoroughly that he often had Smith run the daily practices if there were general manager duties he needed to tend to.

Smith and Imlach were in Punch's office that morning, discussing the previous night's 5–2 loss at home to the Boston Bruins. Imlach asked the 36-year-old about his future plans and whether he was interested in going into coaching. Smith said he had thought about it, and that he'd give it further consideration once the season was over.

But Smith wasn't to be afforded that luxury. Later that same day, Imlach suffered a heart attack that effectively ended his career as a coach. Two nights later, Smith traded in his uniform for a suit and tie to make his coaching debut in a 2–1 loss to the Maple Leafs.

Joe Crozier, a close confidant of Imlach's for years who had been coaching Buffalo's minor league team in Cincinnati, was summoned a day later to coach the Sabres for the rest of the year and, as it turned out, through two more seasons. Smith was sent to Cincinnati to take over the Swords.

When Imlach and Crozier had a falling out during 1973–1974—a disappointing season in which Buffalo failed to make the playoffs after doing so the year before—Imlach fired Crozier and promoted Smith to the head job for 1974–1975.

As a rookie coach, Smith had led the Swords to the AHL's Calder Cup championship in 1972–1973 and then a playoff berth the following year. Imlach felt that not only was Smith ready for the NHL, he also had a great feel for the players on the team, some of whom he'd played with a few years earlier or had coached in Cincinnati.

Sure enough, in his first year at the NHL level, Smith took the Sabres to the Stanley Cup Finals, where they lost to a better, stronger, more experienced Philadelphia team.

"It was a wonderful time for all of us, especially just five years into the club's life the team is in the Stanley Cup Finals," Smith recalled. "The city was so excited. We had a free-spirited, high-scoring team. A lot of young guys who were strong-willed, proud of their skills, and after we started the season with eight or nine wins, we just kept going strong through to the final. It's too bad we didn't win because, as it turned out, that team never got another chance at it."

Indeed, the Sabres endured two decent but ultimately disappointing seasons thereafter, finishing second in the Adams Division but suffering elimination in the second round of the playoffs at the hands of the New York Islanders. Following the second elimination, which came in four straight games, Imlach fired Smith.

Thinking back to what it was like working for the taskmaster Imlach, Smith said, "It was exciting and a little scary at the same time, to be honest, especially with the gentleman there who was my boss. To say he didn't second-guess me more than a few times would be a lie."

Outside of one season with the Leafs (1980–1981) as an assistant coach, Smith was never behind a bench again, choosing to go into scouting instead. He has the distinction of coaching the Sabres to the playoffs every year he was there (even though it was only three).

93 Wear the Colors Proudly

As is the case with the majority of professional small-market sports franchises—and even some greedy big-market teams—the Sabres have had to figure out creative ways to create revenue streams. One of the obvious ones in the 21st century has been to change the look of their uniform to inspire fans to buy the latest gear.

For 26 years, the Sabres stayed true to their roots, wearing the same blue, white, and gold outfits with the recognizable logo featuring a charging Buffalo and two crossed swords (described in a press release by the team's first public relations director, Chuck Burr, as "a clean, sharp, decisive, and penetrating weapon on offense, as well as a strong parrying weapon on defense").

There were subtle alterations made to the uniform through those first 26 seasons, most notably player names being added to the backs of the sweaters in 1978–1979, but the other changes were typically just patches that commemorated the team's 10th, 20th, and 25th anniversaries, the 75th season of the NHL, and a special patch that honored the 1980 U.S. Olympic team.

When the Sabres moved from the Aud into their new home a block away, it signaled a new era for the franchise, and the organization decided to completely overhaul its on-ice look for the occasion.

The Sabres switched to black, red, silver, and white, and a new logo was created that featured a Buffalo head. Fans were initially upset because the Sabres changed everything. Most felt they should have changed the logo and kept the traditional colors, or kept the logo and changed the colors, but not both at the same time. The wholesale switch took some getting used to, but that didn't stop fans from buying the new jerseys.

In 2000 the team recognized a longing for the past and unveiled a third jersey that paid tribute to the original sweater crest while incorporating colors and elements from the newer design. The old circle and crossed sabres logo was imprinted on a red jersey trimmed in the team's black and silver scheme.

In 2006, several years after the transition in ownership from the Rigas family to Tom Golisano, the Sabres felt it was time to wipe away any remnants from the soiled Rigas era and make a return to blue, white, and gold as the team's primary colors. A new logo, which became known as the banana slug, was also devised.

Although the Sabres advanced to the Eastern Conference Finals during the first two years they wore the slug, it ended up having a pretty short shelf life. The Sabres came full circle, going back to their original logo and colors in 2009. They also created a rich blue jersey that is a nod to the old American Hockey League Buffalo Bisons.

The Sabres haven't had the same luxury as the original six teams, who have done very little to their uniforms—if anything at all— over the years. The variety of Sabres gear creates a rather odd scene in the arena these days, as fans sport the many variations on the team uniform and colors. But in the end, it probably doesn't matter what jersey the fans are wearing, as long as their allegiance is with the team. As Jerry Seinfeld once said, all we're really doing is rooting for laundry.

An Imperfect 10, Plus One

The Sabres ascension to elite status in the NHL was remarkably quick, as they joined the NHL in 1970, were in the playoffs by their third year, and played for the Stanley Cup in just their fifth season.

After losing in the 1975 Finals, they were a consistent Cup threat through the end of the 1970s and into the early 1980s. But they never did get back to the Finals until 1999, and one of the main reasons for that was the New York Islanders.

Like the Sabres, the Islanders joined the NHL as an expansion franchise (in 1972–1973), and endured two woeful seasons before shocking hockey observers by reaching the playoffs in their third season. Unlike the Sabres, the Islanders weren't playing for the Cup in their fifth year. But also unlike the Sabres, once that first opportunity arose in their seventh year (1979–1980), New York did not fail. In fact, not only did the Islanders win the championship that season, they also won in the three years that followed.

During this period, when the Islanders were establishing the foundation of a dynasty, the Sabres served as their foil in three play-off series. In fact, at one point New York won 11 consecutive post-season games against Buffalo.

The mastery began in 1976, a year when the Sabres compiled 105 points to finish second in the Adams Division while the Islanders had 101 points to place second in the Patrick Division. Buffalo survived a best-of-three scare from St. Louis, winning Games 2 and 3 in overtime to advance, while the Isles easily swept out Vancouver in two to set up a date with Buffalo. The Sabres were the more experienced team, and it showed early as they won the first two games at the Aud, the second in overtime on a goal by Danny Gare. But things took a drastic turn on Long Island when the Islanders won 5–3 and 4–2, and when they made it three in a row with a 4–3 win in Buffalo, the series was essentially over. They capped it with a 3–2 home victory in Game 6.

The teams met in the quarters the next year, as well, and this time it was no contest. Clark Gillies scored the winning goal in the first three games as the Islanders took a pair of 4–2 decisions on home ice, then earned 4–3 victories in the last two games at the Aud.

When the rivalry was renewed in 1980, the Sabres were the clear favorite. They had won the Adams Division and their 110 points were second only to Philadelphia's 116, while the Islanders had managed only 91 points—all of which ended up meaning nothing.

New York stretched its winning streak to nine games with an easy 4–1 triumph in Buffalo, and a few nights later it reached 10 with a 2–1 double overtime victory in a game that really killed the Sabres. They lost ironman Craig Ramsay, who had played 561 consecutive regular season games, to a broken wrist, and then Rick Dudley went down to a pinched nerve. Missing two key cogs, the Sabres battled hard and had chances to win in overtime. Instead, early in the second extra period, they failed to clear their zone three times. Ultimately, goalie Bob Sauve kicked out a shot by Bob Lorimer, and the rebound went right to the opportunistic Bob Nystrom.

"Think of how they must feel," said New York's star defenseman, Denis Potvin. "They played as well as they could have played and lost in overtime."

The Islanders made it 11 straight with a 7–4 romp in Game 3 before the misery finally ended with Buffalo pulling out a matching 7–4 victory. Energized by that win, the Sabres then played well in a 2–0 victory at home to extend the series. But New York put it away with a 5–2 blowout in Game 6, and went on to beat the heavily favored Flyers in six to win their first Cup.

Danny's Debut

When coach Floyd Smith sent Danny Gare onto the Aud ice with Don Luce and Craig Ramsay to start the 1974–1975 season opener against the Boston Bruins, the diminutive but spunky rookie wasn't quite sure he was ready to play with the big boys.

Eighteen seconds later, when Gare beat Gilles Gilbert to start the Sabres on their way to an eye-opening 9–5 victory, he had his answer.

"That was very exciting for me," said Gare, recalling his memorable NHL debut, which also included an assist. "I guess when it happened, it was kind of like maybe you belonged in the National Hockey League. That sort of took the pressure off me. The Bruins had played the Flyers in the Stanley Cup Finals the previous spring, and here I was facing off against [Phil] Esposito, [Ken] Hodge, [Wayne] Cashman, [Bobby] Orr, and [Carol] Vadnais. The puck went around the boards, Schony [Jim Schoenfeld] took a shot, and I got the rebound."

Former Buffalo Sabres captain Danny Gare shares a laugh with the media during a press conference to announce his and Pat LaFontaine's (behind) jerseys being retired at the HSBC Arena in Buffalo, on October 17, 2005.

Punch Imlach selected Gare in the second round of the 1974 draft after he produced a phenomenal 68-goal season in his last year in junior with the Calgary Centennials. It may have taken a bit longer than 18 seconds—but not by much—for Sabres fans to realize that the 5'9" dynamo with the rocket shot and the feisty fists would become a fixture in Buffalo.

Gare made the Sabres roster after his first training camp and never played a game in the minor leagues during a 13-year career in which he spent seven and a half seasons in Buffalo before a blockbuster trade sent him to Detroit in 1981. When he retired as a member of Wayne Gretzky's Edmonton Oilers in 1987 due to a cranky back, Gare had totaled 354 goals that included two 50-goal seasons, as well as 685 points and 1,285 penalty minutes.

But Gare's career was about so much more than numbers. "Danny was a heart and soul guy, and he brought not only ability and talent to the team, but he brought a work ethic and desire," said teammate Ric Seiling. "He was a nitty-gritty guy who would go to the fence for any guy on his team. The day he got traded, for the first little while there, I was totally lost as far as leadership. He was a guy that I looked up to for leadership, just a great team guy. People look at 50 goals, but there's a lot more than 50 goals with Danny Gare."

That first year Gare scored 31 goals and helped lead the Sabres to the Stanley Cup Finals. During his second season he erupted for 50, scoring a hat trick on the final night against Toronto and his longtime rival Tiger Williams to reach the milestone.

"I'd known Tiger since junior days," said Gare. "Tiger had always been a bit of an antagonist, and before the faceoff, he said, 'You're not even going to get a sniff tonight.' I took the puck [after the 50th goal] and went by Tiger on the Leaf bench and flipped it at him. I said, 'Hey, Tiger, that's 50.'"

After an injury-plagued third year, Gare scored 39, 27, 56 (to tie for the league lead with Hartford's Blaine Stoughton and Los Angeles' Charlie Simmer), and 46 goals during his next four seasons, wearing the "C" for a good chunk of that stretch and earning his reputation as the leader of the team. Said Larry Playfair:

When I got to Buffalo, Danny was the captain and I was just a kid. Danny was the best captain I ever played for. He took the time to come and talk to me on the bus and he made me feel like part of the team. The things that would happen during the year, if we needed someone to address a situation, score a goal, be physical, Danny did it all. He was a great leader in the dressing room.

He was one of the few guys who could look at Perreault, Schony, anyone who wasn't toeing the line, and he'd say something to him. Not many players in the league are capable of calling their friends and teammates out, but Danny could, and he could back it up by going out there and scoring a goal or fighting someone.

96 It Starts with the Kids

Canada may claim that hockey is its national pastime—and no one would argue—but Buffalonians have long had a burning passion for the game, and the Sabres are a primary reason for that.

From their inception in 1970, the Sabres were an immediate hit. Memorial Auditorium was sold out almost every night right from the start. Kids who grew up enthralled with the new team in town have passed that interest down to their own children, who are in turn now passing it along to theirs.

To its credit, the Sabres organization has done a terrific job of catering to its young fans with a number of initiatives designed to help kids understand the game and, ultimately, grow to love it.

The SabreKidz Club was created during the 2003–2004 season to foster a love of hockey in the youngest generation of Sabres fans. The only official Sabres kids club, boys and girls age 12 and under are eligible to join. Membership is free and includes a membership card, a monthly electronic newsletter, and an electronic birthday card from the popular team mascot, Sabretooth. Those who pay for a $20 premium membership also receive two tickets to a Buffalo

Bandits professional indoor lacrosse game (the team is owned by the Sabres), Sabres "logo bandz," a yearbook, and invitations to exclusive SabreKidz Club events such as the Halloween skating party, a spring skate, and a summer picnic.

Youth hockey is a major emphasis for the Sabres as well. Throughout the regular season, the team hosts afternoon children's games at the arena prior to their home games as part of their "Future Sabres" amateur hockey program. It's a thrilling day for the kids, who get to play on the ice that the Sabres will skate on a few short hours later. They and their families also get to stay for that night's game.

The Sabres also conduct periodic hockey clinics run by their director of youth hockey development, former defenseman Grant Ledyard. Ledyard guides players at the Beginner, Mite, Squirt,

Sabretooth

His name is Gene McAndrews—but don't feel bad if you don't know who that is. You're not supposed to.

McAndrews is the man who is Sabretooth, the team mascot who rappels from the rafters to the ice surface—a death-defying 160-foot jump—each game night at First Niagara Center.

According to the Sabres public relations department, there are actually three Sabretooth mascots at each game making appearances in different parts of the arena. But McAndrews is the only one who dons the 80-pound costume and makes that grand entrance from the sky.

"It's pretty hardcore, but it's been a fun experience for me," McAndrews said in a 2011 interview with WNYLaborToday.com. "I've been rappelling as Sabretooth since 2002, and while I haven't kept count, I've done it some 50 times a year for the past six or seven years."

McAndrews has been a professional mascot for more than a decade, having also donned the costumes of Buster Bison and Chip with the Buffalo Bisons triple-A baseball team and Rax, the mascot of the National Lacrosse League Buffalo Bandits.

Mike Gilbert, Sabres vice president of public and community relations, told WNYLaborToday.com that McAndrews has "done a great job" for the team and that he "electrifies and revs up the fans. It's great. He comes down fast and it takes a lot of skill. It's become a big part of the game."

and Peewee levels with the goal of informing and instructing these young athletes. Each one-hour session is limited to 30 participants, and for the cost of admission ($35 in 2011–2012), the kids also get a commemorative jersey.

The team also sponsors several hockey groups, including the Junior Sabres, who compete in the junior-A level Ontario Junior Hockey League as the only U.S.-based franchise. Former Sabre Michael Peca joined the team as its general manager in 2011, and then added the role of coach to his duties when Ledyard stepped down from the position in January 2012.

Founded in 1975, the Junior Sabres also operated as the Niagara Scenics and the Buffalo Lightning before returning to their original name. Through the years, hundreds of the team's players have gone on to play for Division I and III college programs. Some of the graduates include NHL players such as Aaron Miller, Kevyn Adams, Brian Gionta, Bob Beers, Jeff Farkas, Todd Marchant, and Ryan Callahan.

97 Meehan Floors the Flyers

Gerry Meehan can still remember the goal. But he remembers the goal he didn't score a few seconds later in the Sabres' regular season finale on April 2, 1972, against the Philadelphia Flyers even more so.

The City of Brotherly Love was crying that night as Meehan scored a fluke goal with four seconds left. When those final moments expired, so, too, did Philadelphia's season.

The Flyers needed only to beat or tie lowly Buffalo at the Aud to earn a West Division playoff berth ahead of Pittsburgh. That tie appeared imminent when Meehan cruised down the left wing and fired what seemed like a harmless shot at the Philadelphia net from about 80 feet away. Somehow the puck found a hole through goalie

Doug Favell, nestled into the mesh, and just like that, the Flyers were out.

Yet as satisfying as it was to deny the Flyers a trip to the playoffs, Meehan was just as disappointed in the locker room afterward.

"I don't know if it was my most memorable goal," Meehan said of the stunning winner, "but I'll tell you one thing: my next shot was certainly my most memorable miss."

You see, Meehan had a clause in his contract that stated if he scored 20 goals that year, he'd earn $1,500—a big bonus at the time—and the game-winning goal was his 19th goal. On the ensuing faceoff, the desperate Flyers left Favell on the bench in favor of an extra attacker. When Meehan beat Bobby Clarke on the draw, he had the puck on his stick and a chance to make the Sabres show him the money. Instead he flipped the puck down the ice, where it went just wide of the unguarded net as the horn sounded to end the game.

"It's unbelievable," said Flyers owner Ed Snider. "I don't think it would ever happen again. We started the third period in third place and in 20 minutes, dropped out of the playoffs."

The Flyers traded Favell to Toronto for goalie Bernie Parent prior to 1973–1974, Philadelphia won the Stanley Cup that year, and in 1974–1975 the Flyers repeated, exacting their revenge on Buffalo when Parent played out of his mind in the Finals, helping to defeat the Sabres, four games to two.

98 The Voice of the Aud

For those who attended games at Memorial Auditorium, there was one thing even more constant than the excitement Gilbert Perreault provided on a nightly basis: Milt Ellis, the voice of the Aud, announcing the goals and penalties with his perfect diction.

Ellis had a distinct but elegant style, much like other public address announcers of his day who didn't need to over-accentuate every syllable to get a rise out of the crowd.

Whether it was a Sabre scoring a goal or an opponent, Ellis' professional tone was the same every time. He never deviated from the way he announced a goal: "Third Buffalo goal, his 15th of the season, scored by No. 11, Gilbert Perreault; assist to No. 7, Rick Martin, and to No. 14, Rene Robert; time of the goal, 3:42." Perfect.

"Over the years a lot of people have said my voice is distinctive," Ellis told Ross Brewitt, one of the contributing authors to the book *Sabres: 26 Seasons in Buffalo's Memorial Auditorium.* "I don't see what's so unique about it, though I suppose a person hears their own voice differently. It's a nice compliment and appreciated, but my voice is natural. I didn't do anything to cultivate a sound."

Ellis was born and raised in Buffalo and attended Kensington High School before earning a bachelor's degree from Syracuse University in 1953. He served as a corporal in the army from 1953 to 1955 before launching a 41-year career as sales manager for WDCX Radio, retiring in 2004.

Ellis began his PA work with the minor league Buffalo Bisons of the American Hockey League during the 1960s. Stan Barron, a Buffalo radio legend, was the team's public relations director, and Ellis was a friend. "One day he called and said his PA man's work schedule had changed and asked if I'd be interested in filling the job," Ellis told Brewitt. Ellis worked nearly every Bisons and Sabres game played at the Aud for the next 30-plus years until the building closed and the Sabres moved into their new arena a few blocks away at the foot of Washington Street.

"The word *gentleman* isn't used much these days, but Milt was that in every sense of the word," said Budd Bailey, a former Sabres public relations director who now works as a sportswriter for the *Buffalo News.* "He was always in a good mood, always friendly to everyone he encountered."

From "O Canada" to "the Home of the Brave"

Sabres fans at Memorial Auditorium and First Niagara Center have had the privilege of listening to some of the finest anthem singers in the NHL during the 40-plus years of the franchise's existence.

The original owners of the franchise, the Knox brothers, knew that a sizeable portion of the Sabres fan base was going to come from southern Ontario, and the team roster was also made up of almost all Canadian players. So they made a decision to have both the American and Canadian national anthems performed before each game.

At the Aud, organist Norm Wullen and tenor Joe Byron were nearly as dynamic a duo as Gilbert Perreault and Rick Martin. They performed for most of the 26 years the Sabres played in the old building.

Once the team moved into what is now called First Niagara Center, they used a variety of different singers to perform the anthem, but the most frequent was and still is Doug Allen, who belts out the songs in a simple, elegant way night after night. He punctuates the final notes by pointing into the camera that films him for the JumboTron.

Ellis, who was inducted into the Sabres Hall of Fame in 2008, passed away in November 2011 at the age of 81. The Sabres observed a moment of silence for Ellis prior to that evening's game against the Phoenix Coyotes.

99 Blizzard Broadcast

If there was one consistent thing said about Ted Darling during his two-plus decades as the Sabres' lead broadcaster, it was that he was the consummate professional. And never was that more apparent than on the night of January 29, 1977, though this performance had nothing to do with his simple and elegant delivery.

When the famous Blizzard of '77 shut down the city of Buffalo, becoming the first snowstorm to warrant a federal disaster area declaration, the Sabres were scheduled to be in Montreal for a Saturday night game at The Forum.

Only 15 players and the coaching staff were able to get to the airport for a flight that was lucky to depart just before the airport closed. And those on board might have wished it hadn't, as the plane had trouble getting off the ground beginning a harrowing flight into Quebec. Darling was snowed in at his home in Lockport, and there was no way he could get to Montreal, making this the first Sabres game he ever missed. Radio play-by-play man Rick Jeanneret was also stranded at his home in Fort Erie, Ontario.

With the game scheduled to be telecast back to the Buffalo area, Darling came up with as viable a solution as he could. He arranged for a substitute play-by-play man in Montreal to do the television broadcast, then performed the radio broadcast via his telephone while watching the game on TV—with the sound muted, of course. His call was then patched into the studio at WGR.

"Our engineer mixed my telephone report with crowd reactions," Darling told the Toronto *Globe and Mail* years after the game. "My son, Joey, monitored the TV for penalties and time left in the period and would feed me facts on cue cards. The only time I had trouble was on the long TV shots, where player numbers became a little difficult to read. It was the easiest road game I ever worked."

Darling pulled the broadcast off so adeptly that one of his neighbors was convinced he'd actually made it to the game in Montreal somehow.

"I never actually said I was or wasn't in Montreal," Darling said. "Next morning, the snow drifts in Lockport were 20, 30 feet high, but I went down to the store for some milk, and the guy there couldn't believe it. He said to me, 'You were in Montreal last night and we can't even get out of Lockport.'"

Just as incredible as Darling's work was the job turned in by the outmanned Sabres. Montreal was the defending Stanley Cup champion, a dynasty that would end up winning the 1977 championship and the two after that. Yet somehow the Sabres—who were without the stranded Rick Martin, Jim Lorentz, Brian Spencer, and Lee Fogolin—managed a 3–3 tie. The defense limited the high-flying Canadiens to a mere 19 shots on goalie Gerry Desjardins, and the Sabres twice rallied from two-goal deficits to pull even midway through the third period when Jim Schoenfeld beat Montreal goalie Bunny Larocque. Don Luce and Andre Savard also scored for Buffalo.

By the time the storm ended, it had caused 29 deaths and more than $300 million in damage. With the city still in recovery mode, home games at the Aud against Los Angeles (February 1) and Toronto (February 7) were rescheduled for later in the season.

In an Associated Press story commemorating the 20th anniversary of the blizzard, Ed Reich, a meteorologist who was on duty at the National Weather Service in 1977, recalled, "It was the most dramatic storm I ever saw."

It just wasn't dramatic enough to stop the voice of the Sabres from doing his job.

"He said it was the easiest game he ever did because when it was over, he just turned off the TV and went to bed," said Joey Darling.

100 See Ya, Seymour

You would be hard-pressed to find a more unique departure from a team than the one Al Smith choreographed on a February night in 1977 at the Aud.

Aggravated all season by his relative inactivity while playing behind No. 1 goaltender Gerry Desjardins, Smith had decided that enough was enough.

With Desjardins injured, the Sabres called up rookie Don Edwards, supposedly to serve as Smith's backup. Instead, general manager Punch Imlach told coach Floyd Smith an hour before the game against the Minnesota North Stars that he wanted Edwards to play that night.

Smith heard this information and hatched a plan. He went through the normal warm-up routine, came back out of the locker room after the ice was resurfaced, and stood dutifully at attention for the national anthems. As the echo of Joe Byron's voice hummed through the applauding crowd, Smith hopped off the bench, skated over to co-owner Seymour Knox in his lower gold seat, saluted him, and said, "See ya, Seymour." With that, he skated off into the locker room, never to play for the team again.

Edwards, meanwhile, was forced to make his NHL debut without a backup. The Sabres actually tried to sign PR man Paul Wieland—an amateur goalie—to a contract during the game, but it was too late to put his name on the official lineup card.

"I got to the locker room at about 5:00 PM for the game, and we all went out on the ice, and Al Smith took all of the warm-ups," Edwards recalled in Budd Bailey's book *Celebrate the Tradition*. "Then I was sitting next to him in the locker room right before game time and I said, 'Good luck tonight.' He looked at me and said, 'You don't know you're playing?' That sort of ended the conversation right there. I was dumbfounded. So it's my first game in the NHL and I was the only goalie in uniform."

Fortunately for Edwards, it was a pretty easy night. The Sabres dominated the game 6–2, and he was called on to face only 17 shots, 15 of which he stopped.

Center Derek Smith, who knew beforehand that he would be making his NHL debut that night, wondered jokingly afterward if this happened all the time in the NHL.

Al Smith, the ultimate journeyman, had only played in 10 NHL games four years into his professional career. He finally hooked on with Pittsburgh in 1969 and was the Penguins regular starter for two years, then played a year in Detroit before bolting to the rebel World Hockey Association, where he was the primary starter for three years for the New England Whalers before returning to the NHL in 1975–1976 as Desjardins' backup in Buffalo.

Smith played only 14 games that season, and had appeared in only seven in 1976–1977 when he bid farewell. He returned to play for New England in the WHA for two more years, then finished his career back in the NHL, spending one year in Hartford and one in Colorado before retiring.

"I guess Al was disappointed with not playing," coach Floyd Smith said on that strange night. "He left the bench, and that's the last I saw of him. Al and I discussed it before the game, and he knew that I was ordered to play Edwards. People get frustrated in the game."

Sources

Newspapers/Magazines
Buffalo News
Buffalo Courier-Express
San Jose Mercury News
Boston Globe
Boston Herald
Toronto Sun
Globe and Mail
Toronto Star
Sports Illustrated
Welland Tribune
Rochester Democrat and Chronicle
New York Times
Montreal Gazette
Lansing State Journal
Hockey News
Hartford Courant
Newsday
Washington Post
Philadelphia Inquirer
Kitchener-Waterloo Record
Dallas Morning News

Websites
Sabres.nhl.com
Hockey-reference.com
Hockeydb.com
Hhof.com
Sabreslegends.com

Greatesthockeylegends.com
Legendsofhockey.com
Sabresalumni.com
NHL.com
WNYLabor.com

Books

Imlach, Punch. *Heaven and Hell in the NHL*. McClelland and Stewart Limited, 1982.

Maiorana, Sal. *Thank You Sabres: Memories of the 1972–1973 Season*. Quality Sports Publications, 1997.

Maiorana, Sal. *Game Night in Buffalo: A Town, Its Team, and Its Sporting Memories*. Western New York Wares, Inc. 2003.

Wieland, Paul. *Then Perreault Said to Rico... The Best Buffalo Sabres Stories Ever Told*. Triumph Books, 2008.

Brewitt, Ross. *Sabres: 26 Seasons in Buffalo's Memorial Auditorium*. Taylor Publishing Company, 1996.

Schultz, Randy. *Dominik Hasek: The Dominator*. Sports Publishing LLC, 2002.

Bailey, Budd. *Celebrate the Tradition 1970–1990: A History of the Buffalo Sabres*. Boncraft, Inc., 1989.

About the Author

Sal Maiorana is a native of Buffalo, New York, and a journalism graduate of Buffalo State College, class of 1984. He is currently in his 26th year as a sportswriter for the Rochester (New York) *Democrat and Chronicle*, and his primary beats are the Buffalo Bills, college and professional lacrosse and hockey, and golf.

Maiorana is a 2009 inductee into the media group of the Frontier Field Walk of Fame, a two-time Rochester Press-Radio Club Sports Writer of the Year award winner, and has been recognized by the American Legion as Rochester's Sports Writer of the Year. He has also won numerous New York State Publishers' Association and Gannett News Service citations for his work with the *Democrat and Chronicle*.

Maiorana's freelance work has appeared in numerous publications and online websites, including *The Sporting News, Golf World, Golf Week, USGA Journal, USA Today, PGA Magazine, Lacrosse Magazine*, NFL.com, CBS Sportsline, and The SportsXchange.

He is also the author of 17 books, including *Thank You Sabres: Memories of the 1972–1973 Season* (1997, Quality Sports Publications); *Through the Green: The Mind and Art of a Professional Golfer* (1992, St. Martin's Press); *Relentless: The Hard-Hitting History of Buffalo Bills Football* (1994, 1999, Quality Sports Publications, volumes I and II); *Oak Hill Country Club Centennial* (2001, Hasak Publishing); A Lifetime of Yankee Octobers (2002, Sleeping Bear Press); *Game Night in Buffalo: A Town, Its Teams and Its Sporting Memories* (2003, Western New York Wares); *If You Can't Join 'Em, Beat 'Em: A Remembrance of the American Football League* (2003, 1st Books Library); and *Buffalo Bills: The Complete and Illustrated History* (2010, MVP Books).